Praise for
The Science of Successful Organizational Change

"Organizational change is a huge industry filled with buzzwords and fads and suffering from an unacceptably high failure rate. Paul Gibbons applies scientifically founded, rigorous thought and practical wisdom to this charlatan-filled domain, and produces actionable, sensible, evidence-based insights that can make change efforts much more likely to succeed and organizations much more agile and effective."

— **Jeffrey Pfeffer**, Thomas D. Dee II Professor of Organizational Behavior, Stanford Business School

"The best book on change I have read. Paul Gibbons draws from his extensive experience in change management in big businesses and blends it beautifully with his knowledge of philosophy, psychology, neuroscience and even derivative trading to produce a highly readable science-based and groundbreaking study of what has gone right and wrong in managing change in the business arena."

— **David Bennett**, former CEO Alliance & Leicester PLC

"In my 25 years of working with teams and organizations, this is the first book that actually uses science as the foundation of how organizations learn and develop rather than platitudes and well-worn but erroneous beliefs. One of Gibbons' strengths is his willingness to tell it like it is, no matter how sacred the cow. This work will be used by businesses and consultants for many years to come."

— **Curtis Watkins**, Master Coach

"Paul Gibbons rethinks change management with a 21st-century approach that exchanges cargo cult management for an evidence-based approach built on neuroscience and complexity sciences. Time is overdue to replace Kotter's change model for something better suited for a complex world where change is continuous and not a one-time event, and where creative change continuously drives organizational improvement. Paul has succeeded with this, and in the process distills the best research into a book with a framework and ideas that will resonate with the modern leader and the Agile/Lean community. Buy it, read it, and place it on the bookshelf next to *The Halo Effect*, *Switch*, and *The Fifth Discipline*—in easy reach for rereading."

— **Rolf E. Häsänen**, Founder, Value at Work

"Paul Gibbons has made a valuable contribution to the store of knowledge on change strategy and strategic decision making. By applying the latest findings from the science of decision making to his 25 years of practical in-the-tranches experience counseling executive teams, Gibbons has enabled anyone engaged in strategic decision making to raise their game."

—**Dan Sweeney**, Director, IEE, Daniels College of Business, University of Denver

"Few people bring Gibbons' expertise, breadth of scholarship, depth of understanding, and range of experience to that most important of business practices: leading change."

—**Robert Entenman**, Global Head E-business for a major European bank

The Science of Successful Organizational Change

How Leaders Set Strategy, Change
Behavior, and Create an Agile Culture

Paul Gibbons

Publisher: Paul Boger
Editor-in-Chief: Amy Neidlinger
Executive Editor: Jeanne Glasser Levine
Development Editor: Natasha Wolmers
Operations Specialist: Jodi Kemper
Cover Designer: Alan Clements
Managing Editor: Kristy Hart
Project Editor: Elaine Wiley
Copy Editor: Karen Annett
Proofreader: Jess DeGabriele
Senior Indexer: Cheryl Lenser
Compositor: Nonie Ratcliff
Manufacturing Buyer: Dan Uhrig

For information about buying this title in bulk quantities, or for special sales opportunities (which may include electronic versions; custom cover designs; and content particular to your business, training goals, marketing focus, or branding interests), please contact our corporate sales department at corpsales@pearsoned.com or (800) 382-3419.

For government sales inquiries, please contact governmentsales@pearsoned.com.

For questions about sales outside the U.S., please contact international@pearsoned.com.

Company and product names mentioned herein are the trademarks or registered trademarks of their respective owners.

Printed in the United States of America

3 16

ISBN-10: 0-13-400033-1
ISBN-13: 978-0-13-400033-6

Pearson Education LTD.
Pearson Education Australia PTY, Limited.
Pearson Education Singapore, Pte. Ltd.
Pearson Education Asia, Ltd.
Pearson Education Canada, Ltd.
Pearson Educación de Mexico, S.A. de C.V.
Pearson Education—Japan
Pearson Education Malaysia, Pte. Ltd.

Library of Congress Control Number: 2015934399

To my parents and their bequest, the hunger for knowledge; and to science, which reveals both the fragility and vast potential of the human intellect.

Contents

Acknowledgments

It takes a lot to build a career, and many people, mentors, clients, colleagues, and bosses were supportive beyond what was sometimes rational. Thanks to Ray Aldag, Julie Baddeley, Nichola Batley, Sarah Boulton, Aidan Brennan, Richard Briance, Peter Burditt, Cari Caldwell, Simon Collins, Tom Dolan, Maureen Erasmus, Jerry Goldstein, Kelvin Hard, Sigi Hoenle, Dennis Keegan, Kate Larsen, Mike Lewis (consultant), Michael Lewis (author), Jamie Maxwell-Grant, Frank Milton, Steve Oristaglio, AJ Pape, Paul Reyniers, Anita Roddick, Tom Ryves, Makoto Sagi, Bassam Shakhashiri, James Shaw, Rob Shephard, Tim Stanyon, James Shaw, John Stewart, Paul Taffinder, Val Thompson, Mark Wade, Ian Wells, Ian Wilson, Chuck West, Roger Wyn-Jones, Mark Young, and Hyuk Yu.

Many people reviewed early drafts of chapters while they were still unreadable. They were kind enough to say directly when that was the case—a sign of true friendship. This includes Alan Arnett, Charlie Birch, Sarah Boulton, Francis Briers, Olivier Compagne, Pete Cuozzo, Trevor Davis, Geri Gibbons, John Gibbons, Pete Hamill, John Holt, Maz Iqbal, Rob Goathem, Stephen Guise, Akira Hirai, Claire Martin, Larry Pearlman, Tim Ragan, Brian Robertson, Surekha Subramaniyan, Aine Watkins, Curtis Watkins, and Andrew Williams.

A number of researchers were extraordinarily generous exchanging ideas electronically or providing guidance at various stages. These include Rob Briner, Dan Hausman, Helen Hughes, Phillippa Lally, Jan Lorenz, Scott Lilienthal, Mark Keil, James Kuklinski, Brendan Nyhan, Jeffrey Pfeffer, and Nassim Taleb. They bear no responsibility for any wayward ideas in the final product.

Both my agent and publisher were extremely forgiving of this first-time author and his attendant idiosyncrasies. Maryann Karinch and Jeanne Glasser Levine are due the warmest thanks for helping steer this project to completion. Thanks also to Elaine Wiley (Coyote), Karen Annett, and the whole team at Pearson for their extraordinary professionalism.

So many friends offered support in so many ways during the incubation of this book, but some stand above the crowd for their generosity of spirit and support. David Bennett, Robert Entenman, Adam Gold, Jake Simpson, Dan Sweeney, and Guy Warrington, you have my enduring gratitude.

My most heartfelt gratitude goes to my two young boys, Conor and Luca, who handled their dad's distraction and distance during writing with great maturity, and to my own parents, Moira and Willie, who sparked my initial love of scholarship, science, and philosophy.

About the Author

Paul Gibbons has a 35-year career straddling international business and academia. His research and writing explores how philosophy and science can be used to enlighten contemporary business thinking and solve practical business problems, including changing culture, developing leaders, and using analytics and evidence to make strategic decisions. During his 30 years in Europe, he was a derivatives trader, consultant, adjunct professor, and founder/CEO of an award-winning Organization Development consulting firm, Future Considerations. He now writes, teaches, and raises two boys in Colorado.

Introduction

"It is curious how often you humans manage to obtain that which you do not want."

—Spock, *Star Trek: The Original Series*, "Errand of Mercy"

How to Set 3 Million Dollars on Fire

In March 1993, the derivatives market was booming, and banks—although intoxicated by the profits—were worried about the risks of these strange, complex instruments and how to control the armies of traders making all that money. The normally reserved world of British commercial banks had been taken over by brash traders using swarthy epithets as often as the gammas and deltas of the trade. Senior management loved the income, but did not understand the math, hated the new trading-room culture of risk, vulgarity, and aggression, and were at sea with how to manage a business they did not understand.

So they called in the cavalry: consultants.

PwC had assembled a team from MIT, Harvard, and Oxford to help Barclays develop a comprehensive "Risk Management Framework." I was on the team as "a math guy" and because, as a former trader, I spoke the traders' language, the gammas, the deltas, and the epithets.

We worked for months interviewing senior leaders, traders, and other risk experts by day and writing our reports by night. The result was 12 ring-bound volumes of several hundred pages each. The one featuring the majority of my contributions was filled with pages of equations describing how financial instruments behaved under various stresses using advanced statistics. The other volumes were similarly detailed and dense, suggesting what strategies, systems, accounting procedures, processes, and management practices Barclays should use to manage risk.

We charged 1.8 million pounds ($2.7 million), which was a hefty consulting fee for 1993.

And then, nothing happened.

"What?" you say, "surely not nothing?" To be more precise, our findings were presented to the board of directors who nodded vigorously at all the right times. Then we presented to the executive committee, to the managing directors, to the business unit heads, and to their teams. They all nodded and applauded. No PowerPoint slide was left unturned. Almost *none* of our recommendations became real business change.

Although they found our logic compelling, and our recommendations sound, Barclays failed to "mind the gap," the one between agreeing with something and doing it. Barclays might as well have lit a bonfire on Lombard Street with the three million bucks (which, given London's spring weather, would have been better use of their capital).

I was crushed. From Master of Universe Consultant to snake-oil peddler on my first project. The project team remains the smartest and most professional I had ever known. What went wrong? There seemed to be three questions:

1. How could our recommendations not have been implemented when Barclays was so worshipful of them?

2. If our recommendations were as good as we and the bankers thought, what else should we have done to get them adopted?

3. When were they going to blow the whistle on consultants for charging huge fees, producing no results, and hopping off to the next assignment?

Reports in Drawers and Personal Change

Little did I know that such epic fails were more the rule than the exception in strategy consulting; they have a name, "the report in a drawer." Over the next 18 months, I worked on several strategy projects that soon decorated executive shelves and bottom drawers.

This professional epic fail paralleled one in my personal life.

As a teenager in 1980, I worked in cancer research before submitting myself to the sleepless nights of medical education. My research project involved studying the biochemistry of cancer to understand the effect of Vitamin A on skin cancers through its effect on DNA and RNA synthesis—by treating little white mice with a carcinogen from cigarette smoke. Despite this, and since the age of 14, I smoked a pack of Marlboro Red per day. At the lab, I would squirt the cigarette extract, watch the mice get cancer, and grab a quick smoke between experiments. While working at Barclays, I still frequented the parking lot for smoke breaks, so for almost 20 years I had ignored all the science, some of which I produced firsthand, which told me I was killing myself one cancer stick at a time.

The link between the failed project at Barclays and my death wish was not lost on me. There must be a link between how I systematically defied in-your-face rationality, and how Barclays effectively ignored our advice on risk management.

This birthed a tremendous hunger: How do people change, and how do businesses make real change happen? How do good ideas get acted upon in the real world, and how do reports find their way from bottom drawers into hearts and minds? This seemed to be a problem at the root of human happiness, business prosperity, and how we manage ourselves as a society.

The equation seemed to be:

$$E \times X = Change[1]$$

E seemed to be expertise, knowledge, research, statistics, advice, reasons, rationality, and clear thinking. My strategy colleagues and I were good at all that. X was the bit that stumped me completely, that I knew nothing about—the "special sauce" that combined with reasons produced change. X had eluded me in my personal life, and now in

---

[1] Later, in the change management practice, we used $O = E^2$ (output equals excellence times engagement), and others use $R = Q \times A$ (results equals quality times acceptance).

my professional life. I wanted to make a difference, not just espouse grand theories, and to be someone who did not just talk a good game but could play ball. I wanted *X*.

I changed gears. For almost two decades, I lived, ate, and breathed organizational change. My immersion was obsessive: in its academic disciplines (psychology, sociology, Organization Development, and Organizational Behavior), training in Daryl Conner's change toolkit, Californian "self-actualization" workshops, training as a counselor, working as a change manager in dozens of businesses, and teaching the advanced change management program to management consulting partners.

From the Laboratory to the Sweat Lodge

Then another problem reared its head. Little did I know that leaving the solid bedrock of science and reason for the world of change meant journeying to the opposite end of the spectrum—a world where ideas were much harder to test.

At first, I accepted perspectives in books such as Gladwell's *The Tipping Point,* or Goleman's *Emotional Intelligence* uncritically, never wondering how much meat there was on the sandwich, or whether eating marshmallows really predicted success (it does not).[2] My new change colleagues and I talked about emotions, socially constructed realities, presencing, living systems metaphors, ancient wisdom, consciousness, cultural memes, spiritual values, and stakeholder engagement. I loved the writings of 1990's change gurus—for example, John Kotter (Harvard) and Tom Peters (McKinsey)—and at that time, I accepted their ideas uncritically because of their reputations.

Then, as I traveled farther down the change rabbit hole, I encountered notions such as "quantum leadership," "right-brained

---

[2] As with many psychological ideas that are presented as fact by popular media, Mischel's research on emotional intelligence is controversial. How the media popularizes and exaggerates research in psychology is the subject of Chapter 6, "Misunderstanding Human Behavior."

leadership,"[3] and "leading from Source." I attended Organization Development (OD) workshops (also attended by household names in that field) that began with an "attunement" to let in Spirit, and workshops to reveal the collective unconscious (Jung) of a business. One workshop, hosted by consummate change professionals and attended by senior executives from a leading consumer goods company, used a labyrinth (a room-sized carpet that looks like a maze) to evoke insight and creativity. The premise was that if one walked around this ancient sacred structure with a question in mind, insight and creativity would emerge. I just got dizzy. Clients, normally discerning business people, suppressed whatever reservations they might have had.

I was now a stranger in a strange land. I knew there was more to producing organizational and personal change than reasons and "smarts," yet change theories had no science to back them up, and most of my fellow practitioners disdained science in favor of "other ways of knowing."

I had found that the change world (Organization Development and change management) had an overlap in values and methods with humanistic psychologists, pop psychologists, therapists, 1960's counterculture, and New Age spirituality. As great "people-people," they made for outstanding facilitators, but I always had nagging doubts about how reliable methodologies guided by those underlying belief systems might be. Of course, there is no standard belief system that represents the entire people side of business. I had explored the most extreme realms, hungering for meaning, for personal answers, and answers to the question, "How do people and businesses change?" On my search for meaning and insight, in those extreme realms, I had a lot of company; the demand for esoteric approaches from senior business people is enormous. In addition to labyrinths, I hosted Native American drumming workshops, encounter groups, Lego-play workshops, monastic retreats, ropes courses, trust falls and trust walks, improvisational and standard theater sessions, yoga and tai-chi, psychodrama, and workshops with concert violinists and pianists. The

---

[3] There is no such thing as a "right-brained" person or a "right-brained" leader, and psychological dispositions (such as being logical) are unrelated to hemispheric dominance. This, too, is explored in Chapter 6.

clients for these workshops were all in the top 100 corporations in the world and household names. I would wager that 100% of companies in the Global 500 have used and still use at least one of those techniques.

While experimenting with those methods, I also hungered for proof. Clients were happy and came back for more, so I left behind happier workplaces—but was the change sustainable, and did business results follow from the increased engagement? Naturally, in parallel with the esoteric work, I did much "change management" that looked more traditional: stakeholder engagement, team alignment, strategy facilitation, communications planning, organization design, and change-leader coaching. Some of my change experience was on projects with billion dollar price-tags.

Yet, how much better proven were the more conventional tools I favored, such as business cases, process-mapping, organization performance models, risk registers, stakeholder analyses, and criterion matrices, than my friends' labyrinths? Was it just a matter of taste? Although I became skeptical of some of the more esoteric approaches, I had equally little evidence to prove what I did.

The most shocking thing is that during more than 30 years in business, at the most senior levels, in the world's biggest companies, dispensing consulting advice, no client *ever* asked me whether there was evidence to support the models, frameworks, tools, methods, and ideas I proposed using. *Never*. I worry, silly me, about using methods on billion-dollar projects that are based on beliefs for which there is skimpy evidence. Do we just use what looks good, what is in fashion, and what gurus say works? Do we use what methods we know best rather than the best methods? How do we evaluate methods side by side in this science-free world?

I sought to square this circle, in 1999, with some research. I was a pioneer in an academic movement within Organization Development (OD) called Spirituality in Business, which had the very sensible idea that people had a spiritual dimension to their lives—either religion, a deep sense of values, or a commitment to some kind of humanism. By bringing their whole selves to work, they would be more engaged and passionate. Value centered leadership would become the norm. However, my research was aridly called *Spirituality at Work. Definitions, Assumptions, and Validity Claims.* I tried to bring some hard science to where my passions lay, and to the softest part of the soft end of OD. This book, in some ways, extends that project—can we bring some harder-edged concepts and some robust validity testing to the tools and ideas used by change leaders? Can we prove a certain kind of workshop "works"?

Defenders of the Faith—How to Prove Something Works

In this book, I want to shake up our collective certainty that what you do works. As you'll see in Chapter 1, "Failed Change: The Greatest Preventable Cost to Business?," change fails about half the time. Defenders of the status quo say "my methods are tested and proven." They mean, "When I use this change management tool (for example, model, framework, workshop, intervention, process), I *cause* the following result (for example, performance improvement, increased engagement, reduced cycle time)."

The problem is that we cannot easily prove cause and effect and that what we do works. Why? When a car mechanic replaces a gasket and the engine stops leaking, the mechanic has excellent evidence that his craft has worked. There are few, if any, other likely explanations for the engine leak stopping while the car was under repair in the garage.

This is never true in business. As you will see in Chapter 4, "Decision Making in Complex and Ambiguous Environments," businesses are complex systems and complexity theory tells us that cause and effect are *never* provable with *any* confidence in a complex system. When I intervene to improve employee engagement in order to improve financial performance, the causal chain between what I do, the engagement, and the financial performance is far too flimsy for me to make the same claim as a car mechanic can. People who make strong causal claims about what they do and company performance are guilty of two logical fallacies: *post hoc ergo propter hoc* (it happened before it, so it caused it) and *causal reductionism* (reducing to a single cause something that could have been caused by many things). This kind of reasoning is why people buy homeopathic and herbal remedies and over-the-counter cold medications. None of these beat placebo,[4] but people claim to feel better after taking them. They forget that they take them when they feel sick, are doing other things that do work (resting), and that all mild ailments improve on their own.

At the risk of being a bore, in the philosophy of science, if you say some intervention you make *caused* an improvement in performance, you have to at least prove it was a *necessary condition*, meaning the improvement would not have happened without your help. Many consultants make far stronger claims, that what they did was a *sufficient condition*, meaning what they did was enough *by itself* to cause the change. There is too much going on inside a business—too many other variables—that could have produced the result. This problem is solved by scientists using an untreated *control group*, which is then compared with the treatment group. In practice, this is hard to do in business. You will see, throughout this book, but particularly in the final chapter, how this even applies to research conducted by prestigious business schools. It especially applies to research done by consultants who always have something to sell.

Business is a people thing, and the human sciences lack precision and predictive power. We could go along pretending more precision than exists, or we could take a different approach and be far more skeptical (and humble) about what we do.

In this book, we visit some better-tested, more empirically valid theories from the human sciences, debunk a large number of change and psychological myths, and explore some recent discoveries that

---

[4] Placebos can have a very powerful effect; the mind is a better healer than pseudoscience.

advance our understanding of people and consequently change topics such as influencing stakeholder communication, decision making, and behavioral change. Along the way, I also propose some ideas that have not yet been tested, but ought to be.

Spoiler Alert—The Whole Book in One Diagram

Figure 1 divides the change world into valid/not valid and useful/harmful.[5] I believe that the future lies in moving as much to the upper-right quadrant as we can—that is, using practices that are both valid *and* useful. This requires a shift in business culture, toward more scientific validity, more measurement, and greater accountability for results. The shift will take decades, but there are indications that it is already under way with new analytics and data-driven approaches to decision making and a phenomenon called evidence-based management, which is discussed more in Chapter 9, "Leading with Science."

There is much research (upper-left quadrant of Figure 1) that is little known or used, and I hope to offer some of the research I find most interesting that has had little take-up in the change community. Businesses, I hope to show, must move practices (policies, models) from the lower-right quadrant into the upper-right quadrant by evaluating, proving, and testing them. Alternatively, policies, models, and practices that are proven harmful should be moved to the lower-left quadrant and discarded. In many sections of this book, I challenge some of what passes for accepted wisdom in the change world. I also take the liberty of introducing some ideas (on change-agility) that are interesting, useful-looking, but unproven.

---

[5] Both *validity* and *usefulness* are nuanced and contested terms. There are hundreds of books on how we can prove that we know something (in the philosophy of science, epistemology, and books on research methods). In short, by *validity* and *evidence*, I mean (very roughly) that you can prove what you do with the scientific method, and if I did it also, I would get the same results. The final chapter has more details exploring evidence in the section on evidence-based management.

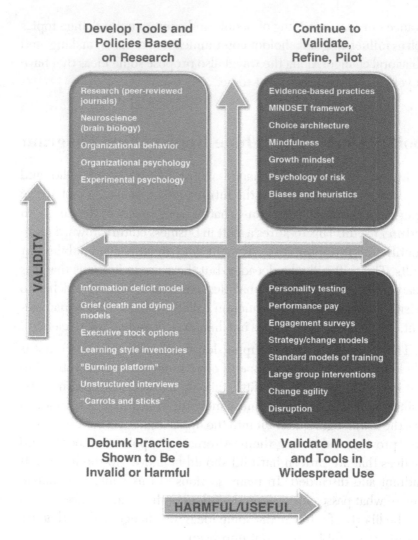

Figure 1 Change management culture needs to move toward increased validity and accountability even though it will take decades.

The War Between Validity and Usefulness

In the business world (especially in HR/change), we have a war, between the "validity people" and the "usefulness people." The validity people berate the usefulness people for lack of evidence and pseudoscience. The usefulness people, when they do not just ignore the researchers, respond, "Leave me alone, I have a job to do." The usefulness people, in their desire to get on with things, are guilty of dropping rigorous evidential standards, hence we get fads, pseudoscience, antiscience, and lack of accountability. They then berate the validity people for not "being in the real world." This theory-practice war destroys value and not just in business. I once asked a criminology professor about the evidence basis for what happens in the criminal justice system. He replied, "Whatever the evidence proves, the system (prisons, parole, courts) does precisely the opposite."

Some topics I weigh in upon are hotly contested. Neuroimaging is an exciting area, but there is much debate around whether brain scans show what they claim to show. (One researcher put a dead fish in a brain scanner and found it lit up when shown images. This did not end the debate about imaging; it was more like putting out the fire with gasoline.) There are volumes—thousands of articles—written about performance-related pay (PRP). When I bluntly say "PRP does not work," this is to act as a counterweight to the "commonsense" idea that paying people for performance increases motivation and performance.[6] The truth is more complex, but the weight of evidence goes against commonsense.

Most of what happens in the change world (and generally in business) has little scientific evidence at all, and we cannot simply switch off the juice until everything is proven. The need do something on Monday morning should not prohibit us from working in parallel on improving the validity of what we do.

Scientific evidence is not necessary for everything: Agriculture existed in preliterate societies as practices developed by trial and error were handed down over generations. However, they also made a lot of mistakes and some rituals they thought worked, such as those to influence the weather gods, were wasteful. Business is more like that than it is like medicine, but even medicine was based on folklore 200 years ago. Doctors had well-established rituals and practices, but they were based on utterly wrong ideas about the body (biochemistry, physiology, and so on) and lack of evidence on whether a treatment worked—because the scientific method had not permeated medicine.

---

[6] This is explored further in Chapter 7, "The Science of Changing Behaviors," but the relationship between incentives, motivation, and performance is not straightforward. If you have to choose between "PRP works" and "PRP does not work," you are safer with the latter claim.

Doctors believed in things such as "humours" and used things like leeches. As with business change today, patients sometimes got better and sometimes died. When they improved, the doctors took the credit (and not the fact that they would have recovered without the leeches). When change fails, do we admit to ourselves that some of our "rain dances" may not work as well as we think, or that maybe our understanding of what make people tick still has "humours"? In change leadership, success has many fathers, and failure is an orphan.

On these contested topics, it matters a great deal less whether we are right or wrong on a particular topic than that we start to ask ourselves the hard questions within the practitioner community (for example, change, HR, or OD people). Business clients can hold the experts' feet to the fire and insist upon higher standards of accountability and evaluation.

The Path Ahead: Change-Agility, Strategy, and Tactics

Although most books on change focus on change tactics, I believe that sound *strategy* in a *change-agile* organization should reduce the need for extensive *tactical* change interventions. Accordingly, *The Science of Successful Organizational Change* is organized in three parts: Change-Agility, Change Strategy, and Change Tactics. The final chapter and conclusion deals with change leadership.

In Chapter 1, the first, context-setting chapter, we look at the scale of the change problem through two questions: How much change happens, and how much does it fail? Leadership is, uncontroversially, the single most important factor in making change happen. The chapter shows that leaders are poorly equipped to lead change because of the structure of business education and because even the expert world is rife with bad metaphors and change mythology.

Change-Agility

One essential capability in a VUCA world (Volatility, Uncertainty, Complexity, and Ambiguity) is the ability to adapt, learn, invent, and build quickly. If every major change project entails bloodletting, over-runs, damaged trust, and unintended consequences, eventually an external threat or internal change will arise that will be too much. In that scenario, each major change leaves the business no better, or perhaps worse, change fatigued, demoralized, and unready for the next change. Change-agility creates adaptive organizations, ones that appear to surf the waves of disruptive technologies, avoid the rapids in turbulent economic times, and set the pace for other businesses to follow.

Chapter 2, "From Change Fragility to Change-Agility," explains those ideas with examples from Google, 3M, IBM, and Shell and four perspectives: agile people and behaviors, agile cultures, agile structures, and agile processes.

Change Strategy

Starting with two premises, that no tactical interventions can fix a flawed strategy and that most of what is written about leading change is tactical, we look at strategy. Chapter 3, "Governance and the Psychology of Risk," examines some of the pitfalls from the realm of where math meets people. Chapter 4, "Decision Making in Complex and Ambiguous Environments," introduces two tools for decision making and discusses the human side of analytics. Chapter 5, "Cognitive Biases and Failed Strategies," covers strategic errors that result from cognitive biases.

Change Tactics

Change tactics are a much better-traveled territory than change strategy. Rather than provide a book of tools, this section looks at twenty-first-century human sciences for insights on leading people through change.

Chapter 6, "Misunderstanding Human Behavior," looks at how we learn what we know about leading people from psychology, the media, popular culture, and gurus. Those concepts from popular psychology lead unhelpfully to *pop leadership* and notions particularly unhelpful to change leaders.

Chapter 7, "The Science of Changing Behaviors," looks at neobehaviorism—how behaviors can be changed without always using persuasion and influencing, but also without resorting to coercion. Chapter 8, "The Science of Changing Hearts and Minds," examines multistakeholder dialogue, influencing with facts, mindfulness, and new ideas on resistance to change.

Chapter 9, "Leading with Science," summarizes the implications for leadership and leadership development, suggesting that the faculty of "farsight" (that seemingly uncanny knack for spotting future opportunities and niches) is an important, although neglected leadership asset, but one that can be developed (so we do not have to run around looking for geniuses). The chapter then discusses ideas on leading with science, or leadership as a science-based craft. First, antiscience and pseudoscience must be stamped out, but then I introduce an intriguing possibility. In the twenty-first century, medicine began to move toward evidence-based medicine. I believe if we can follow the lessons from medicine, evidence-based management could be an exciting paradigm shift.

How to Read This Book and Make It Useful

This is a short book with an enormous breadth of topics, many of which are extremely complex. My ambition is to provoke debate and ask the right questions, not to have the final word (for example, on whether neuroscience is useful). I ask your forbearance in advance should the treatment of a big subject be too abbreviated; many sections of the book, such as mindfulness, neuroscience, complexity, choice architecture, or cognitive biases, have entire libraries devoted to exploring them. I am usually trying to do one of four things on a topic:

1. Challenge the received wisdom in a particular area, such as neuroscience.
2. Bring a newer area to the attention of change practitioners, such as cognitive biases or the psychology of risk.

3. Introduce a subject well understood by the change community to an executive audience, such as large-group interventions or systems thinking.

4. Air some of my own models and ideas, such as the systematic change model, leadership as a science-based craft, or strategic coherence, so they can be challenged and strengthened.

One early reviewer of this book said, "What you suggest is correct, but easier said than done." Everything in the business world is easier said than done! Leadership is as challenging a practical discipline as philosophy and mathematics are as abstract disciplines because technical complexity and social/interpersonal complexity intersect, sometimes making straightforward technical challenges difficult to solve practically.

What I ask of you is that you read with the question, "How might I apply this?" in mind. You will find basic scientific findings on complexity, on analytics, on risk, on biases, on changing behaviors, on influencing hearts and minds, on changing culture, and on creating agile organizations interesting and thought provoking. In a practical discipline, such as business, interesting ideas are the booby prize.

The devil is not in the detail, but in the application. The heavy lifting of applying it to the organizations you lead must be up to you. Mindfulness research has shown that the practice reduces stress, improves emotion control, and betters focus. That does not mean saffron robes at the next executive committee meeting, but it might mean a few private, five-minute sessions per day to reequilibrate, or educating workers in how to practice mindfulness at work. Similarly, you will see how cognitive biases plague high-stakes decision making. You can shrug, and hope they do not affect your teams, or you can design safeguards and new practices that help auto-correct the decisions before they cost money. In short, making these insights *useful* will be your job. *The Science of Successful Organizational Change* will be useful only if it sparks intense conversation *and* alters the way you change.

1

Failed Change: The Greatest Preventable Cost to Business?

The Change Problem—How Bad Is It?

At a time when governments worldwide were desperate to cut deficits, and asking citizens—one way or another, whether by increased taxes or reduced benefits—to foot the bill, the 2011 headline in the British tabloid rag, the *Daily Mail* must have been unwelcome:

"£12bn [$18bn] NHS Computer System Is Scrapped..."

The UK government had, after a decade, canceled the largest civilian IT project in the world at the National Health Service (NHS). Initial cost estimates had come in at a mere £2.3 billion ($4 billion), which presumably seemed a steal at the time. On the other side of the pond, the U.S. Census Bureau canceled the planned automation of the decennial census project after approximately $3 billion in cost overruns. A few years later, the U.S. Air Force canceled a logistics management program that had accrued costs of $1.2 billion. The development cost overruns for Boeing's 787 "Dreamliner" approximated $12 billion, Avon wrote off the entire $100 million of the "Promise Project," Denver airport's baggage system snafus cost $1.1 million per day until abandoned with an estimated cost of $3 billion. Merger failures are even more astonishing—if that is possible. The AOL-Time Warner merger is reputed to have destroyed $100 billion dollars in shareholder value—more than the GDP of a few countries!

Part of that was market timing, but most of the destroyed value arose from cultural and interpersonal conflict that made structural and strategic integration of the businesses impossible.

Visible megaproject failures such as those get plenty of media and political attention, but they are just the tip of the iceberg. Most change failures are below the waterline, either failures of standard change programs, or difficulties with everyday, nonprogrammatic change. Seventy percent of change programs fail is the "statistic" that many gurus and even some experts cite. This seems an extraordinary figure; it should raise eyebrows, yet few people challenge it. Is it true?

Because this is a book on science and change, this is the place to first blow the whistle on a statistic that is neither true nor useful. The statistic "70% fails" was based on survey data published in a non-peer-reviewed magazine and on out-of-context remarks by two well respected Harvard professors (Kotter and Nohria).[1] When I say here that the survey findings are "non-peer-reviewed," why does that limit their trustworthiness? The peer review process means that the methods, data, and conclusions have been scrutinized by a jury of one's peers, and it is the gold standard for quality because of this scrutiny. Despite this, even quality popular business magazines (for example, *Harvard Business Review* and *McKinsey Quarterly*) are not peer reviewed. This is astonishing, unique to business compared to other professions, and very worrying. In medicine or science, the most popular journals also have the *highest* peer-review standards (such as *The New England Journal of Medicine* and *Nature*).

This raises a theme that will recur in every chapter: business has the lowest standards for "knowledge" and the lowest standards for entry among the professions (such as medicine, architecture, science, or law).

Seventy percent is a horrific number. The critical questions are:

- Is it really that bad? What is the quality of the evidence?
- What do we mean by change? Do some kinds fail more?
- What do we mean by failure, complete write-offs, and slight delays?

---

[1] Hughes, M. (2011, Dec. 16). Do 70 per cent of all organizational change initiatives really fail? *Journal of Change Management, 11*(4), 451–464.

Evidence on Change Failure Rates

It seems that 70 percent is only a modest exaggeration: Dozens of surveys place the actual failure rate at around 50 percent, for example:[2]

- Fifty percent of mergers (totaling one trillion dollars in the United States alone) fail to deliver value.[3]
- Seventeen percent of large IT projects go so badly that they can threaten the very existence of the company, and large IT projects run an average of 45 percent over budget, while delivering 56 percent less value than predicted.[4]
- 41 percent of change projects were described as successful in an IBM report.[5]

Perhaps this success rate is something we have to live with. In baseball, a .500 batting average is stellar. Venture capitalists (roughly) expect big returns on only about 20 percent of projects, break even on another 30 percent, and write off the rest. Is change like this? On the other hand, it is hard to imagine driving a car or using a computer that works 30 percent of the time; we expect 100 percent or nearly so.

The challenge that change failure rates pose for C-level change governance is: Are we being honest with ourselves when assessing costs and benefits, return on capital, and risks of major change? Do the firm's accounting and capital budgeting processes reflect these failure rates? Do internal and external management consultants' proposals reflect these failure rates?

---

[2] Surveys of this kind are not robustly scientific, but they are the best that is available in this arena. There are those who downplay the source, saying that consulting firms use the 70 percent number as a scare tactic to persuade clients that they need their services. To me, this seems doubtful. In my mind, these abysmal success rates are a striking indictment of the consulting profession rather than a reason to use them more!

[3] Bain US and European Acquisition Success Study (2007).

[4] Bloch, M., Blumberg, S., & Laartz, J. (2012, October). Delivering large-scale IT projects on time, on budget, and on value. *McKinsey Quarterly* (online).

[5] Jorgensen, H., Owen, L., & Neus, A. (2013). *Making change work*. IBM Future of Enterprise.

The next skeptical question is: What do we mean by change failure? Do failure rates vary by type of change?

Does All Change Fail the Same?

Change failure rates do seem to vary by the type of change attempted. UK researcher Dr. Martin Smith summarized 49 separate studies of change success from the academic and trade press and found the kind of variability we might expect.[6] See Table 1.1.

Table 1.1 Success Rates of Different Types of Change Programs

TYPE OF CHANGE	NUMBER OF STUDIES	MEDIAN SUCCESS RATE
Strategy deployment	3	58%
Restructuring/downsizing	9	46%
Technology change	5	40%
Mixed change	1	39%
TQM (Six Sigma)	5	37%
Mergers and acquisitions	9	33%
Reengineering/process design	7	30%
Software development/installation	6	26%
Business expansion	1	20%
Culture change	3	19%
Total	49	

Surveys of this small number of firms are underpowered statistically and limited as scientific evidence, yet the numbers suggest failure rates just below 50 percent, with culture change (as expected) the most fraught.

Leaders need estimates such as this before attempting something like culture change: Do we expect to do better than the average 19 percent success rate? Why? If I may add to that number anecdotally, I often say that if I had $100 dollars for every time someone said "we have to change the culture" and I had to give back $10,000 every time I saw culture change succeed, I would be well ahead.

---

[6] Smith, M. E. (2002). Success rates for different types of organizational change. *Performance Improvement, 41*(1), 26.

Does Failure Always Mean the Same Thing?

Research including types of change takes us a bit further, but not far enough. What matters even more is the type of change failure. A complete business busting write-off is different than a 25 percent overrun. The lack of definitional rigor of most change surveys produces an average that includes tolerable delays (by the standards of organizational change) and those complete write-offs.

If some executives interviewed for the surveys use the word *failure* to signify "failed to deliver 100 percent of expected benefits," or "overran budget and timetable," and others use *failure* to signify "abandoned project halfway and wrote off entire project expenditure with no positive and many negative results," then even the average estimates from Smith's research conceal some important facts. To get to a more useful statistic, we need a better definition of *failure* and an analysis of outcomes by kind of failure, perhaps using a rough framework such as SOCKS (Shortfalls, Overruns, Consequences, Killed, Sustainable), shown in Table 1.2.

Table 1.2 SOCKS Taxonomy of Project Failures

SOCKS CATEGORY	EXAMPLE[1]	RESEARCH
Benefit **SHORTFALLS**: The project completes, but there are important shortfalls in benefits delivery causing disruption of business processes.	Hershey's **ERP** supply chain system causes $100 million revenue dip.	Little data is available on the average benefit shortfalls by type of change or type of business.
Cost **OVERRUNS**:[2] The project completes, but there are significant overruns (cost or time).	Boston's "Big Dig" overruns by $12 billion.	Average cost overruns are 27% with one in six more than 200%.[3]
Unintended **CONSEQUENCES**: The project completes, but there are costly, unintended consequences.	Fox Meyer Drug $65 million ERP system bankrupts the company. Scott Paper successfully cuts costs, earnings spike, but long-term competitiveness collapses.	Little aggregate data is available on adverse consequences, either the number of projects affected or the type and extent of consequences.
KILLED programs: The project is killed after significant investment.	Denver Airport baggage system first delayed airport opening by 18 months, but was then scrapped at a rough cost of $3 billion.	Little data is available on the number of projects killed and written off completely.
Lack of **SUSTAINABLE** results: Results are delivered, but are not sustained over time.	Following BP's Texas City refinery disaster a new focus on health and safety behaviors brought about short-term gains that eroded as memory of the event faded.[4]	Little data is available on how many projects have benefits that erode over time.

[1] Why projects fail blog. Goatham, R. (Ed.). Retrieved from http://calleam.com/WTPF/.
[2] There is a strong relationship between overruns and benefits delivery. If a system will save $1 million per month, delays extend costs and alter benefit timing.
[3] Based on research we will revisit in Chapter 3, "Governance and the Psychology of Risk," from Professor Bent Flyvbjerg of Oxford.
[4] Based on the findings of Baker, J.A., et al. (2007, January). The report of the BP U.S. refineries independent safety review panel. Retrieved from http://www.csb.gov/assets/1/19/Baker_panel_report1.pdf.

This SOCKS categorization is not a scientific categorization because terms such as *consequences* and *sustainability* can mean a lot of things, but it is considerably better than just talking about "failure." It is a place to start, and every project should have a SOCKS review once completed (or not) using early budgeted costs and benefits as a baseline. This way, businesses can develop internal analytics on how projects fare and how they fail to meet expectations in ways that are useful for capital budgeting. They may be able to draw conclusions such as "When we attempt reorganizations, we exceed budget by an average of 30 percent, and there are often many negative, unintended consequences," or "When we have acquired a new company, the financial returns were, on average, 25 percent less than we had predicted."

As you will see throughout this book, when it comes to measuring change implementation performance, science is lacking, and practitioners are very slow to challenge orthodoxy or urban legends such as the 70 percent statistic. We need much better answers to questions such as: What types of change are riskiest? How much more risky is big budget change than small change? What factors increase/decrease risk? Does performance vary across business regions or functions?

Change Masters and Change-Agility

Even with better statistics on failure rates for types of change (culture change versus IT system implementation), and types of failure (write-offs versus delays), businesses need to go one step further. They need hard, empirical data on their own change performance. IBM, in *Making Change Work*,[7] found enormous variation in change success between organizations that know what they are doing and those that stumble around.

The IBM survey identified a cohort of "Change Master" companies, who claimed an 80 percent success rate for change (almost double the average in the survey) and much better than "Change

---

[7] Jorgensen, H., Owen, L., & Neus, A. (2013). *Making change work*. IBM Future of Enterprise.

Novices" who managed a miserable 8 percent success rate. The next chapters explore some of the facets of these change-agile businesses.

A leader in this is Cisco Systems who, late in the last century, was acquiring one company per quarter. Cisco started to study merger success factors both in the market, generally, and also specifically which factors affected *their* success and failure. They found that mergers of similar-sized firms fail more often, as do mergers where geographical distance is a factor, as do mergers where cultural dissimilarities are pronounced. Although this sort of analysis is observational (only producing correlation, not cause), it nevertheless is a step toward understanding *specific factors* related to a *specific kind of change*, in a *specific business.*[8]

Failed Metaphors—The Fantasy of the Static Organization

Heraclitus, the pre-Socratic Greek philosopher, intoned, "Everything changes and nothing remains still... and... you cannot step twice into the same stream." It is not just a metaphysical truth; it is a practical one for today's businesses. Today's organizations are less static than ever before; staff come and go faster due to shrinking job tenure and the end of "job for life" careers; much speedier information flows have demanded increased reaction times; local businesses have become less local, buffeted by events in faraway lands (for example, car dealers in Kansas affected by the Fukushima Daiichi nuclear disaster).

The kind of change covered by change surveys is called programmatic change, the big CRM system, or the rollout of the new HR policy. In the last section, we saw that about half of programmatic change fails in some respect; what we did not yet consider was how much change that might be! Consider this observation from 2012 while teaching at the University of Wisconsin.

---

[8] From the superb book by Pfeffer and Sutton, *Hard Facts, Dangerous Half-Truths, and Total Nonsense, Profiting from Evidence-based Management* (Harvard Business Review Press, 2006).

If ever a group of businesspeople represented Middle American business, this was it—25 middle-aged managers, from ranks of middle management, of middle-American, medium-sized companies. The middle of the middle of the middle of the middle. What does change look like away from the headline-grabbing failures and $100 million IT projects, smack in the middle of the business world? Our first task of the day was for the managers in attendance to list the change projects running in their companies. After 15 minutes, the whistle blew, and we counted: 585! Each company represented was running an average of more than twenty. The managers were then to "star" the projects in which they were involved: Those 25 managers were involved in 214 projects. These middle-American managers were under constant pressure from the day-to-day business of change—*there was very little that was stable.*

Another kind of change is even more prevalent than programmatic change, and that is continuous, nonprogrammatic change. These managers were affected by centrally driven, big programs as well as programs they initiated themselves (such as a departmental reorganization). They also were expected to continuously improve performance, help staff grow, make their processes more efficient, build new relationships, network, hire new people, and much more. Then, to add another layer of change, they were affected by change in other departments/divisions—what I call *change backwash.* A big change program in HR stretches HR's capacity to serve the business. These managers' experience at work was more or less constant change and its effects, constant pressure, and constant turmoil. The manager who "just keeps things running smoothly and doesn't have to worry about change" is a fantasy, perhaps from a bygone era, but certainly not today. This also casts doubt upon the standard notion that *management* is about efficient running of the status quo and *leadership* is about change.[9]

---

[9] This distinction is from two of the most eminent of leadership theorists, Bennis and Drucker. They are so well regarded that their definitions of leadership and management have essentially never been questioned. In my view, we need to think critically about pat assertions such as this, however impressive their sources might be.

The underlying paradigm, upon which almost all change models rest, is that change is episodic, a disruption to an otherwise static business. I cautiously predict the next decade will hasten the demise (a demise that has been predicted for some time) of the notion of a business as a mechanistic, static entity, with rigid structures, and punctuated by episodic major change. This old paradigm can be seen in two additional canonical (and I think highly inaccurate) change metaphors, Business as Usual (BAU) and the oldest change model, unfreeze, change, refreeze.[10] The first of those metaphors suggests that there are things that are changing and things that are stable. The second of those implies that organizations are stable, and then you have to "unfreeze" them. There is no "frozen" in today's businesses.

The above metaphors and models are sacred territory—rarely are they challenged. From a scientific point of view, metaphors are neither true, nor false—they are either helpful, leading us to consider things in a better light, or unhelpful. BAU, unfreezing, and "management is about efficient running of the *status quo*" are, I think, not just unhelpful, but harmful in three ways:

1. **Management education**—In the way we train managers today, we do not equip them to manage change continuously. As we discuss more fully later, change management is thought of as a specific, discrete set of skills tucked away in a corner of a traditional MBA, or saved for later in management development programs.

2. **The role of the manager and the change specialist**—Managing change is not a small subset of management and leadership; it may be *the majority* of management and leadership—and even if only 20 percent of a manager's role, it may be 80 percent of her headaches. Change is every manager's job every day. Managing change is too important to be outsourced to specialists.

3. **Manager mindset and cognitive dissonance**—Teaching people that change is a disturbance to a stable status quo means that they compare their experience with that nonexistent

---

[10] From Kurt Lewin, a brilliant, pioneer social psychologist and change theorist from the 1940s.

ideal. Change frustrations arise because the world ought to conform to that ideal: stable and predictable. This leads to the widespread (and false) conviction that change must always be difficult.

The amount of change managers deal with, the high failure rates of programmatic change, and the constant challenges of continuous change suggest that that failed (or failing) change is the single largest preventable cost to business. Now we should ask why.

The Change Problem as a People Problem

"'If it weren't for the people, the god-damn people,' said Finnerty, 'always getting tangled up in the machinery. If it weren't for them, the world would be an engineer's paradise.'"

—Kurt Vonnegut, *Player Piano*

One unhelpful, yet commonplace, way of looking at change is as either a technical problem or a people problem: "hard stuff" or "soft stuff." People problems involve engagement, culture, resistance, communication, morale, involvement, skills, attitudes, behaviors, and so forth. Technical problems, on the other hand, involve budgets, planning, quality, risk, controls, change processes, system/user requirements, or other challenges of a technical nature (such as how to integrate two CRM systems during a merger). The insight that belies the false hard stuff/soft stuff dualism is this: The technical dimensions of a change, strategy, tactics, planning, risk management, and design of new processes and structures *become people problems* because people have to solve them. For example, a massive systems project was four months behind schedule because of a *technical* programing issue. Our change team found that this was caused by a shortage of internal C++ programmers with the right skills. The issue then became a *people* issue that found its way to HR (recruitment). Then we found that HR could not simply hire more programmers because it didn't have the budget, or the clout. The problem was weak *HR leadership*. The program delay was eventually (after months) escalated to *executive leadership,* who were irked that the $120 million program was delayed because of inability to hire a few people at 60 bucks an hour. Yet the program governance structure did not permit the program director to easily push such issues up the chain of command. The problem of getting some C++ code written was, in fact, a leadership and governance problem at multiple levels.

The soft/hard (or technical/people) dichotomy has its roots in the canonical writings on organizations in the 1950s. Businesses, of course, are not really hard or soft, but most people see this metaphor as a natural, intuitive, and practical way of looking at the world. The metaphor lives on, like so much in management, unchallenged, as if it were Truth. I am not so sure. The split engenders entirely the wrong kind of thinking about the capabilities needed to implement change. The split leads to people issues (the soft stuff) often being thought of as separate or peripheral from the main objective (getting the "real" change implemented). Indeed, even the word *soft* seems to diminish its importance.

This split often causes the people side of big programs to be undervalued and the change experts to become necessary evils (which would be unnecessary if Finnerty's "god-damn people" did not cause so much trouble). For example, British Petroleum's (BP) Global Head of HR said of the change management plan of a $100 million project, "I certainly do not want my people sitting in bean-bag chairs, next to lava lamps, talking about how they feel during this project." Accenture technical consultants had a nickname for change management experts: "chicks making slides," a stunning, one two combination of ignorance and sexism. When I became a "change guy," more than one PwC colleague challenged my sexual orientation. The soft, in business, is associated with the feminine, and the feminine is still regularly discounted. Sexism is alive and kicking in the twenty-first century, and it affects how both women and people issues (HR) are seen and heard in the workplace, which is a much bigger issue than just change. One IBM partner, who runs billion-dollar projects, described it this way: "When budgets get tight, the first thing to get cut is change management, the second thing is user skills-training, and the third is the program management office." If it is true that the most difficult aspect of change is the people side, then it seems self-defeating that change is the most quickly slashed part of program budgets.

As alluded to earlier, this devaluing of the people side of change is also found in business school curricula. A two-year Harvard MBA has no leading or managing change in its required, core curriculum of about 15 subjects. Managing change is 1 of about 100 electives (although there are one or two that are change-related). The Europeans do no better. INSEAD's MBA also has zero change leadership/management electives, and ostensibly squeezes what leaders need to know about change into their core Organization Behavior (OB) module. It is not a stretch to say that graduates from top business schools emerge with little or no change management theory and (because the courses are theoretical) zero change management experience. If we accept that juggling multiple change programs is part of every manager's job, and that leading major change most severely tests executive mettle, then the content and structure of business education may be part of the change problem.

In summary, technical problems (such as technology, systems, and processes), project problems (such as governance and planning), and people issues (such as stakeholders, engagement, and culture) are all leadership issues. How we educate business leaders in change and how we think about change (technical versus people, soft versus hard) seem to be at fault.

Change Myths

Education in leading change is lacking in standard curricula, but in addition, much of what is taught (canonically) in change leadership programs is untrue—based on dated research, urban myth, or folklore. Study the following list closely. How many of these change myths were you taught, still believe, or ring true? These 20 change myths are merely a sample of misconceptions about change that twenty-first-century science has exposed. Upcoming chapters cover each of these in detail. The specific chapters that deal with these myths are listed in parentheses:

- You need a burning platform to drive change: Negative emotions motivate. (2, 7)
- Trusting your gut is a reliable decision-making strategy. (5)

- Rewards are at least necessary motivators and are sometimes sufficient. Behavioral change involves the right mixture of carrots and sticks. (7)
- Consultant-experts provide an objective analysis of business problems. (5)
- Benchmarking tells us what good performance looks like and fast followership is an effective strategy. (2)
- When stakeholders dissent about a complex problem, bringing experts in to talk to them is essential. (8)
- People know what they want, and will act rationally in pursuit of it. (5)
- There is a natural, inevitable division between people who decide and people who do. (8)
- A concrete budget and delivery plan, from which little deviation is permitted, are essential. (2)
- Changing habits is about having a big goal to get you motivated. (6)
- Giving people more information will alter their point of view. (7)
- In times of complexity and chaos, the best solution template comes from prior experience. (4)
- Change provokes an emotional response that follows the grief model—denial, anger, bargaining, depression, and acceptance. (8)
- Worst case estimates accurately assess the downside risk of particular strategies. (3)
- If you change hearts and minds, behavior follows along. (7)
- Brainstorming (going for quantity of ideas first) is the best way to generate high-quality new ideas. (5)
- Increasing worker engagement increases productivity and profitability. (9)
- Involving many people slows progress. (8)
- If a program goes badly, it is very important to quickly "get back on the change horse." (5)
- When things get difficult, people become more cautious. (3)

Everybody Is an Expert on People Issues— Or Are They?

The change expert has to get his expertise recognized by people who reckon they are "pretty good with people," except everybody reckons they are pretty good with people. As you will see in Chapter 6, "Misunderstanding Human Behavior," it is in this arena that people have the biggest gap between their confidence and their competence.

Change experts can be wet blankets. We make projects more socially complex, raise stakeholder risks, recommend involvement (usually), challenge cultural norms, and require resources and senior leadership time to address those risks. We advocate time-consuming engagement up front: "It is doubtful that engineering will accept that quality control process without extensive involvement in its design." We have to challenge leaders personally: "Your personal style is effective in many situations, but it will be a liability in this one." When we give reasons for things, those reasons are couched in psychological/ sociological language that does not always play with project leaders and budget holders schooled in finance. (What executive under pressure wants to hear, "People may feel threatened and defensive," or "This may conflict with their cultural preferences and preferred communication style"?)

In today's businesses, with change expertise only in the hands of specialists, and top-down change the norm, it is an error to assume people will play nicely. The change expert throws cold water on that convenient error, introducing the near certainty of resistance to change. In Chapter 2, "From Change Fragility to Change-Agility," I speculate that certain business cultures (with the right mindsets, structures, and processes) could make this kind of change resistance a thing of the past.

Putting the Change Manager Out of Work

This makes the expert's job tough. More important, it suggests something hinted at earlier: Change expertise is too important to be left to specialists.

On major projects, change people are called in to sprinkle change pixie dust and make people problems go away. Their efforts are directed at persuading, involving, and communicating in order to align people with the change. However, this is a bizarre circumstance, for is it not the manager's job to persuade, involve, and communicate? Are not change managers, and their tools, a Band-Aid to cover up managerial insufficiency? (In the same way, consultants are sometimes called in to do jobs that more capable teams might well accomplish on their own.) This specialist discipline, practiced by experts (often internal or external consultants), is used to provide tools, models, and expertise that (mostly) ought to be part of every manager's day job.

Imagine an organization filled with leaders at every level who excelled at aligning staff with change strategy. Key change programs become priorities for them; they work hard at understanding the big picture, handle conflict assertively yet gracefully, motivate and align staff, communicate with affected stakeholders (for example, customers), skillfully facilitate cross-functional or cross-cultural teams, facilitate strategy development and planning, and challenge recalcitrant behavior. Would we, if such superstar skills existed throughout the business, need change management?[11] Winning hearts and minds and changing behaviors is the job of leadership; therefore, to some extent, change management is used to shore up shortfalls in leadership and to bring skills that are far distant from business education.

From Change Management to Change Leadership

Following that line of reasoning, I believe that it is time to euthanize change management as we now think about it, and replace it with change-agile organizations and change-capable leaders at every

---

[11] Yes, these activities must be organized, but the change facilitator who parachutes into recalcitrant groups would be unemployed. Most of what I have been asked to do is put the pieces back together of a change program that has fallen apart because of poor leadership or insufficient attention to change issues at the outset. Of course, there will still be high-stakes, critical conflict resolution, strategy formulation and alignment, communication strategy development, and organization design efforts that require deep specialist expertise.

level. There will still be a need for change management skills and knowledge, but those will be widespread, and not concentrated in a few hands.

Table 1.3 proposes some principal differences between change management and change leadership (though there is more overlap than the split suggests).

Table 1.3 Change Leadership Versus Change Management

CHANGE LEADERSHIP	CHANGE MANAGEMENT
There must be an internal leader; this cannot be outsourced to consultants.	Change management teams are often external consultant-experts, especially on big projects.
Engaging with change and leading change is what I do every day, constantly.	Engaging people with change is done through "set-pieces," workshops, "town halls," coaching, and communication.
The main foci are change strategy and building change-agility (removing the need for rearguard change fire-fighting).	The primary focus is change tactics and, more rarely developing change-agility.
"Being" is important (hard to reduce leadership to tasks): day-to-day engagement, inspiration, and challenge ("the happy warrior" metaphor) are key.	Change management is largely process, event, and tool based.
There is a proactive focus on building local change-agility and on business-wide issues.	Change management is often reactive and more narrowly focused.
Modeling leadership behaviors and personal change is critical.	Change manager behavior has less symbolic meaning, and is less important than the behavior of key sponsors.
The critical role is before and during launch (and throughout, but uniquely before).	The critical role is from launch onward (and generally this is a mistake).

Change Leadership and the Human Sciences

"Of all the subjects which he might undertake to formally study, none is more important for the businessman-to-be than human behavior."

—Wallace Donham, 2nd Dean of Harvard Business School, 1919–1942

Some of the change leadership skills required by local leaders are attracting resources, resolving conflicts, streamlining decision making, negotiating, influencing, coaching, removing obstacles, handling risks, motivating people to solve problems, and establishing the right governance structure. Those skills depend on theories of what makes people tick and how they respond in various situations.

The Science of Successful Organizational Change looks at the assumptions and understanding of human behavior that lie behind those skills. Influencing skills, for example, depend upon assumptions about motivation, communication, social factors, power and resistance, how information is processed, what changes beliefs, and how beliefs change behavior. For example, if the underlying fabric of assumptions is flawed, the influencing skills (as recommended by hundreds of books) will be less effective.

Much contemporary understanding of human behavior in business comes to us through the discipline of psychology (and sister field, social psychology). However, human behavior is much more complex than any single field can explain, describe, or predict. Consider the raft of tools used by HR: personality types, psychometric assessments, engagement surveys, emotional intelligence, communications skills, motivational concepts, happiness/satisfaction, trait and behavioral models of leadership, coaching, self-esteem, learning style, and theories. All are based on psychology, and are somewhat useful when used correctly. As you'll see in Chapter 6, "Misunderstanding Human Behavior," the psychology on which they are based is a narrow, young field, whose status as a science is mixed.

Many interesting insights come from the intersection of psychology and other disciplines, such as economics. From just the nexus of psychology and economics, we get economic behavior, decision-science, incentives, predictive rationality, heuristics, cognitive biases, and other insights not always found in traditional psychology texts (nor, may I suggest, in the toolkit of most organizational change consultants). The business leader and change consultant with only psychological insight at her disposal is playing golf with a single club in her bag.

This book promises a science-based treatment of change leadership that takes the newest ideas in psychology but also introduces concepts from other human sciences. The word cloud in Figure 1.1 illustrates just how rich this area is and the sorts of ideas soon to be discussed.

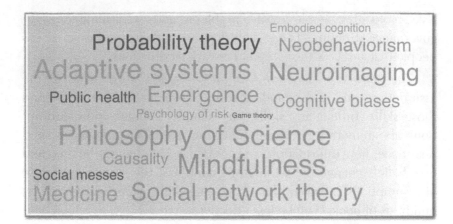

Figure 1.1 Human sciences with essential perspectives on change leadership.

Some of these subjects, such as neuroscience, are already much discussed in the change leadership world. As I will show, neuroscience does not quite measure up in usefulness compared to the amount of media attention that it receives. Other terms, such as complexity and emergence, are thrown around but are very much misused, and I will clarify what they really mean and offer some tools for working with them. Other areas, such as evidence-based medicine, the psychology of risk, and neobehaviorism are relatively underrepresented relative to their usefulness.

Conclusion

The headline "change failures" grabs attention, but change is a substantial portion of what management does today. Businesses need robust data on their (SOCKS) performance to understand realistically where they fall on the Change Master–Change Novice scale. The idea that organizations are static, and that change is episodic, is harmful, and it means that change skills are greatly undertaught in the business community. The soft-hard split between people issues and "real" issues is harmful, and even this language suggests the people stuff is less important.

We should euthanize change management: If we had great, inspiring, change leadership skills through the management pool, there would be much less need for tactical change management.

The world is not ready for that because change management (and related subjects) is just a tiny portion of traditional management education, not reflecting the reality that most of a manager's role today is change-related. While management education remains inadequate in this regard, change management will still be required to cover up the insufficiency.

The next chapter looks at how the world today might be different and how some leading businesses face up to the challenge of change-agility.

Part I
Change-Agility

"An organization's ability to learn, and translate that learning into action rapidly, is the ultimate competitive advantage."

—Jack Welch

The VUCA World and Change Strategy

Around 1990, U.S. military strategists began to use the expression VUCA (Volatility, Uncertainty, Complexity, and Ambiguity) to describe the context for their strategic thinking. Looking back on the first 15 years of the twenty-first century, it is easy to see how VUCA might be an apt description. There were spectacular successes, such as Twitter, Apple, Facebook, Google, Amazon, and YouTube; transformation in the media and entertainment sphere; and the rise in prominence and power of BRIC countries. There were also spectacular corporate failures, such as Lehman Brothers, Enron, AOL-Time Warner, WorldCom, and nearly General Motors; the dot-com collapse and the Great Recession of 2007; bailouts of U.S. corporations and Southern European countries; appalling natural and humanitarian disasters, such as the Fukushima Daiichi nuclear disaster, Hurricane Katrina, the 2010 Haiti earthquake, and the 2004 Indian Ocean tsunami; and the Deepwater Horizon explosion, SARS, and Arab Spring.

It certainly seems that we live in VUCA times, but every generation thinks its epoch unique, perhaps due to the *availability bias,* overweighting what is in front of us, which is covered in more detail in Chapter 5, "Cognitive Biases and Failed Strategies." It is not easy to compare epochs, but we are probably not as special as we think: The first few decades of the twentieth century saw the Spanish flu; World War I; the Titanic; and breakthroughs such as flight, movies, radio, the theory of relativity, and the Model T.

What *is* special about our time is information speed and volume. Although matter, such as a tanker full of oil, moves at roughly the same speed as it did a century ago (in order of magnitude), information moves hundreds of millions of times faster—from days to microseconds. Data storage technology means the U.S. Library of Congress (about 10 terabytes) can be put into a device the size of a toaster. Information flows, as well as the movement of people and goods, have increased connectivity, so that "domino chains" of events are more intricate and longer.

Part of thinking about how VUCA changes the business context involves thinking about the effect of that volume and speed of information on how much and how fast businesses need to change, but it also means that strategies can become obsolete before they are even realized. Entrepreneur Luis van Ahn, known for crowdsourcing, reCAPTCHA, and Duolingo, claims his biggest error was investing heavily in a Web-based product when apps on mobile devices were quickly making those "traditional" channels irrelevant. One sign of the times is that we can talk about Web-based/Internet-based business models as obsolete when many of those are much less than two decades old!

When there is a mismatch between the pace of external change and the pace at which an organization can innovate or adapt, the business is always playing catch-up, always being disrupted rather than doing the disrupting, and its long-term viability is at risk. Many businesses have felt this tectonic crunch, including one-time market leaders, such as Nokia and Research in Motion, and once-successful retailers, such as Borders and Sears. Yet some businesses do the disrupting, forcing their competitors to adapt. IBM used to make industrial time recorders and meat slicers, then cash registers, typewriters, and card punches, then digital mainframes, then personal computers, then supercomputers, and now nanotechnology, solar technology, smart cities, smart grids, cognitive systems, Big Data, and much more. In its 130-year history, there have been a few times when IBM has been on the ropes, but for the most part, it is a leader in the turbulent of technological and competitive environments.

The concept of *change-agility* captures the spirit of what businesses need to do to prosper in a VUCA environment. While "agile" is in everyday use in the project-management context, the concept merits exploration on a business scale, and not just a project scale. Unlike other unhelpful change ideas—such as "unfreezing," "burning platforms," and "carrots and sticks"—I believe change-agility better captures the reality of today's businesses and will prove useful as an ideal at which business can aim.

Change-agile organizations have the following characteristics:

- The business structure is more like a portfolio of change programs with a smaller, supporting core (rather than a large core, with episodic change projects).

- Change readiness and change capability are differentiating competitive advantages, and this is reflected in HR structures, particularly in learning and development.

- Businesses are "antifragile," i.e. strengthened—not traumatized—by major change, that is, businesses are not change-fatigued or change-overloaded.

- Businesses have a dynamic flow of knowledge, ideas, problem solving, initiative, and innovation—including more bottom-up, and not just top-down change.

- Businesses are operationally adaptable and strategically nimble—doing the disrupting rather than being disrupted.

- Resistance (on today's scale) is largely a legacy of the past because leadership, structures, processes, and skills for engagement are widespread.

As foreshadowed in Chapter 1, "Failed Change: The Greatest Preventable Cost to Business?," the contention is that an organization with those change-agile characteristics will need many fewer professional change managers. There will be fewer "change fires" to put out with change tactics. Those skills will still be vital for business prosperity, and they will be more in demand than before, but they will be provided by rank-and-file leaders, rather than by specialists intervening in "set pieces."

Table I.1 suggests some of the shift required from the change management paradigm to the change-agile paradigm.

Table I.1 From Change Management to Change-Agility

CHANGE MANAGEMENT PARADIGM	CHANGE-AGILE PARADIGM
Leaders lead change initiatives.	Leaders create change-agile organizations, a context within which change happens with greater fluidity.
There is limited, or overstretched, change capacity; the business is underprepared for major change.	There is ample change capacity and a state of constant change readiness.
Change is episodic.	It is all change, always...
Business is highly structured but punctuated by major change.	Structures are more dynamic and the business can be viewed as a portfolio of change, supported by core business functions.
Employees are resistant to change; the organization's change mindset corresponds to "grief models" (denial, anger, bargaining, depression, acceptance).	Employees have the attitude of "Change is why I love to come to work..."
Specialist change managers are assigned to projects.	Change management is too important to be left to specialists.
Project planning is more static, and less adaptive. Implementations are "big bang."	Business plans include iteration, experiments, pilots, and prototypes.
Business change is top-down, centrally planned, and centrally driven.	Some business change is driven by grassroots hacktivists and bottom-up innovation.

It's possible that the single, biggest answer to change failure is the creation of change-agile organizations, hence its early position in this book. The following single chapter on change-agility—Chapter 2, "From Change Fragility to Change-Agility"—sketches out a few concepts that, at this stage of thinking about change-agility, seem most relevant. The evidence in this chapter is much more anecdotal and much less scientific than in other chapters because agility is a newer idea and happens on a scale where controlled experiments are hard to do.

2

From Change Fragility to Change-Agility

"Wind extinguishes a candle and energizes fire. You want to be the fire and wish for the wind."

—Nassim Taleb

One of the most radical thinkers of our era is the iconoclastic Nassim Taleb, some of whose ideas you'll read about in the next chapter, who through applied mathematics and statistics has made a surprising contribution to understanding how structures—including business structures—respond to volatility and uncertainty. Into the tidy world of statisticians, prognosticators, economists, stock analysts, marketing professionals, futurists, and data scientists has walked Taleb the Usurper who, if you believe his bark, would fire them all.

Taleb coined the term *antifragile,* which became the title of his fourth book. In that book, he gives examples of systems that *gain from disorder,* that is, that profit from uncertainty. His premise is that in business (and in economics, in nation-states, and in life), we struggle earnestly to make the world predictable, or at least to make it resilient or robust in the face of randomness. In doing so, we shoot ourselves in the foot, making it more fragile.

What if, asks Taleb, our structures prospered and strengthened when under stress? What if there were a science of decision making not so reliant on prediction in an unpredictable world? The project is not complete, but Taleb categorizes structures according to those abilities: *fragile, robust,* and *antifragile.*

You can easily imagine *fragile* business models that are like champagne glasses, prone to crack and break under modest stress, start-ups with limited capital, and highly leveraged banks. *Robust* business strategies can include diversification, so that a single stressor can never break the bank, or sound portfolio and financial management to weather market downturns. (Nevertheless, notice here how overly conservative business strategies—that is change averse, reluctant to experiment and take risks—are also fragile because they are vulnerable to disruption.) *Antifragile* structures do not just survive—they *prosper* under stresses. We may have a sense of how personal mishaps have made us more capable and emotionally resilient, how breaking down muscle tissue by weight lifting makes muscles bigger and stronger, how some damage to an ecosystem can help the system flourish, and how vaccination (a low dose of a virus) strengthens the immune system.

Taleb does not offer individual business examples with these antifragile (much stronger than robust) properties, but Silicon Valley is an example of an antifragile business ecosystem. Nearing its 75th anniversary, Silicon Valley attracts one third of all U.S. venture capital funds, and hosts Intel, AMD, Google, Pixar, Facebook, HP, Oracle, Cisco, Symantec, and eBay (and thousands of smaller enterprises). However, the technology industry has been subjected to *more* disruptive influences than any other since 1940 (it began with vacuum tubes and radios, nearly 20 years before electronic calculators and 40 years before the personal computer). Yet the region surfs these disruptive threats and (seemingly) becomes stronger each decade (despite the extraordinary costs of office and residential space). Contrast this with the textile or auto industry "valleys," which were concentrated in the Northeast and Detroit, or perhaps the world of print media today.

Of course, much ink has been spilled on establishing a narrative for Silicon Valley's success, but antifragility is a new way of looking at the business ecosystem and seems a plausible interpretation. Can businesses be structured in antifragile ways? What follows are some early ideas and experimental practices from some successful businesses.

The Systemic Change Model

Any radical transformation, from change-fragile organizations to change-agile ones, requires a holistic approach to change, one that reflects the structure and dynamics of complex systems. The systemic change model, shown in Figure 2.1, illustrates those elements. The greatest weakness of much writing on agility is that it focuses on just one element, but each element provides a partial understanding of agile system performance. The complex system can be understood only when regarded as a whole. The system output depends on progress across all four quadrants, and is limited by the weakest link. If you want to change strategy, then behaviors, culture, and mindset must support that change or regress is inevitable. To try to change culture without changing structures, mindset, or behaviors will similarly fail. Each element of the system depends on each other element, and the system performance cannot be understood by reductionist thinking or be changed by changing just one element.[1]

Figure 2.1 Systemic change model.

---

[1] There are other useful organizational performance models such as McKinsey's 7S, the Burke-Litwin model, and the EFQM (European Foundation for Quality Management) model. I think this model better captures which features are subjective, which are measurable, and the emergence of group properties from more basic, individual units.

The insight that businesses are complex systems that only change as fast as the weakest link is not radically new; it is, however, radically ignored. The examples throughout this book—such as trying to change structure without changing processes, changing reward without changing management behavior, or changing IT systems without considering users or culture—show specifically how that has failed.

While the last thing the change world needs is a new four-box model, this one is extremely useful and has been used for culture change, large-scale IT implementations, and in leadership development.[2] Here, we use it to summarize four elements of change-agility and show their interdependencies: agile people, culture, structures, and processes. The treatment of each area is much abbreviated—this is a canter through each of the various elements. Just the topic of agile people merits a book in its own right—harvesting not just what is written about agility but earlier research on related topics that did not use the name (for example, flexibility, resilience, creativity, and so on).

Business theorists are often accused of "putting old wine in new bottles"—that is, re-invigorating old concepts with a new word. "Agility" may be such a villain, and I may be her accomplice. I think the term gets business leaders (in a VUCA world) thinking along different lines, and if the concept proves a useful way to think about twenty-first century businesses, then there is much more work to be done to harness the best earlier ideas under the newer agile rubric!

Agile People

"In times of change, learners inherit the earth, while the learned find themselves beautifully equipped to deal with a world that no longer exists."
—Eric Hoffer

---

[2] I developed this in 1999 to help explain why culture change often failed and have used it extensively since as a simple way to help businesses understand the holistic nature of change.

A key part of change-agility means agile people will have the right *agile mindset*. John Kotter (of Harvard Business School) describes this sort of mindset as a "get-to" rather than a "have-to" orientation. The agile mindset includes concepts such as resilience, that is rising above bumps in the road and returning to one's best in the face of hardship. The mindset also includes a "plays well with others"; a "we" rather than "me" orientation; and an ability to build trust quickly, to work on diverse teams, and to rise above interpersonal frictions to focus on the big picture. Finally, the notion suggests an attitude toward learning and self-development that reskills rapidly: what I call a "grower and not a knower."

Those general, intuitive ideas about agile people are supported by two recent research paths that give us specific, measurable ways to look at the agile mindset that have implications for recruitment and development.

Growth Mindsets

For most of psychology's history, it has used static measurements (intelligence, personality) that describe capabilities that are stable (or fixed). From this point of view, you either "have the right stuff" or you do not. Newer ideas suggest that static measures of personality (general intelligence or personality inventories) are an incomplete answer. We should also be interested in the slope of the curve, how fast a person can grow and change, and not just how they are now.

Professor Carol Dweck, of Stanford, has proposed that there are two belief systems related to this fluid view of capability and that determine long-term performance and learning: the fixed mindset and the *growth mindset* depicted in Figure 2.2.

Dweck's central idea is descriptive, that intelligence and personality are fluid, and also prescriptive, that some mindsets are more productive and psychologically healthy. She describes the fixed mindset this way: "Every situation calls for confirmation of intelligence, personality, and character...."[3] That is, we view the range of performance

---

[3] Dweck, C. (2006). *Mindset: The new psychology of success*. New York: Random House, p. 8.

available to us as fixed. Then, Dweck says, the fixed mindset type tries to prove itself right—looking for confirming evidence of our talent or not trying when we lack talent. For this reason, the fixed mindset responds poorly to challenge and setbacks because if success or failure results from a fixed talent, there is little more to do.

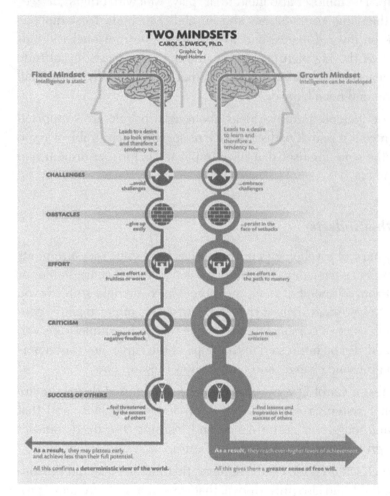

Figure 2.2 Growth versus fixed mindset (from Nigel Holmes, with permission).

The fixed mindset is evident culturally, in the way we talk about children, how we educate them, and how we think about success and failure in life. People such as Stephen Hawking ("genius"), Steve Jobs ("maverick"), or Warren Buffet ("Wizard of Omaha") are seen as "gifted," rather than the product of some talent, but mostly effort, resilience in the face of setbacks, and an attitude toward continuous learning. In parenting and education, Dweck says, "Emphasizing effort gives a child a variable that they can control. They come to see themselves as in control of their success. Emphasizing natural intelligence takes it out of the child's control, and it provides no good recipe for responding to a failure."[4] Dweck's fixed versus growth mindset has wide business and societal implications for how we think about talent and how and what we reward, coach, and recruit in business.

She suggests four steps to shift a fixed mindset, shown in Table 2.1. As with all personal change, this requires a level of awareness—an ability to catch yourself in automatic patterns of thought that hinder performance.

Table 2.1 Carol Dweck's Steps to Self-Coach Yourself from a Fixed Mindset

SELF-COACHING STEP	EXAMPLE
Learn to hear your fixed mindset "voice."	"This is too difficult."
	"I've been doing this for ten years; I've got it nailed."
Recognize you have a choice.	Realize that beliefs are habitual and not always right, and predetermine if you will succeed or learn.
Challenge that fixed "voice."	"You have mastered more difficult situations than this one by taking one step at a time."
	"There is always more to learn."
Choose the growth mindset action.	Grab the challenge with both hands, taking baby steps if you have to.

Our second "agile people" concept is *learning agility,* the ability and willingness to learn from experience and subsequently apply those lessons to perform optimally in new or first-time situations.

---

[4] Ibid, p. 14.

Learning Agility

Talent consulting firm Korn Ferry's survey-style research suggests that learning agility is related to selection as a "high potential," to career flexibility, and to career advancement.[5] The firm suggests that learning agility has five dimensions, as shown in Table 2.2.

Table 2.2 Dimensions of Learning Agility (from Korn Ferry)

DIMENSIONS OF LEARNING AGILITY	DESCRIPTION
Mental agility	Thinking critically to penetrate complex problems and expanding possibilities by making fresh connections
People agility	Understanding and relating to other people as well as tough situations to harness and multiply collective performance
Change agility	Enjoying experimentation, being curious, and effectively dealing with the discomfort of change
Results agility	Delivering results in first-time situations by inspiring teams, and exhibiting a presence that builds confidence in themselves and others
Self-awareness	Being reflective and knowing themselves well; understanding their capabilities and their impact on others

The important idea here is that organizations reward experience, but not everybody learns equally from experience. An executive with a 25-year track record may have learned a great deal from each experience (especially setbacks), or very little, justifying such setbacks by blaming others or circumstances. You cannot assume that just because someone is senior, they are any good. Now we can move beyond using experience as a proxy for ability, and assess ability *and* the slope, or growth potential, of that ability. Using the growth mindset and learning agility concepts is, I believe, part of a shift to a more dynamic view of personality, and a very intriguing way of looking at talent.

Few people would dispute that the growth mindset, or learning agility, looks valuable. How do you build a workforce with more of these growers, not knowers?

---

[5] Dai, G., De Meuse, K., & Tang, K. (2013). The role of learning agility in executive career success: The results of two field studies. *Journal of Managerial Issues, 25*(2), pp. 108–131.

One organizational solution is hiring decisions, as exemplified by Korn Ferry's use of the learning agility tool to assess the slope of an executive's potential. Another solution is developing the workforce we have with learning agility and growth mindset as part of your culture, a culture of "growers not knowers." Part of how that can be accomplished is discussed in the upcoming sections, "Agile Structures," "Agile Processes," and "Learning 2.0." Finally, you'll see in Chapter 8, "The Science of Changing Hearts and Minds," that mindfulness practices improve mental faculties—such as cognitive flexibility, impulse control, and emotion management—that are related to the growth mindset. Harvard's Bill George, a former CEO, claims mindfulness practices have shaped his own resilience and were "the single best thing to improve my effectiveness and sense of well-being."[6]

So that we can treat agility as a systemic issue, we should wonder whether there are *growth cultures* that correspond to the growth mindset—that innovate, adapt, and learn more quickly, and whether they can be fostered by leadership action.

Agile Culture

"I came to see, in my time at IBM, that culture isn't just one aspect of the game—it is the game."

—Lou Gerstner, IBM

Gerstner voices the idea that, in business, culture is primary in explaining performance. Many writers, in books such as *In Search of Excellence* (by Peters and Waterman) and *Good to Great* (by Collins), imbue culture with almost magical powers as in, "...architects of visionary companies... build cult-like cultures around their core ideologies."[7] According to this notion, from getting culture right, great results flow.

---

[6] George, B. (2013, Mar. 22). Resilience through mindful leadership. *Huffington Post*. Retrieved from http://www.huffingtonpost.com/bill-george/resilience-through-mindfu_b_2932269.html.

[7] Collins, J., & Porras, J. (2004). *Built to last: Successful habits of visionary companies* (3rd Edition). New York: HarperBusiness, p. 7.

The notion of "agile culture" is central to change-agile businesses in two respects. If we believe culture is primary in explaining performance, then a change-agile business must be able to change its culture. Culture can change, but it is harder work than anyone cares to admit. The failure rate (from Chapter 1, "Failed Change: The Greatest Preventable Cost to Business?") of culture change is over 80 percent, which testifies to the difficulty. Second, some cultures will have values more closely aligned with agility, say creativity and curiosity rather than stability or control.

Culture Change Maxim—The Fish Rots from the Head

Culture is an emergent phenomenon *produced* by structures, practices, leadership behavior, incentives, symbols, rituals, and processes. All those levers have to be pulled to have any chance of success. However, one driver of culture change is more important than the others. Culture change fails when the most visible symbols of it fail to change. Those key symbols are almost always the top leader's behavior, which speaks much louder than anything they might say. Unless they radically alter their own behaviors and dramatically embody the culture they wish to create, there is zero chance of successful change.

When I have seen culture change succeed, it was when culture change focused on changing very *specific* and *tangible* aspects of top team behavior and then cascaded those downward. At KPMG for example, I helped them shift their culture from one where feedback was a rare formality, to one where it was a daily practice, and from a culture where a public face of joviality and camaraderie masked toxic private discussions of colleagues' performance (such as, "He is rather poor at closing the bigger deals and will never make it in the new role"). This happens many places, but KPMG decided to get honest about it. Their culture change focused on those very specific behaviors and the beliefs that kept them in place—they became highly skilled at having those tough conversations directly, and thus helped each other grow and learn.

The next section focuses on just one aspect of culture—the culture surrounding innovation and ideas—at the heart of agility. How do the most innovative companies create and sustain their cultures?

Agility and Innovation

Agile organizations have to innovate, and the literature on business innovation stretches back (at least) to the 1960s. Interest in innovation waxes and wanes, but it is enjoying a rebirth similar to one that it enjoyed in the 1990s with best sellers such as Christensen's *The Innovator's Dilemma.* My research[8] discovered that some large companies had more than 50 percent of revenue from products and services invented in the last five years, and some innovation laggards closer to zero. PwC's found that not all the high innovators were in technology; some were in fusty old industries such as paper and packaging and logistics distribution. Our research showed three other things. The first is that the high innovators are nimble in *every* function, finance, operations, HR, and not just marketing, strategy, or R&D. The second is that high innovators have highly structured processes for managing every stage in their innovation pipelines, from harvesting ideas across the business, to filtering a small number for investment and support, to processes for prototyping. The third finding suggested a climate (an organizational mood) exists for innovation, and that there are *learnable* individual leader behaviors to create that climate.

Expecting Innovation Everywhere—Google and IBM

Consider Google's 17-year history. From its humble start, an algorithm for ranking Web sites, it has innovated in personal productivity (Gmail, Google Drive, Google Docs, Picasa, Google Voice), social networking (Google+, Google Cloud Messaging), operating systems (Android, Chrome OS), hardware (Chromebook), location services (Google Earth, Google Maps), and much more. We encounter so many of Google's innovations in our digital day-to-day that it is easy to take for granted that one company has produced so much.

---

[8] Conducted with colleagues Trevor Davis, Frank Milton, and Alan Arnett.

If these were not breathtaking enough, consider Google's current suite of innovations:[9]

- **Calico**, which is a spin-off company, working to extend the human life span
- **Google's autonomous vehicles**, which reached the 500,000-mile (driver-free) benchmark—incident-free
- **Google Fiber**, which is bringing gigabit Internet service to Austin, Texas and Provo, Utah, inspiring Los Angeles, California, and Louisville, Kentucky, to follow
- **Google Glass**, which is making wearables the next computing trend
- **Shopping Express**, which is an experiment in same-day delivery with national and local retailers
- **Google Now**, which reminds users when their favorite band or author has a new release and when the last train is leaving—before it is too late

Self-driving cars, human aging, drone delivery, and fiber optics? Google's hunger for innovation transcends traditional industry boundaries. To get a sense of how remarkable this is, imagine the stock market's reaction if General Motors went into biotechnology, if Glaxo SmithKline went into telecommunications, or if Lufthansa started making computers.

Google is primarily in the innovation business, and this applies (perhaps to a lesser extent) to other greatly admired companies, such as Apple, Samsung, Microsoft, 3M, IBM, and Amazon. All these companies defy historical business logic in the way they manage their business portfolios, and destroy the notion that small companies are necessarily more agile. The thread that seems to link these companies is the value they put on innovation. Boston Consulting Group, in their 2014 analysis of the world's most innovative companies, found exactly as my research did a decade earlier. The most innovative companies place "a high value on innovation. They demonstrate

---

[9] Collated from Wikipedia (http://en.wikipedia.org/wiki/List_of_Google_products and http://en.wikipedia.org/wiki/List_of_mergers_and_acquisitions_by_Google) and from Google (www.research.google.com).

a consistent commitment, even—or especially—in the face of failure. They encourage collaboration, they reward ideas, and they seek to capitalize on good ideas both quickly and with an appropriate level of support."[10]

The question for everybody who does not work at Google is: Can you make yourself into a Google? Or, can a large company reinvent itself and out-invent IBM—which leads the world in patents filed for 22 years running (through 2014)? How? There are no panaceas, pixie dust, or glib answers, but there are a few consistent leadership practices that some of these businesses seem to have in common.

Do Corporate Mission Statements Help?

In the beginning, there was the word. There is a leadership practice at the heart of this innovation culture—crafting a corporate purpose and mission with innovation front and center.[11] The message is that we *expect* innovation, and that produces a shift in individual identities and how people construct their roles at work, so that they see themselves foremost as innovators and avatars of change.

The following are some examples of admired companies and their "innovation statements":

- **IBM**—"Innovation that matters—for our company and for the world."
- **3M**—"...a global innovation company that never stops inventing."
- **Toyota**—"Always better cars. We continually reinvent ourselves, introduce new technologies, and stay ahead of our competition."

---

[10] Wagner, K., Taylor, A., Zablit, H., & Foo, E. (2014, Oct. 28). A breakthrough innovation culture and organization. *BCG Perspectives*. Retrieved from https://www.bcgperspectives.com/content/articles/innovation_growth_digital_economy_breakthrough_innovation_culture_organization/.

[11] We cannot distinguish cause and effect here. It could be that innovative companies *describe* themselves in such statements. I believe, but cannot prove, that those inspiring, well-communicated statements help create the right kind of culture.

- **Google**—"Our mission is to organize the world's information and make it universally accessible and useful. We strive
to maintain the open culture often associated with startups, in
which everyone is a hands-on contributor and feels comfortable
sharing ideas and opinions."

Corporate mission statements are sometimes the object of considerable, well-founded cynicism. One reason, to borrow from John
Kotter, is that they are undercommunicated by a factor of 1,000. In
my experience helping business create these inspirational messages,
the leaders rarely work hard enough to translate the lofty words into
changed business practices. The birth of a corporate mission statement is like the birth of a child. Much hard work and pain may have
gone into the labor, but, as parents know, their job has just begun—
the other 99.99 percent is yet to come. Nothing breeds cynicism faster
than a lofty mission statement with no follow-through, no leadership
modeling, or no alignment of business practices. Mission statements
have to be linked to specific behaviors, structures, and practices. Only
with this behavioral specificity (a theme discussed in more detail in
Chapter 7, "The Science of Changing Behaviors") do they have a
chance of shifting corporate culture, and even then, many years of
sustained effort are needed.

Communicating Culture and Mission—The Power of Storytelling

Many years ago, I was due to lead a session on leading change
for some senior executives at one of the world's top-three oil and gas
companies. The divisional leader welcomed the group, pointed the
way to fire exits and lavatories, and then asked, "Who would like to
share a safety story?" Three executives chimed in, with two telling stories of accident prevention, and one told a story in which a safety lapse
had caused a death. This seemed a bizarre way to start a conference,
until it dawned on me—this is how they are creating and transmit-
ting a safety culture, through stories. Upon investigation, I discovered
they started every half-day or longer meeting in this way.

The symbolic message, conveyed through this seemingly strange
ritual, is "we put safety first."

The power of storytelling to create and transmit culture is very well documented, yet this practice never happens, to my knowledge, with innovation at its heart. "Who has an innovation they are working on, or an innovation success story they would like to share?" is a very simple way to get people thinking and talking innovation all day, every day. The symbolic nature of starting with innovation first, and the creation of a culture-building ritual that shares innovation practices could, in my view, be a very powerful cultural shift.

Innovation stories are inspiring: the history of the 3M Post-it; Sony's cofounder (Masaru Ibuka) tossing a paperback book onto a table and saying "make it (the Walkman) this size";[12] Virgin's Richard Branson selling records from a church basement and making deals in London's red telephone booths; and Henry Ford's classic "If I gave customers what they wanted, I would be making faster, stronger horses." Companies need to develop their own stories (like Ford's), and those well-communicated stories have powerful effects on people. When I asked one IBM consulting partner why he didn't move for three times the money to a competitor, he quipped, "I work for the company working on the neurosynaptic chip. Why on earth would I move?"

Specific Leadership Communication Behaviors Toward Innovation

> "Many great product ideas come from stumbling, but you can only stumble if you are moving."
> —Paul Carleton, 3M

If it were just about having the right mission statement, and telling the right stories, we might have a world full of Googles. It starts there, but leaders have to behave toward innovation and ideas, in ways aligned with their loftier aspirations, to create the right *climate* for innovation. (Climate is, as it sounds, a collective mood—sweltering Houston, rainy London, or balmy San Diego.) There is high-quality

---

[12] There is some debate whether this was the original Walkman or a subsequent compact disc player.

research that strongly suggests, moreover, that climate dimensions were "especially effective predictors of creative performance in turbulent, high-pressure, competitive environments."[13] Research also suggests that "creative people" are particularly sensitive to organizational climate.[14]

One very useful measure of climate comes from Swedish researcher Goran Ekvall whose climate for innovation framework is summarized in Table 2.3.

Table 2.3 Climate for Innovation (Ekvall)

RESOURCES	1. Challenge	How challenged, emotionally involved, and committed to the organization are staff?
	2. Idea Time	Do staff have time to think things through before being obliged to act?
	3. Idea Support	Are there enough resources freely available to give new ideas a try?
SAFETY	4. Trust and Openness	Do people feel safe speaking their minds and offering different points of view?
	5. Playfulness	How relaxed is the workplace and is it okay to have fun?
	6. Conflict levels	To what degree do people engage in interpersonal conflict (negative effect)?
CURIOSITY	7. Debates	To what degree do people engage in lively debates about issues?
	8. Freedom	How free are staff to decide how to do their job?
	9. Risk-Taking	Is it okay to fail?

The useful thing about Ekvall's model is that it points to some very specific leadership communication behaviors around ideas, risk-taking, and trust. The model suggests "hands" (resources), "heart"

---

[13] Hunter, S. T., et al. (2007). Climate for creativity: A quantitative review. *Creativity Research Journal, 19*(1).

[14] Ibid.

(trust and emotional safety), and "head" (curiosity and lively debate) are important features of climate. Although those pro-climate behaviors are habitual (how leaders relate to novelty and risk), they can be taught and practiced so that they become part of the culture.

Two of the first dimensions are *idea-time* and *idea-support*. (Are people given the time and the resources to develop ideas?) Google has institutionalized a 70-20-10 rule: 70 percent of time is spent on innovations that improve core products, 20 percent is spent on next-generation products and "adjacent growth," and 10 percent is spent on exploration of new markets. Emotional safety is a critical climate dimension, and includes the dimensions of trust and openness, and playfulness and humor. Contemporary neuroscience research suggests that stress and interpersonal conflict affect both decision making and creativity. A healthy climate for innovation is fun—and includes people feeling safe to volunteer new ideas and safe from interpersonal attack. Finally, the last three dimensions on the climate scale mean that new ideas are debated constructively, that risk-taking is expected, and that roles are not so structured that people do not have the latitude to try things out.

This has been a short summary of some anecdotal and research findings on organizational culture and climate from the last few decades. Although culture is produced and reinforced by leadership practices, and organizational structures and processes, it is transmitted through communication behaviors (including symbols and rituals). We looked briefly at *what* could be communicated (that innovation is central to the business's purpose) and *how* it can be communicated through stories. Finally, research suggested that leadership behaviors that produce a pro-innovation climate can be learned and practiced.

Agile Structures—Beyond Hierarchy

Hierarchy gets a rough ride today, especially from progressive management thinkers. The criticism is overdone. Indian National Railways employs 1.4 million people and transports 8.5 billion per year. Hierarchies can be immensely stable in some instances, for example, the Catholic Church has been doing its job for nearly 2,000 years,[15] perhaps the longest lived unified hierarchical organization on the planet, and has a billion "customers." Hierarchies do some things well, delivering scale and stability. In static strategic environments, this may work best.

Hierarchies function through specifying power relationships and information flows. This is the source of their stability, but their silos, rigidity, and formality also restrict those flows. This leads to reduced communication speed, rules and policies that do not change quickly enough, people clinging to roles and turf, and people closest to the customer having the faintest voices. These rigid roles can restrict people's creativity; worker disengagement entails a loss of freedom, a sacrifice of control, and navigating the political jungle. Today's hierarchies may be flatter and matrixed, but the basic concept of power cascading from the top and people being boxed into specified roles and single functions is still commonplace.

Organization theorists have postulated since the 1950s and 1960s that there is no "one best way" to structure an organization,[16] and that the correct structure depends on environmental contingencies: The faster the environment changes, the less a rigid structure can cope. We have all felt hierarchy's limitations, but knowing those limitations is a far cry from knowing which structures are better and how to get there from here. Furthermore, people with the power to change hierarchies (restructure organizations) tend to live near the top and they lose the most in a new order of things. My prediction is that the next quarter century will see a proliferation of different organizational forms as we search for the stability and scalability of hierarchy, without the lack of agility and loss of human energy that hierarchies engender.

The following sections look at three alternative forms of organization: the project-based organization, self-managed work teams (SMWT), and holacracy. These structures are theorized to be much more adaptable and agile than traditionally structured businesses, and

---

[15] This is not a theological or moral endorsement, just a reflection that it is very hierarchical, very structured, and very long-lived.

[16] For example, Joan Woodward in *Industrial Organization: Theory and Practice*, or summarized in Gareth Morgan's *Images of Organization*.

there is anecdotal evidence that they remove many of the issues associated with hierarchy (for example, worker disengagement and lack of
organizational responsiveness).

Project-Based Business

Project-based business (PBB) models predate the corporation: In
the seventeenth century, merchants, monarchs, financiers, ship cap-
tains, and owners formed partnerships based around a single expedi-
tion, which dissolved upon return of the vessel. Today, the paradigm
example is the movie industry.[17] In the middle of the last century,
actors, directors, financiers, producers, publicists, distributors, cam-
era operators, and lighting experts were all employed by a single stu-
dio. Today, those experts are from different business entities who
collaborate on a project-by-project basis. Research suggests that those
networks tend to be stable, but they also display great flexibility.[18]

The question is whether, in a more connected and faster-
changing world, we require a middle ground between the PBB and
the traditional corporation: a PBB-*hybrid* organization, with a traditionally structured core but a substantial number of staff engaged in
dynamic, strategically critical projects. All organizations have multiple
projects running (and so all of today's organizations are hybrids to
some extent), but in a PBB-hybrid organization, projects comprise a
much greater proportion of how work gets done. These hybrids would
be a more dynamic and agile way of organizing and a better way to
implement major strategic thrusts and low-cost experimentation. The
"core" of the PBB-hybrid manages the portfolio of projects providing stability, capital, and supporting functions (communities of practice and centers of excellence). Kotter, in his new book *XLR8*, uses
the metaphor of "dual-boot" operating systems that "create agility

---

[17] Other examples include industries such as construction and software
development.

[18] Powell, W. W. (1990). Neither market nor hierarchy: Network forms of
organization. *Research in Organization Behavior, 12*, pp. 295–336.

and speed with projects" and "free the hierarchical core to do what it is optimized to do well."[19] Because of Kotter's unmatched access to senior business leaders, his book provides some excellent examples of this hybrid form in action.

The unsolved problems of this newer model are scaling project results (transferring them to the more stable core), getting the mix of projects and traditional structure right, managing human capital, creating sufficiently dynamic HR processes, and building sufficient project (and change) leadership capacity.

Self-Managed Work Teams—Industrial Democracy

Interest in self-managed work teams (SMWT) dates back to the 1940s where many of the pitfalls of traditional organization structures began to be studied. SMWTs are given considerable autonomy for the outputs, planning, resourcing, and monitoring of their outputs. They are given latitude to solve day-to-day problems and normally control over some central HR functions (performance management and learning). To summarize an enormous amount of research, SMWTs can produce extremely high levels of engagement, innovation, and efficiency. They work especially well when parallel structures require less collaboration, such as service delivery or sales teams where territories do not overlap. Problems arise in coordinating the activities *between* autonomous teams—when several teams must accomplish something together, they must sacrifice some autonomy for the sake of collaboration. This can lead to conflict between them, and in most SMWT structures there is a supervisory core (management) that sets parameters and standards for the work they deliver. SMWTs have considerably more liberty, but only within the team—that is, only up to a point. SMWTs are yet another area where custom trumps science. Research suggests they are an extremely viable alternative, but we might well speculate that hanging on to power gets in the way.

---

[19] Kotter, J. (2014). *XLR8: Building strategic agility for a faster moving world.* Boston: Harvard Business Review Press, p. 25.

Holacracy

More innovative still is a new, more ambitious form of SMWTs developed in the last ten years called *holacracy*. Holacracy is a pastiche of ideas from networked organizations, project-based organizations, self-managed work teams, decision science, and personal effectiveness practices. Inside the holacracy team (called a circle), they have the same liberty to structure and direct their own work as in a SMWT. Coordination and communication between the circles are achieved by their representation in those interdependent circles (so-called links). Unlike SMWTs, there are no bosses (anywhere), but there is a great deal of leadership and accountability—but granted from the bottom up, rather than from the top down.

Each circle decides who does what and plans its work using structured meeting and decision-making processes. In holacracy, once someone has a role-based accountability, that person has full (autocratic) authority to make relevant decisions. (The nightmare of consulting every single person on every single thing does not happen.) As in SMWTs, this method harnesses the power of people to self-organize around their passions and talents—and to produce results they care about. This process means that although power is diffuse, there is substantial alignment behind those who lead. Circles have flexible life spans, so can dissolve or form in response to threats and opportunities. This allows the dynamic restructuring that an agile organization needs.

There are two further principles that make this form of organizing intriguing. First, everybody is accountable to the purpose of the business. They are all playing the same big game so that petty differences (ego and turf) tend to disappear. Second, everybody is expected to be actively sensing any gaps (tensions) between that purpose and what is going on. That gap might be strategic, it might be structural, or it might be operational, but when that discomfort is felt, the "partner" (Holacracy's word for employee) is expected to discuss how to close it. It is unacceptable to suffer in silence while a threat, opportunity, or inefficiency is being overlooked. This begins to solve one of the most acute problems with hierarchy: the restricted flow of information from those at the coalface to those with the power.

In any human group, there is the political problem of who decides what, and who decides who decides what. The third intriguing aspect of holacracy is that power lies not with people but with purpose and process. The purpose is the ultimate authority, and the governance process (set out in a constitution) sets out how the business organizes to deliver that purpose.

Holacracy is new, and still largely untested in larger businesses, but Zappos (an online shoe retailer with $1 billion in revenue and 1,500 staff) adopted the model to much media fanfare in 2013. Since then, a number of Silicon Valley companies have emulated the Zappos way.[20] CEO Tony Hsieh, who gave much of his formal authority to this structure and to Zappos' new constitution, says,

> Research shows that every time the size of a city doubles, innovation and productivity per resident increases by 15 percent. However, when companies get bigger, innovation and productivity per employee generally go down. So Zappos is trying to figure out how to structure itself more like a city, by switching from a normal hierarchical structure to a system which enables employees to act more like entrepreneurs and self-direct their work instead of reporting to a manager who tells them what to do.[21]

PBBs, SMWTs, holacracy, and hybrid types are experimental organizational structures. It is important to remember that hierarchy has a long history. Our models of organization are derived from the Church, the military, and monarchical and feudal societies where power is vested at the top.

However, we are still learning how to structure decision making in democratic societies, centralized versus devolved power, and the rights of groups versus the rights of individuals. Although we like to think in terms of "revolutions," fundamental changes to ideologies and the structures that support them take many centuries. Whatever rational arguments and research may say about the efficiencies

---

[20] The consulting firm that I founded began to experiment with organizational democracy and the holacracy model in 2009.

[21] From the Zappos website: http://www.zapposinsights.com/about/holacracy.

of self-organization, agility, and organizational democracy, mental models change slowly, and power rarely concedes without a fight. As someone who experimented, in my own company, with democratic decision making in a holacracy type model, I can attest to the fact that my emotional unease about ceding power to "the masses" vied with my theoretical commitment to an agile democratic workplace.

Agile Processes—Ideas, Execution, Learning

Our final section is agile processes, but with a narrow focus on enabling processes: idea management, change execution, and learning processes.

Agile Idea Management

Management of ideas includes harnessing the creativity of the entire workforce and outside entrepreneurs, which Shell achieves through an "open innovation" process they call GameChangers[22] that "identifies and nurtures unproven ideas that have the potential to drastically impact the future of energy." Shell claims that GameChangers has worked with over 1,500 innovators and turned more than 100 "big ticket" ideas into reality—some with great potential. One of those success stories was Shell's Floating Natural Gas technology, which liquefies natural gas at −162°, which condenses its volume 600-fold. The 2012 prototype, Prelude FLNG, has just one quarter the surface area of a similar onshore LNG plant.

A second breakthrough GameChanger was using solar power to create the steam injected into oil reservoirs (called Enhanced Oil Recovery), which reduces greenhouse gas emissions from the process by 80 percent. GameChanger ideas are funneled into the process through an open-access portal, where entrepreneurs and Shell insiders can pitch their ideas to a team of 12 scientists and engineers. Ideas are vetted and developed through an exacting process, financed and

---

[22] http://www.shell.com/global/future-energy/innovation/innovate-with-shell/shell-gamechanger.html

resourced, and developed through to the pilot implementation stage and final commercial implementation.

GameChangers is an example of a world-class idea-management process that harvests ideas widely (the open innovation concept), uses hard-edged analysis to select a few, then supplies ample resources to those selected (meaning that they have a chance), and rigorously evaluates returns and its own effectiveness.

Agile Execution

In organizations that are increasingly organized around projects, mere competence at running projects is no longer sufficient—a much greater level of mastery is required. At the highest level, the business must excel at managing a portfolio of projects, the way an investment manager manages a portfolio of securities. Echoing the views in Chapter 1, it would be bizarre for a bank not to have an aggregated view of its investments, and because most of the investment capital, and a great deal of the risk of a contemporary organization, exists in its change portfolio, a centralized view is essential.

In many globally diverse organizations, even a single function, such as HR, may not have centralized oversight (and risk management) of all the projects under its wing. Even a middle manager in HR might have a half-dozen projects she leads, and there might be a few hundred like her in a big company. An aggregate view and risk analysis are even more important for projects, or thousands, than for securities because securities do not interact (bump into each other and compete for resources) the way projects do.

In the Chapter 3, "Governance and the Psychology of Risk," I suggest that this portfolio approach would allow analysis of variance from planned benefits and from estimated costs—the "leaks" in the system. It would allow a more statistical approach to change competence as well as allow a comparison of different capabilities in leading change between business units, geographies, and functions.

Agile Change Management

Although I think change management (as a specialist discipline) should go the way of corded telephones, *change management skills* will be more important than ever, Harvard's John Kotter agrees saying that the number of change-management competent people needs to increase "not by 50%, but by 500% or 1000%."[23] If organizations must adapt more quickly in response to VUCA environments, and if change now dominates the manager's day job, then how much education in leading change is the "ante" for a change leader? What should be the content?

My finger-in-the-air answer to "how much" is about 20 days to be minimally able and about 40 days to be capable, perhaps spread over several years. By comparison, a specialist Master's degree in Change Agent skills (or OD, or OB) takes about two years of full-time study, and this largely theoretical education must be supplemented with advanced training in coaching and facilitation—or about a five years of full- and part-time education.

Of these days, perhaps 20 percent might be conceptual, 50 percent reserved for skills (such as facilitation, understanding power, navigating politics, diagnosing organizational problems, creative problem solving, coaching, conflict resolution, stakeholder events, and negotiation), and 30 percent on personal development, (building personal change-agility, vision/values resilience, creativity, and cognitive flexibility). A great deal of the most important work that change experts (OD consultants) are paid to do is facilitation of various kinds—team development, strategy formulation, team alignment, conflict resolution, and stakeholder engagement. Facilitation, if I had to pick just one skill, may be the most important of all of these. Facilitation permits getting the best from groups of people, so that the ideal of "all of us is smarter than one of us" or the "wisdom of the crowd" can be realized. (Any experienced manager will know that in a dysfunctional group, "all of us" is quite a bit dumber than "one of us.") Facilitation also helps navigate what can be the most destructive force in business—badly managed conflict. From my point of view, this skill is more *practically* valuable than most of what is traditionally taught in an MBA.

---

[23] Kotter, J. (2014). *XLR8: Building strategic agility for a faster moving world.* Boston: Harvard Business Review Press, p. 60.

Agile Learning Processes

We are at the dawn of a new era for the nexus of learning and technology: the democratization of knowledge. This is an extension and acceleration of a trend established by the printing press, and the advent of public education, before which only a few scholars and priests could access the repositories of human knowledge. Massive Open Online Course (MOOC) technology means that, today, someone in Kigali can take a course in machine learning from a Stanford professor for free. Some MOOCs attract over 100,000 learners. In years to come, we may see this infant technology grow further and see million-person courses. There are still problems to be solved, such as certification, completion rates, and cheat-proof testing, but these are relatively trivial when compared with the potential for low-cost, self-directed, high-quality education. MOOCs are delivered in bite-sized chunks, of 10 to 20 minutes, which can be watched on iPads in airports, or listened to in podcast form while driving—in other words, to suit a learner's lifestyle.

This will destroy the brick-and-mortar business models of all but a very few business schools (and perhaps universities). Why should someone attend an expensive course (in, for example, business strategy) at the University of Wisconsin–Oshkosh, delivered by a local instructor, when, for next to nothing, she can attend a program delivered by one of the world's leading experts? Students often claim that the principal benefits of a business education are the networking opportunities, but we are in the midst of a social transformation where relationships with friends, colleagues, and collaborators are formed and maintained without ever having met "IRL" (in real life). As baby boomers leave the workforce, and GenY and GenZ, who are online from adolescence, take up leadership positions, the notion that people have to be colocated to "connect" will continue to fade.

New learning technologies also disrupt the hub-and-spoke nature of education, where an expert communicates (mostly talking) to a group of learners. The extraordinary, and sometimes overlooked, property of the Internet is that strangers from around the world can collaborate to create and share knowledge—a web, not a hub-and-spoke model. Open source development projects (such as Wikipedia) involve over 30 million different contributors—a far cry from the model where tiny groups of archivists and researchers or single individuals produce repositories of knowledge.

Web-based "communities of practice" mean that expert communities transcend organizational and geographical boundaries. Leading businesses now use enterprise social networks (ESNs), such as Yammer and Jive, to develop those communities of practice and problem solving in-house.

The old model, where learning and application were separated in time and place (you go to school for a long time, then you apply what you have learned later and elsewhere) will soon die. In the "mobile era," knowledge can be accessed "just-in-time" to find solutions it might have taken days or weeks to solve earlier.

The sum of this new approach to learning and knowledge is called "learning 2.0" (after Web 2.0). The two hallmarks are integration and multiple modalities. Integration means that learning, collaboration, and knowledge management work together, whereas these were traditionally separate. Formal learning was the province of learning and development, collaboration relied on formation of formal teams, and knowledge management was formal (not tacit) knowledge, and often considered an IT "thing." In this world, learning and collaboration are facilitated by technology, but the presence of technology means that the creation of knowledge happens at the same time. (The frustration with old-school knowledge management systems is that IT had to persuade the people to spend time updating the system. In consulting, that usually meant a time-consuming, extra piece of work done principally for the benefit of others.)

Varied modalities include specialized wikis, user-generated content, social networking, micro blogging, webcasts and webinars, videoconferencing, podcasts, e-learning, virtual instructor-led training, as well as traditional methods (conferences, workshops, classroom-based learning). Accenture's "performance workspace" is an example of a portal that combines, for the worker-learner, these three dimensions—learning, knowledge, and collaboration—and integrates the various modalities.

There is much more that can be added—technology (such as cloud computing, or Software as Service) is making IT platforms more agile (lessening the need for multimillion dollar systems and similar implementation budgets and headaches). Enterprise social networks are harnessing the creativity and passion for virtual connection, but enabling connections around a company's mission and projects.

Although agile idea management, agile portfolio and change management, and agile learning do not exhaust the possibilities for creating innovative and agile processes, these are three of the most exciting contemporary possibilities.

Conclusion

The most important message of this chapter is that a change-agile organization cannot be created by a single variable change, either to HR processes, to organizational structure, or to mindset and behaviors. Some of the ideas discussed from the four quadrants are:

- The notion of *agile people* looks not so much at their current capability, but at their growth potential (the slope of the line). Mindfulness practices (covered in more detail in Chapter 8) are possibly useful for developing that capability rather than recruiting it.
- Creating an *agile culture* requires whole-system change, and cultural change must be anchored in specific changes to behaviors, systems, and practices for it to have any chance. We looked at specific research-based, pro-innovation leadership behaviors.
- There are new experimental forms of *agile structures* that are a long way from traditionally organized businesses. Project-based *hybrids*, self-managed work teams, and holacracy are such experimental models.
- *Agile processes* include agile idea management, agile portfolio and change management, and agile learning. Learning 2.0 blends learning, collaboration, and knowledge management in ways not possible even a decade ago.

Creating an agile organization from a sluggish one is the kind of change that will probably take a decade of experimentation, of prototyping, and of development of long-term capabilities. In the twenty-first century, we have some template organizations the likes of which did not exist three decades ago, I realize that "the market," including business writers and business school professors, tends to fall romantically in love with certain companies only to find out their multiple infidelities later (as with Enron). Perhaps I suffer slightly from "Google eyes," and perhaps Google will one day stumble, having proved strategically overambitious or having spent too much capital developing its much-lauded capabilities. Even if the company does, they (and the many companies experimenting with their practices) will have taught us a tremendous amount in their short 17-year history.

Part II
Change Strategy

"Tactics teaches the use of armed forces in the engagement; strategy, the use of engagements for the object of the war."

—General Carl von Clausewitz, *On War*

Change Strategy

What is commonly called change strategy is not very strategic because strategy properly focuses on *goals* and not on *how to deliver those goals*. Many publications on change strategy unhelpfully define it as stakeholder management, communications, HR alignment, short-term wins, benefits realization, people development, and organization design. All of those are *how* to deliver a strategy—and in my view are tactical, not strategic. Change strategy should be at a level above those *how* questions.[1]

However, change strategy must also sit below business, market, operational, and corporate strategies (we do not need another word for those). Does this leave a void, or is there a place in the middle for change strategy?

In international relations, there will be the highest-level strategic objectives (for example, containing the Soviet Union or supporting African development); there will be a portfolio of activities (military,

---

[1] One could argue that change management includes change strategy and change tactics, but surveying what is included in change management, even by this definition, is often all tactical. The activities normally talked about as change management are called change tactics in this book.

diplomatic, trade) that must be coordinated to deliver those objectives; and then there will be the tactical specifics (how we conduct diplomacy and trade). That middle level captures the idea of change strategy, making the business's grand strategy (the whole portfolio of change) cohere—that is, "add up" to the bigger picture.

Strategic Coherence

Strategic coherence is more important than strategic precision in an uncertain world. It is impossible to get everything right because of market volatility, but we can ensure strategies do not collide. In large, complex organizations where many executives are empowered to launch major change, strategic incoherence can be a big problem.

One of Silicon Valley's iconic companies recently sent an executive committee member to London to ask why costs had not fallen in response to a mandatory 20 percent head-count reduction. The full-time staff had been cut, but another initiative (aimed at rolling out a new product and improving customer service) had hired contractors to fill the void! As this involved more than 1,000 workers, it was roughly a $100 million clash of strategies. Similarly, in one of the world's top-five banks, its digital/mobile strategy was fragmented across IT, marketing, retail banking, and operations and several geographies, each with a piece of the pie. (They were falling behind in delivery because some things fell between the cracks, and there were overlaps and conflicts.)

Change strategy is, by this definition, the way a business (1) manages the portfolio of change to make sure that the parts deliver the whole business strategy, (2) creates the context for change, and (3) monitors change risk and change performance across the entire business. Table II.1 contrasts change strategy and change tactics.

Table II.1 Change Strategy Versus Change Tactics

	CHANGE STRATEGY	CHANGE TACTICS
Purpose	Ensuring strategic coherence Managing portfolio interdependencies, returns, and risks Creating change-agile business	Aligning the organization, its culture, and its people with a specific strategy or program
Worldview	Adapting and innovating in a VUCA world (Volatility, Uncertainty, Complexity, Ambiguity) "Doing the right things"	Delivering more static objectives and focusing on the *how* "*Doing things right*"
Accountability	Integrating portfolios of projects to deliver business success	Delivering project results
Scope	Monitoring how programs deliver business strategy Assessing change portfolio risks, coherence, and returns Developing change agility	Focusing on single-project effectiveness and value-for-money
Time horizon	Delivering long-term change capacity and medium-term program synergies	Delivering short-term term value (for example, one year or shorter)
Mindset	Challenging conventional wisdom Adopting contrarian mentality Ensuring strategy-project fit	Accepting conventional wisdom for the sake of expedient delivery
Virtues	Balancing risk-taking and prudence	Balancing pace and quality of engagement
Constraints	Weighing tactical considerations and the business' change capability and capacity	Optimizing use of program resources
Unique risks	Conflicting programs Mistiming implementation, Overlooking unintended consequences, Overloading stakeholders/ change agents	Overlooking stakeholders Underestimating resistance Failing to challenge and develop leaders

How Change Strategy and Change Tactics Interact

Naturally, these are generalizations, and many change managers are aware of the demands of the change strategy column. What is most interesting is the interplay between the change strategy and tactics. Strategy that takes no account of tactical practicalities is doomed, and great tactics without strategy produce incoherence and nonalignment. Despite this, the strategy-tactics dialogue happens too rarely in organizations. Many of the strategic questions are handled out of sight of the people who best understand the people side of change, engagement, and alignment. Senior executives can feel that such conversations are "above the pay grade" of the change expert, who, especially if internal, will be many layers farther down the hierarchy. The tacticians then do not understand the full strategic picture, and the strategists do not understand what it will take to get change implemented on the ground. This has consequences.

Consequences of the Strategy-Tactics Split

Change consultants are frequently called in midproject when change is going badly and asked to supply tactical means of resolving people and culture problems. As with aid workers surveying a posthurricane scene, they may find one or more political conflicts, unhappy stakeholders, culture clashes, dysfunctional project teams, skills issues, or sponsorship troubles, all causing delays and overruns.

This is often caused by the misguided (and ubiquitous) strategic mindset, "Figure out what to do, and then persuade people to follow us." This causes the following problems:

- Strategies that do not include knowledge from the "coalface" make strategy mistakes, such as a clash of cultures in a merger, a poorly chosen technology solution (at least from a user/manager's point of view), or distance from understanding changing customer needs.

- Strategies substantially underestimate and underinvest in the people dimension of the change (hearts, minds, behaviors, skills), especially early in the project.

- Strategies insufficiently consider tactical implementation issues such as change load or how possible a strategy implementation is in the *realpolitik* of the business.

Favor Continuous, Rather Than Discrete, Involvement

Involvement of the right people, at the right time, and in the right way solves all three of those problems. Tactical change solutions are limited in their ability to fix a flawed strategy, and skimping on change management early costs more than it saves. (On a big project, each month's delay may cost $1 million.) Senior leaders must begin to think involvement and engagement up front, when strategy is being formulated.

Where orthodoxy on involvement falls short is when that involvement traditionally takes place via *set pieces*,[2] such as workshops, communications, facilitated sessions, and other interventions. These set pieces are, as in soccer, planned and distinct from the normal free flow of the game (the free flow of work and information). The involvement set pieces are performed to get around barriers to information flow, either horizontal (cross-functional) or vertical (between senior decision makers and the front line). It is easy to picture a small organization (for example, fewer than ten people) where set pieces are unnecessary because consultation and communication are unrestricted (the exchange of inputs between the top and the front line are part of daily work life). The problem, which change-agile organizations try to solve, is constant involvement and engagement with strategy, and continual flow of high-quality information from the whole (big) organization to decision makers. Technology, such as enterprise social networks, can help, but strategists require the right mindset also—that involvement produces better decisions and more engaged workforces.

The goal is to create continuous, everyday, deliberative strategic processes that build engagement while capturing the best shared thinking—the opposite of "figure it out and then persuade them to do it." This section introduces the possibility of change strategy that harnesses the power of group deliberation, cognizant of human limitations, informed by analytics, and guided by science.

Change Strategy—The Road Ahead

"Strategy is fog, friction, chance," said von Clausewitz, perhaps the most famous military strategist of all time. Fog limits the ability to see far ahead and dictates more agile approaches, friction suggests

---

[2] A military and soccer analogy, meaning a setup confrontation. In soccer, it is a free kick or corner kick where both teams have rehearsed positioning and strategy, as opposed to the free flow of the rest of the game. Gridiron (American football) is all set pieces by this definition.

that strategy execution is never flawless, and chance tells us that there are always risks. The first chapter in this section, Chapter 3, "Governance and the Psychology of Risk," examines the governance implications of strategizing in a VUCA (Volatility, Uncertainty, Complexity, and Ambiguity) world. This includes treatments of how poorly humans understand probability, biases which affect risk assessment and planning, solving problems in complex environments, and leading through the "fog of war" (ambiguity).

Chapter 4, "Decision Making in Complex and Ambiguous Environments," examines what complexity is and reveals that it requires two new problem-solving approaches for strategists. Then the chapter turns to ambiguity, and looks at some of the emerging challenges on the human side of analytics and Big Data.

Decision making has always been confounded by error, but during the last few decades, the kind of mistakes, their frequency, and their impact were not well understood. Today, they are. The final chapter of this section, Chapter 5, "Cognitive Biases and Failed Strategies," looks at cognitive biases and the systematic change strategy mistakes that result from them. You'll see how perceptual and reasoning flaws color which problems are selected, distort views of current reality, and skew solutions. This is in combination with decision making based on myths, fads, and shaky data, powered by egos and hubris, and driven through senior executive teams who were cowed into compliance by the "great man" [sic] style of leadership—the root of much change failure.

3

Governance and the Psychology of Risk

Volatility, in the VUCA world, means greater frequency and scale of the uncontrollable, unpredictable events that alter the competitive landscape. In less-connected times, a local business might only be affected by local or national events. Today, because of connectedness, there are more pesky competitors, suppliers, regulators, stakeholders, and discontinuities in customer preferences in far-flung places that can buffet the business.

Faster business change is a necessary adaptation to this volatility, but that introduces *additional business risk,* which from my point of view is the natural volatility of change outcomes (SOCKS: shortfalls, overruns, consequences, killed, and sustainability). Change risk is usually analyzed qualitatively, using a *risk register.* The best versions of risk registers include a risk classification (for a simple example, people, process, technology, environment, and financial risks), a qualitative grading, and a pointer to an action/accountability (who is going to fix it, by when).

A robust *change risk register* and a process for guaranteeing risks are addressed as part of Change Management 101. As with most Change Management 101 basics, change risk registers are vastly underused (when compared with their usefulness). However, our specific interest in change risk is not just technical, but where the mathematics of risk meets the psychology of people and the culture of organizations. Are businesspeople, and business cultures, set up to prosper in a volatile world, where risks are greater? Are change management specialists sufficiently informed about risk and risk psychology? In exploring these questions, this chapter explodes a number of myths:

1. Most business risk (volatility) is from ongoing operations (rather than projects).
2. The "gut feel" that is used to complete Change Management 101 risk registers is accurate enough.
3. Risks can be measured and normal distributions track reality.
4. Risk management is a technical discipline, confined to specialist functions, or specialist frameworks (such as enterprise risk management).

Psychology of Risk—Knowing the Mind of God?

"Randomness is so difficult to grasp because it works against our pattern-finding instincts...sometimes there is no pattern to be found...randomness places fundamental limits on our intuition..."

—Charles Seife

Part of business is peering into the future, looking for patterns, exploiting unexplored niches, and betting on them. Starting a business is gambling that people will buy what you sell in the future, and significant investments rely on the gamble that cash flow will continue be able to finance them. Life is full of predictions as well as big and little gambles, such as taking an alternative route because you predict rush hour will be busy, playing a risky shot to the green in golf rather than laying up, and training for a job entails gambling that those skills will be in demand, and that you will enjoy it.

Nobody calculates probabilities in these situations, but all decisions rely on intuitive estimates (a gut feel) of how different choices will fare in a predicted future. Is that gut feel any good?

The answer is: No. Our minds, especially our intuitions, are not equipped to deal with a probabilistic world. Risk and prediction are widely misunderstood, and gambling is seen as something restricted to Las Vegas rather than part of what we do daily, sometimes for trivial stakes, and sometimes (personally and corporately) for very large ones.

All decision making in a probabilistic world involves estimating the likelihood of an event and how much we will value it (affective forecasting). Humans are bad at both—particularly at the former.

Six Systematic Flaws in How Humans Think about Risk

This century's research in psychology and economics has shown how deeply flawed human intuitions are *especially about probability*, and this lack of intuitive savvy and of risk education compromises the human's ability to make important personal decisions (for example, about health). In the business context, where the stakes are much higher, leaders need to build institutional and decision-making safeguards to protect their business (and the communities and environment they affect) from risk-oriented mistakes.

First, humans believe in trends and patterns in events that happen randomly. We believe in "winning streaks," "hot hands," "due for some rain," or that seven black spins increases the change that the next spin will be red.

Second, we place our faith in small samples. Our exquisite pattern-finding apparatus causes us to leap to conclusions about the world based on flimsy data. An institutional sampling error in business is the "case study"—a single data-point that cannot be extrapolated to other businesses without caution.

Third, in troubled situations, our attitudes toward risk change. Rather than hunkering down until the storm passes, we tend to get more aggressive and risk seeking. Suppose I offer you the choice of two boxes. One contains $1,000 and the other contains a surprise—50 percent of the time, it contains $2,000, and the other 50 percent of the time, it contains nothing. You take the sure thing; in fact, you might take $950 rather than a fifty-fifty chance of $2,000, giving up

some economic value for some certainty. This is called risk aversion.[1] However, when Kahneman and Tversky produced their famous
paper, *Judgment Under Uncertainty*,[2] they showed that in neutral and
positive situations (things are going well, or as planned), risk aversion dominated. However, when things became difficult, risk aversion
gave way to risk-seeking behavior. This explains why people who are
"stuck" stay much longer in casinos than people who are "up." When
their stocks go down, people risk-seek to "get it back." When change
projects go awry, even sensible leaders can try desperate measures.

Fourth, humans are particularly bad at relative probabilities. After
9/11, people left the skies and took to the roads, sending fatalities
soaring because road travel is substantially more dangerous than air
travel. People will pay more for antiterrorism insurance than regular
travel insurance despite the fact that terrorism is a vanishingly small
probability when compared with less emotionally charged events such
as losing luggage or missing a flight. This is especially acute in situations where qualitative judgments of risk are used, such as the project
risk register described previously.

Fifth, when dealing with tiny probabilities with catastrophic consequences, people sometimes make irrationally conservative decisions. This has had a dramatic effect on parenting norms in the last
decades. Modern parenting is dominated by "abduction monsters,"[3]
despite the fact that the chance of stranger abduction, especially non-
family members, is minuscule[4] (about 2,000 times less likely than

---

[1] When I offer this puzzle in programs, there are always executives who object,
saying they would always take the highest expected value. Try the thought experiment with a sure $9,000,000 or a fifty-fifty chance of $20,000,000 to test your
own risk aversion.

[2] Kahneman, D., & Tversky, A. (1974, Sep. 27). Judgment under uncertainty:
Heuristics and biases. *Science, 185* (4157), pp. 1124–1131.

[3] Hoffman, J. (2009, Sep. 13). Why can't she walk to school? *The New York Times*,
p. ST1.

[4] Despite the prevalence of this fear, and the extraordinary measures to prevent its
occurrence, in the United States, there are about 100 abductions per year from
a population of 16 million children. About 75 percent of those are by estranged
spouses, leaving 25 out of 16 million. The risk of stranger abduction is just greater
than one in a million, approximately the same as being killed by lightning—an
example of emotions clouding risk assessment.

Black Swan

dying in a car accident). Paradoxically, in business, the opposite sometimes happens in these low-probability, big-catastrophe scenarios. Leaders pretend there is no risk at all. This is called the *zero-risk bias,* that bias that turns small risks into zero risk or, as I like to call it, the "it could never happen to us" bias. Big events with significant, but low probabilities are completely discounted—like two of Wall Street's oldest and finest declaring bankruptcy within a 13-month period or housing prices collapsing 75 percent in some areas. Yet events such as these make or break countries and corporations (taking families and communities along with them).

Sixth, we misunderstand "risk of ruin." Suppose you have $1 million in capital. I offer you a coin toss where you get $1.2 million if you win, but you can only lose your $1 million. This is obviously massively profitable, what is called *plus EV (expected value).* How much should you wager on the first coin toss? If you "bust," you lose the ability to make future massively profitable investments. Even with this very large plus EV situation, only slightly more than 10 percent of the capital should be risked at any one time to avoid risk of ruin. This calculation (called the Kelly Criterion) applies to change projects and how much capital should be invested in risky ventures. Lack of attention to risk of ruin brought down Long Term Capital Management, a firm run by some of the biggest brains in investment banking.

We have those six kinds of irrationality in the realm of probability, and two proposed corrections. The first is a wider education in qualitative probability theory and the psychology of risk, beginning long before university. Everybody needs to know which things in life are random, which are cyclical, and which are linear. We also need to know (qualitatively) which risks produce great probability of harm (such as texting while driving), which are moderate (dietary factors, such as salt and trans fats), and which are negligible (risk of harm from vaccination) to avoid collective irrationality around everyday decisions. Professor Gird Gigerenzer, in *Risk Savvy,* says that risk literacy is the basic knowledge required to deal with a modern society. From the business strategist's perspective, we make risky bets all the time mostly when risks are impossible to quantify. Most of the time, we are using "gut feel" rather than statistics to estimate risk. Given how bad humans are at estimating risk, business leaders need to be aware of those systematic errors that we (and our followers) will make with our capital. <u>*In business, understanding the psychology of risk is more important than understanding the mathematics of risk.*</u>

The second class of arrangements (to protect ourselves from our risk *naïveté*) has to be institutional (either in business policy, project governance structures, or government legislation) to protect us from the zero-risk bias, risk-seeking behavior under pressure, or spotting trends in random events. The Wall Street meltdown of 2007 brought the world face-to-face with financial Armageddon. Negative GDP growth for a short while is relatively minor compared with complete economic collapse, such as Weimar Germany, or the near 30 percent unemployment of the Great Depression (that would be nearly 50 million unemployed people if it happened today). In today's connected economy, the runaway domino effects would have been felt around the world and for decades. The situation was a case study in the psychology of risk, but also revealed how poor our governance structures were (and are).

The remainder of this chapter focuses on the implications of the volatility of change outcomes and how leaders are equipped (or not) to deal with that volatility. We will look at

- How human psychology and business culture produce planning errors
- How standard ways of estimating (point-estimates) are inadequate
- How different kinds of probability distributions require different risk protocols
- How creating a risk culture achieves outcomes that risk systems may not
- How it is important to think about change risk across entire change portfolios to capture the risk to the whole business

Planning Fallacy and Consulting Fictions

"'What is a management consultant?' asked the MBA candidate, of the consultant. 'We're a Breed Apart, and only the very best of you could become one.'"

—Lewis Pinault, *Consulting Demons*

Professor Bent Flyvbjerg, of Oxford's Saïd Business School, specializes in analyzing major projects. He studied 1,471 such projects and found an average overrun of 27 percent. That number may strike you as tolerable, perhaps good? However, Flyvbjerg also found that *one in six* projects had a cost overrun of 200 percent or more and a schedule overrun of almost 70 percent. Some overruns can be grotesque in stature (see Table 3.1).

Table 3.1 Illustration of Major Project Overruns[5]

ORGANIZATION	CHANGE PROGRAM	OVERRUN PERCENTAGE (SIZE)
U.S. Air Force	Expeditionary Combat Support System	100% ($600 million)
U.S. Census Bureau	Field Data Collection Automation	250% ($2.2 billion)
NHS (National Health Service)	Connecting for Health	700% ($15 billion)
City of Boston	Big Dig	190% ($12 billion)
Denver Airport	Infrastructure, new baggage system	100% ($3 billion)

The *planning fallacy* is the systematic tendency for project plans and budgets to undershoot. Lest we be seduced by thinking that the fallacy applies only to projects of enormous complexity, recall that Flyvbjerg studied 1,471 projects. It equally applies to projects with tiny scales. One study asked students to estimate how long it would take to complete a term paper (1) if everything went as well as it could, or (2) if everything went as poorly as it could. They provided a range of 27 to 49 days. The actual average time to complete was 55.5 days—quite a bit worse than their worst-case estimates.

---

[5] The Web site www.calleam.com maintains a robust database of failed change programs and case-study analysis. I thank Rob Goathem for this analysis and for fruitful conversations.

Daniel Kahneman[6] summarizes as follows,

[Executives] make decisions based on delusional optimism rather than on a rational weighting of gains, losses, and probabilities. They overestimate benefits and underestimate costs. They spin scenarios of success while overlooking the potential for mistakes and miscalculations. As a result, they pursue initiatives that are unlikely to come in on budget or on time or to deliver the expected returns—or even to be completed.[7]

Psychology of the Planning Fallacy

The reasons for the planning fallacy are partly psychological, partly cultural, and partly to do with our limited ability to think probabilistically. Psychologically, the optimism biases (discussed in Chapter 5, "Cognitive Biases and Failed Strategies") create a tendency toward hopeful and best-case estimates. Paradoxically, the planning fallacy may be very useful from an evolutionary standpoint. How often have you said "If I had known how hard this would be, I would never have begun"? Naïve underestimates may mean we take on bigger and more complex challenges that would otherwise seem too daunting. Cologne Cathedral took over 600 years to complete, and Notre Dame, 200. Had Louis VII known that, would he have started?

In boardroom cultures, executives pitch for resources providing business cases for projects. And who, seeking project approval, would not want to suggest the most optimistic view of benefits and costs? The incentives are skewed toward getting projects approved, and there is very rarely real accountability, post-project, for having been overoptimistic before launch.

Consulting Fictions

The planning fallacy is institutionalized by the structure of the management consulting industry. Buried within every consulting

---

[6] Professor Daniel Kahneman, Nobel Prize laureate and author of *Thinking Fast and Slow*, whom we will visit often in this and coming chapters.

[7] Kahneman, D. (2011). *Thinking fast and slow*. New York: Farrar, Straus and Giroux.

proposal are two works of fiction: the price for the project and the plan for achieving it. They are fiction because they are based on an EGAP (Everything Goes as Planned) scenario.[8] Sales situations are highly competitive, so the price and plan are the consulting firm's Sunday best. Consultants know, empirically, that things never go that well. Yet, competition destroys realism as consultants bid for major projects. Of course, buyers of $50 million IT projects are sophisticated and experienced enough to understand the game, but there are strong *game theoretical* forces that steer choices toward the cheapest and the fastest. Suppose IBM decided to submit a bid (time and cost estimate) that realistically weighted those 27 percent average overruns and highlighted the possibility of 200 percent overruns as documented by Flyvbjerg. Meanwhile, the competition, EDS, Accenture, and SAP, stick to standard practice of EGAP estimates. IBM, by refusing to align with EGAP practices, unless dealing with a very enlightened client, shoots itself in the foot and loses the deal.

When the reality of a project hits the overoptimistic (planning fallacy) estimates provided by consultants during the proposal/contracting phase, the ABC rule of management consulting applies: *Always blame the client.* The client culture, client leadership, lack of client stakeholder engagement/cooperation, and lack of client resources and expertise are prime targets. Consultants evade responsibility for those features of a project even though they (1) are of critical importance, and (2) are factors at which consultants competent at change management should excel! Consulting contracts cherry-pick the easy stuff (technical) and duck responsibility for the harder stuff (culture, politics, internal leadership, building commitment, and engaging stakeholders). Although there are sometimes lawsuits that try to hold consultants accountable, they are usually only in cases of extreme failure, and almost never for "standard" overruns. Because consultants are contractually protected, shareholders or taxpayers usually pick up the tab for the consultant's failure to manage the people side of change, and therefore failure to deliver results.

---

[8] It's not that consultants do not build contingencies into estimates, but rather that those contingencies themselves are far too optimistic.

Estimating Better

Better than the optimistic EGAP is MLD (Most Likely Development).[9] The graph shown in Figure 3.1 depicts the effect on ROI of EGAP, MLD, and returns that (empirically) are not unlikely—that is, returns below the hurdle rate ROI, or even breakeven. As you have seen, people are motivated by economic structures to skew estimates strongly toward the optimistic, and whether an endeavor remains profitable depends on how much those estimates deviate from real-world outcomes.

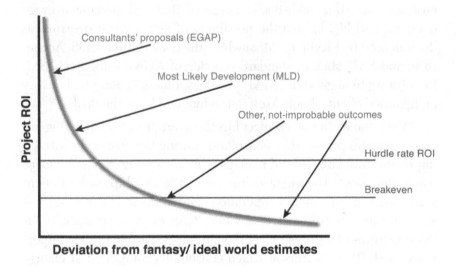

Figure 3.1 Graph of project returns showing EGAP and MLD.

Daniel Kahneman's pioneering research on the planning fallacy proposes a method for arriving at more realistic estimates under conditions of uncertainty. He suggests the following procedure for "grounding" planning in reality:

1. Identify an appropriate reference class (for example, ERP implementation, acquisition, Six Sigma program).

---

[9] Professor Bent Flyvberg's term.

2. Obtain the statistics of the referenced class (for example, percentage by which expenditures exceeded budget, project delays, benefit shortfalls). Use this objective research to generate a baseline prediction.

3. Adjust the baseline prediction based on your estimate of your competence relative to the average estimates.

In Chapter 1, "Failed Change: The Greatest Preventable Cost to Business?" you saw the variability between various organizations' change success rates—some achieved 80 percent and some 20 percent. As well as general benchmarks of overruns, leaders must begin tracking how well their business's projects fare relative to initial plans and budgets. It would be unwise, for example, unless you have Cisco Systems's exceptional acquisition capabilities, both in selection and execution, to expect greater-than-the-market-average success rate (around 50 percent). If, empirically, every IT project that you have launched costs, for example, 40 percent more than initial estimates, then that added cost must be factored into cost-benefit ROI calculations. Few organizations are honest with themselves in this respect.

The Deterministic Fallacy—Point Estimates

"The illusion of control deludes leaders into banking on a single outcome in situations that are highly risk dependent."
—Daniel Kahneman

Although better estimation improves governance and risk management of major projects, even good *point estimates* (such as MLD) are a fictitious view of reality. Reality is probabilistic, and chance is sewn through the fabric of the universe from how subatomic particles behave, to how baseballs bounce, to whether a chance encounter provides a business opportunity.[10] Every nontrivial project task has a range of outcomes, and as every seasoned project manager knows,

---

[10] The two biggest business deals that I have ever done had completely serendipitous origins from randomly bumping into the right person at the right time.

one-week tasks never take two days, and sometimes take three weeks. Create a project of 10,000 tasks with those distributions and you have the sort of high-variance outcomes change programs produce.

To see just how deterministic boardroom culture is, and how much we rely on fictitious point estimates, imagine an ambitious vice president who presents a 30-slide presentation of a business case as follows:

- "This project will take 18 months and cost $65 million dollars; however, there is a 40 percent chance that it will take twice as long and cost 75 percent more."

- "This $10 million investment clears our hurdle rate, but 30 percent of the time we will only break even and 15 percent of the time we will write off the entire amount."

- "35% of the time we will break even on this investment, but only 15% of the time will it generate returns that justify the risks."

This VP will not last long. People do not talk like that, we communicate point estimates, and corporate culture does not applaud probabilistic analyses. The failure/overrun rates presented by this hypothetical VP are the sort of overruns we should expect. Even though this soon-to-be-fired executive painted a more-accurate picture, it is not one senior teams typically like to see. In fact, U.S. President Truman once moaned, "Can someone please find me a one-handed economist," apparently fed up with nuanced "on the other hand" reasoning. Truman wanted a certainty that the world just cannot deliver.

Recall the experiment with college student term papers. Their worst-case estimates were a very long way from worst-case outcomes. They estimated 49 days as the worst case, but the actual average was 55 days to deliver the paper. Yet, with a 55-day *average*, some students delivered much later—the average conceals the fact that some students may have taken 70 days! Governance needs to reflect this error in risk psychology. When project teams use risk registers to "traffic light" risks, they are using their gut, and systematically underestimating what things going badly wrong means.

To make sense of this probabilistic world, mathematicians created simplified ways of understanding distributions of outcomes. One way is to reduce a distribution to a simple number, a mean, median, mode, variance, or range. The MLD is such an average. However, any time a complex pattern is reduced to a single number, there is a loss of information. To illustrate, if you cannot swim, walking across a river that is an *average* of four feet deep will get you into big trouble. The river's depth is a distribution and using just one number to describe it creates a perilous situation. Just as a range of depths helps clarify whether crossing the river will be safe, a range of outcomes is a better way of looking at how a change project might unfold.

A great example of the paradigm shift, from point estimates to distributions, comes from the work of Nate Silver, a polymathic statistician, and author of *The Signal and the Noise*. Election punditry in the United States is big business and the historical paradigm used to be for experts to make point estimates, to call a race one way or the other. Usually, the degree of confidence far overstates the precision of the estimates and even in recent decades, there have been spectacular failures of prediction. Silver's real contribution, though, is not in the math that underlies his analysis, but in the way he communicates his estimates. Rather than communicate a point-estimate (that is, who wins), Silver's communications show a range of outcomes. For example, during the 2014 U.S. elections, his research showed the probability that Republicans would hold each exact number of Senate seats (45 through 60) in 2015—not blunt forecasts such as "they will control the Senate." Even though they were big favorites to do so, there remained a 10% probability that they would not. Silver became famous by being more often right than wrong, but (paradoxically) he does not attempt to "get it right"—he tells his stories in probabilities.

The questions we must answer are: What are some nonaverage situations? How probable are those nonaverage situations? Can our capital, resources, and strategy withstand the worse, but not-improbable variations in project outcomes?

Understanding Project Variance Using SOCKS

The SOCKS framework (shortfalls, overruns, consequences, killed, and sustainability) can be used to drive conversations at the leadership team level. This will not reduce risk, but the team will have looked each other in the eye and acknowledged Most Likely Development and other much worse, but not-improbable outcomes. Use SOCKS[11] (or something more elaborate) to get an approximate handle on the range of ROI/outcomes you can expect (as shown in Table 3.2).

Table 3.2 Using the SOCKS Framework to Understand the Range of Project Outcomes

SOCKS CATEGORY	QUESTIONS	SAMPLE ANSWERS
Shortfalls	How much volatility is in our benefits expectation?	Cost savings of $10 million MLD, 25% of time $6 million, 25% of time less than $3 million.
Overruns	How much volatility is in time and cost estimates?	50% of time within 10% of MLD estimates, 25% exceed estimates by 25%, 15% exceed estimates by 50%, 10% exceed estimates by more than 50%.
Consequences	What are possible unintended consequences, how likely are they, and what are their effects?	Service levels in the call center may suffer during implementation increasing attrition: probability 50%, cost $500K.
Killed	How often have we written off a project like this one? If we had to do that, what the consequences be?	Yes it could happen to you, perhaps it has happened before?
Sustainability	How much will benefits be reduced by relapse?	This is particularly important where behavioral change is a key part of project success.

The more complex the system, the more variable (risky) the outcomes. The profound implications of this essential feature of reality still elude us in all the practical disciplines. Sometimes variance averages out, but more often fat-tail events beget more fat-tail events because of interdependencies. If there are multiple projects running, outlier (fat-tail) events may also be positively correlated—one IT project falling behind will stretch resources and increase the likelihood that others will be compromised.

---

[11] Some very sophisticated firms may have much more elaborate and quantitative methods for having these conversations. I do not intend this simple analysis to augment the very best risk/governance/leadership practices in the world. Having said that, I have consulted to 20 of the world's biggest and most admired companies, on projects with eight- and nine-figure budgets, and never seen even the simplest SOCKS-like analysis on the client side. By doing this, leaders begin to create a culture that thinks probabilities, not deterministically.

CHAPTER 3 • GOVERNANCE AND THE PSYCHOLOGY OF RISK

In a volatile world, where outcomes are not deterministic but probabilistic, we need both better ways of estimating probabilities and (crucially) better ways of talking about probabilities and communicating probabilities. In boardrooms, that means giving up the pretend certainty of a point estimate for a less certain looking, but more realistic distributions of outcomes.

The section on volatility offered some ideas on provisioning for (probable) deviations from estimates, and for better planning and provisioning based on the psychology of risk, the cultural norms around project estimation, and the institutional features of the competitive consulting industry. We also need a way of understanding catastrophic events, which will bring us to VUCA's *U* (uncertainty).

Uncertainty—What to Do When Risks Are Unmeasurable

"Without an understanding of randomness, we are stuck in a perfectly predictable universe that simply doesn't exist outside of our own heads."

—Charles Seife

If volatility adds unpredictability to the decision environment, uncertainty is more difficult still. According to the traditional distinction from economics,[12] risk is measurable, whereas uncertainty is indefinite or incalculable. In truth, risk can never be measured precisely except in dice rolls and games of chance, called *a priori* probability. Risk can only be **estimated** from observations in the real world, but to do that, we need to take a sample, and estimate the underlying distribution. In a sense, our estimates of real-world volatility are themselves volatile. Failure to realize this fundamental untidiness of the real world is called the *ludic fallacy* from the Latin for games.[13] This could be called semantic pedantry. However, when

---

[12] Knight, F. (2008). *Risk, uncertainty, and profit*. Evergreen Books. Online edition.

[13] Another Taleb neologism.

the term *risk measurement* is used as opposed to *risk estimation*, a degree of precision is suggested that is unrealistic, and the choice of language suggests that we know more than we do. Even the language "risk management" implies we can do more than we can.

Normal Distributions Do Not Help with Abnormal Events

"...as far as the propositions of mathematics refer to reality, they are not certain; and as far as they are certain, they do not refer to reality."

—Einstein

In Chapter 2, "From Change Fragility to Change-Agility," we introduced Nassim Taleb to view his ideas on fragility and "anti-fragility." However, Taleb's ideas on risk are what have made this mathematician, and Lebanese options trader a celebrity author. *The Black Swan: The Impact of the Highly Improbable* sold three million copies and spent 36 weeks on the *New York Times* best-seller list (not bad for a book on statistics). The book is rich philosophically, aesthetically, and mathematically (although equation free) and, if I may risk a forecast, Taleb has likely gained a place as one of the most significant thinkers of this century.

In brief,[14] Taleb says that while we continue to run businesses, banks, and economies according to mathematical fantasies, as described above by Einstein, of which the bell curve is one example, we can expect events such as the meltdown of 2007 (and much worse) to forever be with us. In essence, says Taleb, every regression, correlation, bell curve, t-test, mean, confidence interval, and standard deviation are little lies we tell each other that grotesquely mischaracterize reality.

Taleb gives us two concepts that are essential to understanding uncertainty. First, *black swans* are events of very low probability and

---

[14] Taleb has four books, each of which is entertaining in its own way. The most valuable (so far) is perhaps his most recent *Antifragile* that looks at practical means of exploiting the ideas in his first books.

that the normal distribution (the bell curve) underpredicts by factors of a thousand or a million. In a normal distribution, an event that occurs five standard deviations (five sigma) from the mean has about a 1 in 3.5 million chance (or one day in every 10,000 years). Over the past 56 years, the S&P 500 has seen 52 (!) days with five sigma or greater movement,[15] and three days in 1987 with changes that were ten sigma or greater. In the words of Taleb, "model error swells when it comes to low probabilities."[16] In other words, we are reasonably good at predicting events in the middle of the distribution that make little difference, and atrocious at predicting events that really matter.

Black swan events can trigger further black swan events. Connectivity is (again) our enemy because the domino effects may be multiple and may be nonlinear (such as the heat from a forest fire increasing the flammability of surrounding foliage). The magnitude 9.0 earthquake (according to some probability models a five sigma, one-in-ten-thousand year event) off Japan's coast triggered a tsunami with 40-meter waves that triggered a meltdown of three of the Fukushima six reactors. The area affected is home to high-tech manufacturing and scarcity of those products rippled across the world, affecting motor industry supply chains worldwide and computer manufacturers up and down the coast of Asia. Thus, a rare event 10,000 kilometers away affected a Kansas car dealer's livelihood.

Second, Taleb coins a heuristic for understanding fundamentally different probability distributions: *extremistan* and *mediocristan*. Follow Taleb's thought experiment. Take 1,000 people you know and line them up. Now add the heaviest person you can imagine (for example, 400 pounds) to the group. The average weight of our 1,001 people will not change much. That is mediocristan and the world of normally distributed outcomes. Single events do not matter much.

Now take those same thousand people, and add the wealth of the richest person you can imagine (for example, Bill Gates) to the group's wealth. Gate's wealth is now 99.9 percent of the group's total,

15 October, what a month! (2012, Oct. 22). *The Quant Monitor*. Retrieved from http://www.quantmonitor.com/october-what-a-month/.

16 Taleb, N. N. (2010). *The black swan: The impact of the highly improbable*. New York: Random House. Kindle edition.

and the combined total wealth of the original thousand is a rounding error. Welcome to extremistan. Book sales also live in extremistan: The mode book in the United States sells about 500 copies per year, J. K. Rowling sold several hundred million—dwarfing the combined sales of the thousands of hopeful authors (like yours truly). Remember our river that was four feet deep in most places? In extremistan, it would have a Grand Canyon–sized drop-off.

Black swans and extreme events can also be positive. The tiny UK publisher, Bloomsbury, who took a risk on Rowling sold 400 million books and launched the $15 billion Harry Potter black swan. Taleb's ideas suggest that the conservative assumptions used in many strategic forecasts and scenario planning are misguided because they greatly underestimate the probabilities of the things with the biggest effects. (In other words, our predictions are reasonable, except when it matters most.)

Because prediction is a fragile enterprise, businesses that rely heavily on predictions are necessarily fragile (for example, highly leveraged banks). Change projects have fat tails and sometimes produce black swans. This risk is asymmetric—mega projects can cost multiples of initial estimates, but never surprise by costing one quarter of what was budgeted. This involves knowing which of those two kinds of distributions (extremistan and mediocristan) affect different aspects of the business and managing them differently. In a connected world, there are few hiding places, but Taleb gives examples of industries, such as publishing, R&D (drugs), and venture capital, with black swan upside and banking with lots of black swan downside. In Taleb's words, business models that are susceptible to black swans are like "collecting nickels in front of steamrollers."

Taleb's ideas are so important that every strategic decision maker should be familiar with their essence, and every board should consider how their portfolio would fare in extremistan. His major books are—besides being essential business reading—great entertainment as he pops the balloons of social scientists and philosophers of various stripes, while peppering his stories with contemporary and classical-era examples.

Managing Uncertainty—Pre-Mortems

How do you think about the unthinkable black s
and consider what highly improbable risks would break
What practical tools are available to deal with this mos
matical abstraction: uncertainty? Decision-making exper ...y Klein
has proposed a stunningly simple strategy, called the *pre-mortem* that
short-circuits weaknesses in the psychology of risk, and most risk cultures. In a pre-mortem, change strategists and key decision makers
imagine themselves in a black swan future where their program has
failed spectacularly. They then work backward to examine the causes
of failure and use that learning to inform their forward-thinking program risk management.

This works better than "forward" risk planning because, according to Klein, it "removes pressure from those who are worried about
seeming disloyal by voicing concerns, creating a competition to find
ever more convincing reasons for failure."[17] The method counteracts
social psychological processes, such as groupthink and the planning
fallacy, and legitimizes dissent and contrarian thinking.

IBM has another practical tool similar to the pre-mortem, which
again sidesteps the cultural tendency to avoid doom-saying. IBM's
project dashboard evaluates projects along seven dimensions: Stakeholders, Business Benefits, Work and Schedule, Team, Scope, Risks,
and Delivery Organization Benefits. Every consulting firm has one of
those. However, IBM made the observation that starting projects on
Green led to insufficient focus, attention to detail, and energy when it
matters most, at the beginning. If one starts with the assumption that
all the lights are green, people may be reluctant to turn them to red
or amber. Now projects start on Red, until they prove themselves, and
the default setting is Red, unless evidence suggests otherwise.

---

[17] Klein G., interviewed by Burkeman, O. (2014, May 10). This column will
change your life: Hindsight – It's not just for past events. *The Guardian*. Retrieved from http://www.theguardian.com/lifeandstyle/2014/may/10/
hindsight-in-advance-premortem-this-column-change-life.

Risk Governance Is a People Problem, Not a Math Problem

Every decade or so, there is a good financial crisis to get the blood boiling: 1973, 1987, 1997, 2001, and 2008. In between those, every year or two, there is a good billion-dollar (plus or minus) minicrisis/ fraud that does not quite make the same global impact:[18] Madoff's embezzlement, Baring's $1.4 billion loss, the "London Whale" LIBOR fraud, Société Générale's $5 billion loss, Bank of China, BCCI, National Westminster, the Savings and Loan Crisis, and Allied Irish Bank.

In my previous professional life, I was a quant, providing equations (the kind Taleb is critical of) to help manage financial risk. What struck me most was how my analytical/mathematical approach seemed to make no difference at all. The biggest risks were not in equations—they were people risks! From the early 1990s, the major banks would have had (at least) the following well-staffed functions overseeing risk: compliance, risk management, middle-office, back-office, internal audit, credit and market risk, and legal. Add to this the external oversight of auditors, regulators, and other government bodies (many), and the bank's chicken coop was very well guarded.

Time after time, the fox got in. In a complex, labyrinthine organization, formal systems, which anticipate every eventuality, cannot be designed. In macabre terms, on 9/11, despite the U.S. $250 billion defense budget, the mainland proved vulnerable to attack by a few zealots with screwdrivers. Because the perfect system cannot be designed, there will always be weak spots that human ingenuity and resourcefulness can exploit.

This suggests that more than formal systems are required. Businesses need an ethical and risk-aware culture from top to bottom in the bank. For example, the two fraud investigations in which I was involved, Barings and National Westminster Bank ($150 million loss), were effectively carried out by one or two people who flew under the radar of the banks' formal systems. On both occasions, there was

---

[18] This is far from an exhaustive list, but many of these are in the billions of dollars, and most make the headlines only briefly before passing into the archives of business history.

plenty of smoke circulating on the trading room floor long before someone bothered to yell fire. As with an itinerant spouse, the most interested party was the last to know. Many people at these banks knew long before the bank's officers and regulators that something was amiss, but the risk culture allowed the misdeeds to go unchallenged for months. With the right kind of ethical culture, many such frauds might have been avoided.

Sometimes it is easier to identify the opposite of a sound risk culture. At PwC, we observed the following cultural attributes of poor risk cultures:

- The thought that risk compliance is "somebody else's job"
- Groupthink: "If I know about it, they must know about it, so it must be ok..."
- Poor risk intelligence/education, particularly in the psychology of risk
- Failure to clarify risk appetite and communicate permitted levels of risk-taking
- Insufficient attention to risk at board level
- Lack of upward communication of risk events and risk potential (shooting messengers)

A culture of managing risk needs to exist from the boardroom to the assembly line and employees have to have the accountability, attitudes, tools, and skills to manage risks, including operational risks, but also the risks associated with major change. This risk culture is not commonplace: More than half (58 percent) of corporate board members and internal auditors surveyed by KPMG said that their company's employees had little or no understanding of how risk exposures should be assessed for likelihood and impact.[19]

Managing uncertainty and risk require the understanding that risk is a people game, and not just something managed through formal structures. Risk-taking is an essential part of business, and as with change management, risk management is too important to be left to

---

[19] Many enterprise risk management programs lack fundamentals. KPMG's Survey of Internal Auditors and Boards, 2008.

specialists. This suggests that education in risk and the psychology of risk, understanding volatility and uncertainty, and creation of a risk culture are business education imperatives.

This chapter now turns to how uncertainty affects management of a portfolio of change, where some of the risks may be very highly correlated.

Managing Aggregate Change Risks

The scariest thing ever said to me by a CEO was that he had no idea, on aggregate, how much change was happening in his organization, nor how much they spent globally on consultants.

Consider three premises that are from my observations of global multinational corporations:

1. Rarely does a central body has oversight of the overall portfolio of change projects, except for a few exceptionally large projects that get C-level attention. Change is initiated and monitored in functional silos. The CIO will have a portfolio of IT projects, the CHRO will have a portfolio of HR projects, and other functions (or regions) will also have portfolios of dozens of projects running simultaneously. In addition to centrally driven initiatives, regional and country heads will have their own initiatives.

2. Change projects comprise most of the discretionary spending, are where most of the risk is taken, and (if failure rates are right) are where many losses are realized.

3. Change project outputs are very hard to measure—for example, how much a system is used, how much increase in throughput for a process redesign, how much quicker to market, the customer relationships the new CRM system should deliver. As McKinsey says,[20] "With big money and possibly the company's competitiveness at stake, why do many application-development

---

[20] Huskins, M., Kaplan, J., & Krishnakanthan, K. (2013, Aug.). Enhancing the efficiency and effectiveness of application development. *McKinsey Quarterly*. Retrieved from http://www.mckinsey.com/insights/business_technology/enhancing_the_efficiency_and_effectiveness_of_application_development.

(IT) organizations fly blind without a metric in place to measure productivity?"

When you add those premises together, you might conclude that businesses have no central, aggregate oversight of where they take the most risk and spend the most money, and (if we believe McKinsey) are limited in their ability to measure returns on investment. This competence in understanding, with data, how change fares in your business is, I think, one of the first steps toward improving change performance. As organizations are increasingly project-based, competence at evaluating and comparing returns across an entire portfolio of projects is vital. I think that business must get aggregate analytics on projects, probably at the CSO level, to answer the following questions:

- How much do we spend, on aggregate, on change projects (big and small) across the whole business?
- How good are we at measuring project outputs? (How much, exactly, did this save us, or increase revenue?)
- How good are we at predicting and estimating costs and benefits? (Variance)
- How are we doing over time? Is spending increasing? Are returns increasing or decreasing?
- How much do we use consultants? How do we assess value for money of every single project?
- How often are we in a SOCKS category? What are our normal overruns and benefit shortfalls? How much do we write off? How much volatility is there in project returns?
- How does change capability vary across functions and regions?
- What are our aggregate risks? What is the aggregate change load on the business? (For example, Asia-Pac has two big HR projects and two major IT projects and several smaller ones being implemented at the same time.)

The idea of portfolio management for a portfolio of businesses, comparing ROI, risks, and variance is nothing new. Venture capitalists and private equity do the same thing for their portfolios. Businesses can also be seen as a *portfolio of projects* (and are increasingly structured this way), so portfolio management at the project level seems an essential capability. This is even more important for projects than for separate businesses (or private equity investments) because projects in the same business can bump into each other and compete for resources, and increase the demands on managers dealing with implementation.

Conclusion

"We have minds that are equipped for certainty, linearity, and short-term decisions that must instead make long-term decisions in a non-linear, probabilistic world."

—Paul Gibbons

Understanding volatility and uncertainty, and how people behave and make decisions under those conditions is, I believe, an essential capability for twenty-first-century businesses. A few important ideas for leading change in volatile and uncertain times are:

- Change programs are where the risk is; risk and risk psychology are not part of the change management canon. We need to go beyond the risk maps and risk registers of Change Management 101.
- The planning fallacy means that estimates systematically under-shoot outcomes; leaders need to adjust for this as a yachtsman adjusts for a strong tide. The competitive structure of the consulting industry, and their excellence at managing their risk exposure, means businesses bear too much of the brunt of the planning fallacy.
- Point estimates do not represent reality; they are fictions that provide false certainty in risky situations.
- Uncertainty manifests itself through black swans and extremistan; leaders need an understanding of risk and business models that takes into account these kinds of events.

- Risk culture and risk education (including the psychology of risk) are essential to plug the gaps in formal risk management systems.
- Because most of the discretionary expenditure and risk lies in a business's change portfolio, an aggregate view of performance, risk, and SOCKS failure rates is the ante for improving change performance.

The leadership implications of these systematic faults in risk psychology are threefold. First, leaders must be able to adjust their risk judgments to take account of the mathematics and psychology of risk. Second, education in how math and psychology interact to determine human risk behavior seems to be more important than the obscure courses in econometrics and statistics that were part of my own business education. Third, business leaders must understand the specific psychology of projects and some of the systematic errors that happen around change: the planning fallacy and consulting fictions.

Volatility and uncertainty are just part of the VUCA package; we are still left with the problem of how to solve problems, analyze cause and effect, and make decisions in complex and ambiguous environments.

This is one of the hottest areas of research in management science today. In the coming chapter, we clarify what complexity and ambiguity mean, and then steal ideas from the environmental sciences, information theory, and analytics that suggest practical tools for decision makers in complex and ambiguous environments.

4

Decision Making in Complex and Ambiguous Environments

"Today the network of relationships linking the human race to itself and to the rest of the biosphere is so complex that all aspects affect all others to an extraordinary degree. Someone should be studying the whole system, however crudely that has to be done, because no gluing together of partial studies of a complex nonlinear system can give a good idea of the behavior of the whole."

—Murray Gell-Mann, Nobel Prize, Physics, 1969

Numerous CEO surveys (for example, from IBM and the Conference Board) cite complexity and analytics as their number-one and number-two challenges. Both complexity and analytics have difficult technical dimensions. Modeling a complex system, such as the climate, requires as much super-computing power as we can muster. Reducing ambiguity with analytics is at the forefront of computer science and artificial intelligence. The most interesting aspect of these challenges is where "math[1] meets people," or how non-technical leaders can capitalize on the opportunities and avoid the risk. Accordingly, this chapter looks at the human side of complexity and ambiguity for non-quantitative tools and to see what the leadership challenges may be.

---

[1] Not just math, but also computer science, cybernetics, and econometrics.

Complexity

The word *complexity* is often confused with *complicated*; people often use complex just to mean "difficult." This book derives the concept from mathematics, cybernetics, and systems theory. There is not just a pedantic difference between complicated problems and complex ones. Complex systems need different decision-making tools than complicated ones.

Complex systems have three features that combine to make them particularly challenging:

- *Multiplicity* means many moving parts, but that alone only creates complicated[2] systems. If parts of a system interact predictably, or are exhaustively known, the system is merely complicated, not complex, and behaves deterministically. For example, an aircraft engine may be complicated, but the parts interact in predictable ways and the behavior of the engine can be explained if you understand the laws of physics that govern interactions between those parts. The next two features are required for complexity.

- *Nonlinearity* means that inputs are not proportional to outputs, small changes may produce big results, and big changes may produce no results. A few examples of nonlinear relationships are cyclical, random, discontinuous (structural, or step-change), logarithmic, and exponential. Nonlinearity is the default setting for cause and effect in business: Linearity is rare.

- *Emergence* is the least intuitive, but also the most interesting feature. Emergence describes behaviors that arise out of more fundamental entities and yet are novel or irreducible with respect to them. For example, poker has simple rules that can be learned by a six-year-old, yet the dynamics of an expert poker game—bluffing, betting patterns, psychology, game theory, and the metagame that emerges from those simple rules—cannot be understood just by knowing those simple rules. A second example of emergence is an ant colony. Again, the colony

---

[2] Experts contrast *complicated* with *complex,* whereas in casual speech they might be used interchangeably.

displays extremely complex community behavior: finding food sources, responding to threats, and building and rebuilding the habitat. Yet, individual ants are not clever, and there are no central directives ("the food source to the south is exhausted, go find another"). Nevertheless, the overall effect of some simple rules is colony-level behavior that looks just like a purposeful attempt to solve certain problems.

Complexity theory provides a way to understand the behavior of a wide range of dynamic systems, ranging from traffic flow and economics to weather. In business, it explains consumer behavior, the psychology of markets, and aspects of business and operations management and strategy. The plentiful computing resources available today have made it far easier to study these sorts of systems and to begin to understand the rich patterns and dynamics that the mathematics of emergence produces.

Inadequate Ways of Dealing with Complexity

One way of managing complexity is to constrain the freedom of the parts: to hold some of those nonlinear interactions still. Businesses accomplish this with tight rules, processes, hierarchies, policies, and rigid strategies. Gathering people together under a corporate roof reduces complexity by constraining individual autonomy. The upside, of course, is collaboration, alignment of goals, and faster exchange of information. As you saw in Chapter 2, "From Change Fragility to Change-Agility," this highly structured approach works as long as the external world is stable. Reliance on structure and hierarchy to reign in complexity may explain why of the original dozen Dow Jones companies, only one (General Electric) has not been dissolved, or acquired—a 90 percent attrition rate in a century. Compared with ecosystems and some species (sharks, invertebrates) that endure for hundreds of millions of years, corporations are very fragile entities indeed. This creative destruction may be necessary for the survival of economy (as a competitive ecosystem), but it also speaks volumes to the lack of adaptability of individual enterprises.

Another method of analyzing complex systems is reductionism. For example, individual performance can be analyzed in terms of individual motivation and skills, but this misses causes such as team dynamics, culture, and organizational constraints, *and* the feedback looks between these different variables. It is a very commonplace error, covered in more detail in Chapter 5, "Cognitive Biases and Failed Strategies," to quickly attribute cause to a single factor in a complex system. (This also explains why such strategies fail.)

Two Tools for Solving Complex Problems

There are two practical tools for applying complexity theory to problem solving. The first suggests that different types of thinking are required in complex and other systems; the second helps solve problems in complex systems by analyzing cause and effect.

The first tool comes from a Welsh scholar, David Snowden, who divides systems into four types: simple, complicated, complex, and chaotic. The first step in problem solving and decision making is to decide which of those four *causal logics* apply to the system in which you are trying decide.

Simple Systems

Simple systems are stable, familiar, well defined, and have clear cause-and-effect relationships: We do A, and we get B. *Categorization* is what solves simple problems: This is that category of problem, we have successfully solved it this way in the past, let us do this. They are every manager's bread and butter. Experience tells us the category, and our responses are well practiced. The risks for the leader are assuming one understands the problem well enough to categorize it. We would often like to see the world as simpler, or more certain than it is—"we don't see things as they are, but rather as we are."[3]

Complicated Systems

Complicated systems knit many simple systems together, and this layering and combining of systems means complicated systems might not resemble each other enough to categorize problems.

---

[3] Attributed to Anaïs Inn.

Categorization thus prevents deeper understanding of the system's logic. In complicated systems, the key is *analysis*, and reductionism can be a good strategy. The system's parts—and the relationships between them—can be studied.

Complex Systems

"To really understand a [complex] system, you have to try to change it."

—Donella Meadows

Complex systems are complicated systems where the parts misbehave: Human parts are particularly prone to responding differently to the same stimulus because they learn and adapt. A microchip is complicated, but not complex—you can predict how it will behave once you understand its logic. As you have seen, in a complex system, behavior emerges that is ornate and even "intelligent," without orchestration from a top-down hierarchy. Complex systems include things such as businesses, the economy, ecosystems, the weather, networks, flocks of birds, and our brains.

Complex systems require *experimentation* and *prototyping*: To understand it, you have to change it. Why? Committing resources to a system you do not understand is foolish; you have to dabble, tinker, and hack the system to see how it works.[4] In fast-moving consumer markets, long-term strategy and short-term experimentation pair up. For example, despite its unassailable market leadership, Amazon keeps running experiments, today with drone delivery, and paying the U.S. Post Office to deliver on Sundays. Some Amazon experiments stick. How many of these have you heard of: 1-Click, Amazon Marketplace, Customer Reviews, Amazon Recommendations, Amazon Wish List, Kindle Direct Publishing, Amazon e-reader, Amazon Cloud Drive, Print-on-Demand, Amazon Prime, Amazon Instant

---

[4] The weather is an interesting contrast; we cannot intervene and see what happens. The difference is hundreds of thousands of weather stations each measuring (at least) dozens of variables, modeled by the finest applied mathematicians, and then crunched on a supercomputer.

Video, and Amazon Studios. Leading-edge digital marketing uses the experimentation and prototyping mechanism to their advantage by running multiple trials (called *split-testing*) and modeling customer responses. According to Google's chief economist, Hal Varian, Google conducts about 10,000 experiments per year and has 1,000 running at the same time.

Brick-and-mortar firms can also take advantage of this experimental (scientific) mindset and methods. Another recipe for failure can be "big bang" style implementations, that is, programs rolled out in haste and globally with disastrous consequences. Time is money, and projects are often behind by the implementation stage—it is tempting to allow hope to triumph over experience and pray all will all go swimmingly. To misquote another Prussian strategist,[5] "no project plan survives contact with the enemy." The stunningly simple pilot or staged implementation uncovers organizational complexity that is hard to imagine during planning.

Chaotic Systems

In a chaotic system, cause-and-effect relationships break down completely, creating the high turbulence associated with chaos. This context is characterized by multiple, parallel decisions, little time to think, heightened emotional tension, and requirement for quick action. The archetypal situation is crisis where the situation can tumble further out of control if no action is taken.

Chaotic situations prohibit analysis, and there is little time to experiment, but quick categorization of problem subareas and a "fix what you can fix attitude" nudge the system back toward order and mere complexity. The key to chaotic decision scenarios is to "act quickly and learn." This method prevents destructive *analysis paralysis* in situations that defy analysis. A U.S. Senate inquiry after Hurricane Katrina found that "failure of initiative" exacerbated the disaster's consequences. The inquiry found fault in government at many levels, including the White House ignored dire expert warnings days before, the mayor ordered evacuation too late, the governor refused foreign

---

[5] Field Marshall Helmuth von Moltke—"no battle plan survives contact with the enemy."

ald that would have saved lives, and the president continued his vacation for two days rather than use the power of his office to mobilize federal resources. In crises, where fast action is called for, having a template (checklist) of things to quickly do is useful and much disaster response planning provides such checklists to get action quickly under way.

A simplified version of Snowden's model appears in Table 4.1. One can still make errors of categorization or analysis, but by using this powerful yet simple rubric, the right sort of logic can be brought to bear.

Table 4.1 Systems with Different Logic Require Different Decision-Making Styles

SYSTEM LOGIC	DECISION STYLE	EXAMPLE
Simple	Categorize	Some day-to-day management challenges
Complicated	Analyze	Traditional reductive strategic and operational analysis
Complex	Experiment, prototype	Rapidly changing markets, start-up environments
Chaotic	Act quickly, learn	Crises

How to Understand Cause and Effect in Complicated and Complex Systems

"We need systems thinking more than ever, because connectivity and complexity make it harder to understand cause and effect."

—Peter Senge

Our second tool, systems thinking, is conceptually understood by all change experts. Despite this, very few executives seem to have heard of it, and only a small fraction of those will have used it. Even change experts deeply familiar with its concepts use it rarely. Systems thinking is an idea with its roots in cybernetics and modeling of ecosystems in the environmental sciences. In my opinion, despite being widely understood by change experts and despite the method's enormous power, very few executive and project teams use it to understand cause and effect. It is the most powerful yet underused tool in the change toolbox, and the hope here is to further its interest and adoption as a way of addressing VUCA challenges.

In the words of Peter Senge, who wrote the 1996 change classic *The Fifth Discipline*, "*Systems thinking* [is] a way of thinking about, and a language for describing and understanding, the forces and interrelationships that shape the behavior of systems." The biggest strategic mistakes happen when four different kinds of mathematical relationships are confused: linear, nonlinear,[6] cyclical, and stochastic (random). When the housing bubble burst across the world, there were, until the banks and stock market collapsed, experts still arguing that the market had "changed structurally." The experts were sure that "ownership culture" had transformed housing, that the structure of the mortgage industry had created new liquidity, and that urbanization would propel asset prices ever higher. The hyped *structural* change, that asset prices had entered a new era, gave way to a *cyclical* collapse. In contrast, Research in Motion (RIM), makers of the Black-Berry, missed the *structural* changes in the smartphone market from the iPhone and Android launches thinking their competitors' success was short-term and cyclical. The stock now trades at 10 percent of its peak value.

Systems thinking helps predict the type of mathematical relationships between variables even when it is very hard to calculate those exactly. Getting precise predictions from a complex system requires very advanced mathematics and a supercomputer to crunch the numbers, but business leaders can avoid big mistakes by understanding qualitatively the sort of behavior the system will produce.

The Systems Archetype Tool

One of systems thinking's tools, the *systems archetype,* can be used at a number of levels, from "back of the envelope" modeling, to extended systems mapping done by teams in a workshop environment,

---

[6] Exponential, power law, logarithmic, polynomial, and so on.

to mathematical modeling of behavior. Systems archetypes are built out of *causal loop diagrams*. The two simplest loops are *balancing loops* and *reinforcing loops*, which parallel *diminishing returns* and *increasing returns* in economics. Balancing loops happen when markets saturate, or when systems approach constraints, meaning substantial efforts will yield little or no improvement. Just understanding this system type and being able to spot it can prevent much banging of heads against walls. Who in a leadership position has not pulled multiple levers to fix a problem to no effect?

One example of a balancing loop from my own industry is driving profitability by increasing consultants' billable hours, called *utilization*. This seems to be irrefutable logic—fixed salaries plus more billing equals more profits—but it's only in the short term. Driving up utilization has the effect of driving down practice-building activities, such as selling, networking, product development, and marketing. As a result, many consulting firms find themselves insanely busy, only to be followed by periods of extreme overcapacity because the activities that drive medium and long-term value slowed.

The opposite type, the reinforcing loop, can create a "virtuous circle," which might happen as a new product gains market share, attracting attention and word-of-mouth publicity, thus further increasing sales and market share. This is the essence of the nonlinear behavior called *virality*, and understanding the drivers of viral phenomena is an area of serious research for network modelers and theorists. It explains a common pricing strategy in the e-commerce world (sometimes called a "land grab") where market share is built rapidly at very unprofitable prices to capitalize on virality. Reinforcing loops also form vicious circles where the system begins to collapse upon itself. During the 2007 mortgage crisis, housing prices fell, banks became more cautious, mortgage lending dried up, and housing prices fell further (as much as 80 percent in places where the bubble had been most extreme).

Many natural systems and many business systems combine these two, producing an S-curve that explains phenomena such as diffusion of innovations, product life cycles, and start-up returns (shown in Figure 4.1). Reinforcing causal loops dominate the beginning of a life cycle (increasing returns), and balancing loops dominate the latter stages (saturation, diminishing returns), as seen in Figures 4.2 and 4.3.

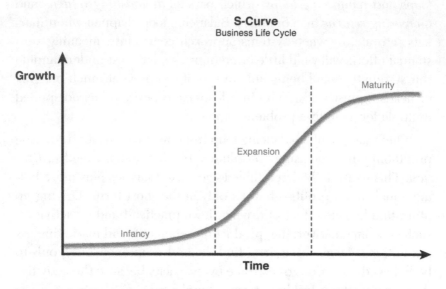

Figure 4.1 S-curves model interesting natural and business phenomena.

More Advanced Systems Modeling

"The harder you push, the harder the system pushes back."
—Peter Senge

Most experienced businesspeople have a deft, intuitive grasp of these two typical nonlinear relationships and build those intuitions into decision making. Systems thinking gets much more interesting: Balancing and reinforcing loops are just the building blocks of modeling very complicated (and complex) systems. With just those, we can draw systems on the back of beer coasters, create wall-size models with entire teams in a strategy workshop, or even build computer models.

Some of the ways those two loops combine produce systems such as the "Fixes that Fail" archetype (which is one of about a dozen). Figure 4.2 shows a "fix" reducing a problem (loop B1), but increasing other consequences (loop R2), which make the problem worse.

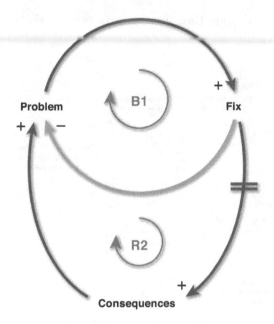

Figure 4.2 Fixes that Fail archetype—quick fixes make things worse (produced with Vensim software).

Some examples of this system are:

- Borrowing money to "fix" a debt problem without addressing chronic overspending

- Using consultants to solve business problems that managers ought to solve, which therefore prevents the business from developing problem-solving skills and change expertise

- Taking pain relievers to "fix" chronic back pain, allowing continued aggravation (rather than trying stretching, yoga, better posture, or more exercise)

- Kicking the can down the road in politics with superficial, populist policies whose adverse effects will be felt by the next incumbents (or generation)

Figure 4.3 shows a commonplace situation (in many departments and teams), called *project overwhelm*. The figure shows balancing (seesaws) and reinforcing (snowballs) loops that keep adding projects to an already overbusy team despite their best efforts to clear their backlog.

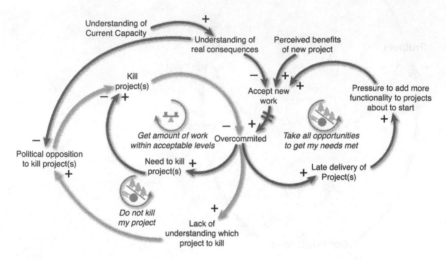

Figure 4.3 Systems thinking diagrams can help us understand why things do not change despite our best efforts (courtesy of Rolf Häsänen).

If doing this seems burdensome and overcomplex, it is, in my view, more burdensome to attempt change that is strategically misguided based on naïve views of the situation. Although Figure 4.3 is a complex diagram, the diagram is still *less* complex than the system it represents! There is not a seasoned leader who has not thrown the kitchen sink at a problem to zero effect, nor a leader who has not seen an aspect of the business spiral out of control despite attempts to rein it in. Systems thinking explains why. Yet, when I have taught this in business school classes, some leap upon it, and others roll their eyes seemingly craving a much simpler way to understand something very complex. Frequently, the greatest benefit that teams derive from creating these diagrams is sharing views of the problem, discussing cause-and-effect business drivers, challenging assumptions, unearthing important missed variables, developing shared understanding of dynamics, enabling team learning, and building a consensus around a solution.

Systems thinking allows the user to see patterns and to visualize the whole system. As such, it is a better solution to complexity than reductionism, which destroys information in the system. Systems thinking is also dynamic and allows picturing the whole system "in motion" rather than, for example, a table or graph showing how just two variables may be related. Systems thinking also begins to explain phenomena that befuddle experts, such as bubbles, crashes, virality, domino effects, life cycles, and structural market changes.

VUCA's ambiguity now leads us to a consideration of whether analytics helps with the ambiguity problem and what the human and leadership challenges are with analytics implementations.

Ambiguity and the Human Side of Analytics

"The fog prevents the enemy from being discovered in time, a battery from firing at the right moment, a report from reaching the General; the cavalry from charging effectively..."

—General Carl von Clausewitz, *On War*

Ambiguity, von Clausewitz's "fog of war," prevents seeing clearly, and hence deciding wisely. Today's business ambiguity is different than the ambiguity of bygone days, when East India Company traders had to wait years until ships returned to see whether ships were full with booty from faraway lands, were empty, or had been sunk.

Today, executives face a deluge of data and the problem is not lack of data, but rather distinguishing the signal from the noise and creating information, insight, and wisdom from the data. The problem is that this data deluge hits businesses with the same formats and the same speed of decision making as hundreds of years ago: human beings sitting in a room talking about things, using rigid, hierarchical organizational structures to decide and execute. We need a way of converting the petabytes of data into kilobyte-sized graphs and tables that human beings can process.[7] There are then two sides to

---

[7] Charts, graphs, and tables do not exhaust the possibilities for information display. These 2D and 3D methods are limited, and there have been recent advances in visual display that make column-and-row charts seem dull.

the human side of analytics implementations: teaching people to use analytics wisely in decision making and leadership of the technology side so that investments in analytics pull their (expensive) weight.

Twenty-First-Century Analytics—Big Data and Beyond

"There is now a computer in the middle of most economic transactions. These computer-mediated transactions enable data collection and analysis, personalization and customizations, continuous experimentation, and contractual innovation."

—Hal Varian[8]

The story of using computers to support business decision making is barely in adolescence when compared with commerce, which has been around for at least 5,000 years. We can now do in a nanosecond, with a silicon wafer no larger than a potato chip, that which used to take a room full of people several years. The armies of clerks in a 1930s office each performed a few calculations per minute. The Intel I7 (probably the chip in your laptop) performs 70 billion operations per second, which is crawling compared with the 30 quadrillion operations per second of a Cray supercomputer. Although the information age may be 70 years old, we have seen nothing of its potential.

Since the 1960s, there has been a progression of terminology, from management information systems, to decision support systems, to enterprise information systems, to analytics, and now the nomenclature is *Big Data*, with which only a very few companies have come to grips. Big Data expert, Jeanne Harris, advocating for Big Data approaches, says that "mere" analytics is now a hygiene factor and is no longer a source of competitive advantage.

Humans connect to digital devices every day, and devices connect to the Web every day. Walmart processes one million customer transactions per hour, and Facebook processes one billion posts per day. This creates a "digital exhaust" we leave behind that, if combined with

---

[8] Chief economist, Google, and Professor Emeritus at the University of California, Berkeley

static data (such as genomic data or archival data on habits), creates opportunities to understand human behavior in unimagined ways.

Big Data is more than just an incremental change; it is radically different in these ways:

- **Volume**—Forget "gigs" and "teras." Today, data is processed in petabytes (one thousand trillion), and stored in exabytes (one million trillion). Google processes about 24 petabytes of data per day, and may store in the region of 10 exabytes. As Trevor Davis, IBM futurist and distinguished engineer, puts it, "the future is yottabytes" (that is one billion trillion bytes or 10^{21}).

- **Velocity**—Data no longer sits nicely still (static data waiting on a server). Real-time image parsing—used in some experimental retail environments—requires extremely powerful hardware and algorithms.

- **Variety**—Numbers are old hat. Data now comes from sensors, from mobile phones, from cars, from cameras, and from genomes.

- **Required tools**—New data technologies and development environments (for example, ML, Hadoop, F#, R, and WEKA) change quickly making even year-old technologies obsolete. That pace means data scientists' skills age quickly, and companies that want to remain at the leading edge need agile HR processes and shifting skill sets of data scientists to keep up the great demand.

What are the new uses of Big Data?[9]

- **Price optimization**—Retailers can accurately model their demand elasticity (how demand responds to price changes), which allows real-time repricing according to market conditions. Airlines and hotels have mastered this ability in the last decade; others will follow.

- **Customer intimacy**—Why bother advertising new cars to families who have just bought one, or mortgages to consumers

---

[9] Adapted from the excellent book by Tom Davenport, *Big Data at Work*.

in their 70s? Customers can be offered only products they might need and not be inundated with offers that irritate.

- **Contract compliance**—Car rental agencies, insurance companies, and automobile financing companies can assess driving behaviors and risks, and reprice accordingly.

- **Customer service improvement**—Sensors allow General Electric to monitor the performance of heavy machinery (such as generators) and more quickly anticipate and resolve maintenance issues.

- **Predictive analytics**—Data mining and machine learning can help analysts test hypotheses and make much more accurate business forecasts than previously.

- **Better customer targeting**—Netflix now knows what I want to watch before I do, and my phone company knows when I am fed up and about to switch providers. By contrast, my cable provider still offers me special deals on *Monster Truck Challenge* (not special enough).

- **Business process improvement**—Experimentation allows continuous business process improvement, supply chain optimization, predictive analytics to anticipate demand, and HR analytics.

The Human-Machine Interface—Where Data Becomes Wisdom

The model shown in Figure 4.4, based upon one from information sciences, illustrates what has to happen to data before it becomes a decision—petabyte information flows turn into "we are going to do X."

The first step is to structure *data* into *information* so that it may be visualized and understood by people who are decision makers. The leading edge of this is accomplished by machine learning, one of the hottest areas in computer science and statistics. Machine learning reverses the historical practices of the business dictating the information it requires, and then securing relevant data to data-driven approaches where algorithms mine information in a sea of data.

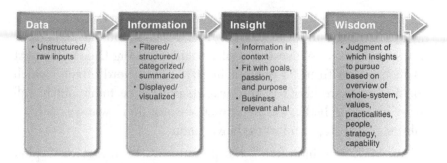

Figure 4.4 Knowledge hierarchy—from data to wisdom.

The translation from *information* to *insight* involves in-context application, and requires human expertise although artificial intelligence is encroaching on this aspect also. This step is where the strategic context, purpose, and passion come in. Caesars Entertainment, for example, had behavioral *information*, gained through data mining, that customers stop spending money after a casino loss. The *insight* was that they could distribute perks (shows, meals, hotel rooms) at those times (when they will make the biggest difference to customer mood) and thus increase goodwill and retention. (This works much better than the less-targeted allocation of rewards based purely on annual spending.)

Not every business insight, or idea, is worthy of attention and implementation (all things considered). To translate *insight* to *wisdom*, executives must consider wider strategy, organizational capability, values, and implementation practicalities. The insight has to "fit" with the big picture, and only executive judgment (wisdom) can evaluate the insight in that context and choose whether to execute or not. Computers cannot do that, at least not yet.

What are the consequences for the organization and the role for leadership along that journey?

The Human Side of Analytics

"It is becoming apparent that without extra executive horsepower, stoking the momentum of data analytics will be difficult for many organizations."

—McKinsey & Company

Investment in Big Data technologies continues to expand, according to a late 2014 survey by Gartner, Inc., which found that 73 percent of respondents have invested or plan to invest in Big Data in the next 24 months, up from 64 percent in 2013. The "herd effect," which you'll learn more about in the next chapter, is certainly out in full force, and done badly, for the wrong reasons, there will certainly be substantial missteps and wasted investment.

As McKinsey indicates,[10] the pressure on businesses to exploit analytics (Big Data) falls to senior leadership, and success or failure depends most heavily on their ability to adapt themselves and their organizations to the challenge. Table 4.2 suggests organizational and leadership capabilities are required.[11]

Big Data and "Pilot Error"

Our interest in Big Data, and this abbreviated treatment, in this book is because businesses are increasingly trying to solve the ambiguity problem with Big Data implementations. Big Data also promises a way to get science-based, decision-making tools into the hands of strategists and are a part of the passion for science-based craft that drives this book.

There are pitfalls from early adoption of any technology that go beyond the risk of a large systems implementation failing (recall that success rates for this type of change hover around 70%). Senior executives will have to understand enough about the underlying science to know how far to trust information from Big Data applications. Predictions are model dependent, however much data they make use of. Observational data alone does not produce causal conclusions—experiments must be run to turn those observations into cause and effect. In summary, there are limits to how much senior leaders can treat such systems as "black-boxes." (The Wall Street crash of 2007/2008 revealed the weakness of unquestioning acceptance of banks' risk models and failure to ask the hard questions of the "quants.")

---

[10] "Big Data: The Next Frontier for Innovation, Competition, and Productivity," from McKinsey Global Institute.

[11] Based partly on the scholarship of analytics experts Tom Davenport and Jeanne Harris.

Table 4.2 The Human Side of Big Data: Staff, Skills, Culture, and Capabilities

HOW KNOWLEDGE CHANGES	THE HUMAN SIDE OF KNOWLEDGE
Data to information	**Staff:** Hiring and managing data scientists and adopting HR practices appropriate to that community, such as rewards and constant technical training. **Skills:** Helping data scientists understand the business context, strategy, and needs. **Culture:** Creating a small-company, hacker-style culture that fits data scientists. Having product managers and marketing value analytics approaches. **Capability:** Understanding which information, in which formats, produces maximum value for the business decision makers.
Information to insight	**Staff:** Having data/information–literate executives who understand the opportunities, the risks, and the process. **Skills:** Generating insight from information, asking data the right questions, blending intuition and experience with data-driven methods. **Culture:** Having a culture that values "open questions" as much as "closed questions"—that is, values and uses data-driven experiments. **Capability:** Having management and senior leadership who understand data-science methods, culture, and possibilities.
Insight to wisdom	**Staff:** Overseeing a Big Data capability requires a blend of deep technical knowledge that changes rapidly, and also robust knowledge of the industry and company culture (a rare blend of young skills in a seasoned body). **Skills:** Having analytics governance and a hacker/experimental mentality. **Culture:** Balancing art and science in decision making, that is, the Moneyball approach. Shifting technology organization from operational focus to customer/strategic focus. **Capability:** Utilizing faster, more data-driven decision making and strategic processes to avoid human bottlenecks.

Conclusion

Complexity and analytics (our partial answer to ambiguity) are two of their biggest worries, CEOs say. To work with complexity, we saw we had to use the term correctly, particularly to distinguish it from merely complicated. Snowden's decision-making rubric helps suggest the kind of causal logic we should use depending on whether a system is simple, complicated, complex, or chaotic.

Systems thinking (and the systems archetype tool) helps model non-linear effects, especially feedback loops in systems with many parts. For a tool with its power (both analytical power and the power to drive the right kind of conversations about what is really happening) it is sorely underused, even by experts who understand it well.

Tera- and exa-byte information flows still hit human decision-making systems that have not changed a great deal in the last century. This creates a different kind of ambiguity which requires that the data morph into information, insight, and then wisdom. Each step of the process requires an organizational and leadership capability. New technologies, such as Big Data, will provide better information on which to base decisions, but the final word is always human. The next chapter, the final chapter in Part II, "Change Strategy," looks at the human side of decision making, how error-prone it can be, and what can be done about that.

5

Cognitive Biases and Failed Strategies

"Truth is confirmed by inspection and delay; falsehood by haste and uncertainty."

—Tacitus

The VUCA context produces conflicting demands for decision-makers. Volatility suggests a need for speedy response, but uncertainty, complexity, and ambiguity suggest greater deliberation.

High-stakes decision making is never easy, but the toughest decisions often surround major change. Outcomes are uncertain, significant capital is at risk, the emotional and career stakes are high, and relationships may be strained. We would like to be at our best, but humans are fallible and get less rational under pressure. For an individual, a decision error could mean a bad financial, career, or other type of decision, where the costs are painful, but contained. When leaders of major corporations make errors, sometimes lives and livelihoods are at stake. While there are conflicting voices, the center of gravity today leans toward speed, trusting one's gut, and decisiveness. I believe this to be a flaw, and this chapter explains why.

Cognitive Biases in Business

"We are more like Homer Simpson than Superman."

—Dan Ariely

Human fallibility has been around long before Alexander Pope said, "... to err is human." Only in the last 50 years has research begun to systematically study human error. The mistakes people make in decision making are not random, sometimes overshooting, and sometimes undershooting. They are systematic and called *cognitive biases,* or *logical fallacies,* and are among the hottest areas in psychology, neuroscience, and economics during the last four decades. The fact that humans are error-prone is not news, but the fact that the errors are systematic allows us to correct for them or be skeptical about how certain we ought to be.

Some biases may have their roots in the evolution of our brains. Hunter-gatherers, on the savanna, might discern a threat and it was better that their threat-discernment yielded *false positives* (there is no real threat, but protective steps are taken anyhow) than *false negatives* (you see no threat and you are eaten). Some biases are shortcuts, or snap judgments, and systematically incorrect because our overactive pattern recognition apparatus sees patterns where none exist. Other biases result from emotions and motivations affecting judgment. As you saw in Chapter 3, "Governance and the Psychology of Risk," people will pay much more for antiterrorism travel insurance than general travel insurance policies because the emotion associated with the first is so much stronger.

How many of each animal did Moses take onto the ark? Most people answer quickly and wrongly, saying "two." The correct answer is, "None. It was Noah, not Moses, on the ark." Even when the question is asked in a class called "cognitive biases and decision making," people still get it wrong. That fast-and-frugal reasoning is an example of what Daniel Kahneman,[1] in *Thinking Fast and Slow,* calls System 1 thinking. System 1 is fast, automatic, frequent, emotional, stereotypic, and subconscious. System 2, by contrast, is slow, effortful, infrequent, logical, calculating, and conscious. System 1 is most useful in very familiar situations, but when we have misclassified the situation as familiar, and fail to engage System 2, we make mistakes.[2]

The list of biases and fallacies is very long. There are more than 100 that have been classified and studied. Table 5.1 classifies and names the most important of these for business decision makers.

---

[1] Kahneman shared the 2002 Nobel Prize in Economics with Amos Tversky.

[2] There is an alternative, misguided view, that our "guts" make better decisions, covered at the end of this chapter.

Table 5.1 Cognitive Biases Affecting Change Strategy

BIAS/FALLACY	CHANGE STRATEGY ERROR
Perception Biases	
Overconfidence bias (Chapter 5)	Telling us we are right when we are wrong—confidence without competence
Deterministic fallacy (Chapter 3)	Using point estimates for resources, risks, and planning
Halo effect (Chapter 5, Chapter 9)	Allowing the glow of one success from something (company, project, individual) to prevent diligent appraisal
Ludic fallacy (Chapter 3)	Underestimating fat tails and skewness of distributions, where the biggest risks lie
Ostrich bias (Chapter 5)	"Groundhog Day"—failing to learn from past errors and improve change capability
Zero-risk bias (Chapter 3)	Assuming small risks are zero risks ("It could never happen here")
Problem-Solving Biases	
Egocentric bias/fundamental attribution error (Chapter 5)	Curing symptoms, ignoring the disease, and playing the blame game
"Is-ought" fallacy (Chapter 5)	Using analyses to drive change without requisite guiding narrative or emotional commitment
Narrative fallacy (Chapter 5)	Constructing neat and tidy cause-and-effect narratives that are simplistic and wrong
Hyperbolic discounting (Chapter 5)	Underweighting future costs, or discounting future benefits—short-termism
Availability/confirmation biases (Chapter 5)	Thinking that the data we see is all that is important, or only seeing data that confirms how right we are ("We observe what we believe, not believe what we observe")
Solution-Selection Biases	
Action bias (Chapter 5)	Fire, ready, aim. Acting too quickly and considering too few options, sometimes to give the appearance of being "action-oriented"
Institutional bias (Chapter 5)	Following the herd and jumping on the fad bandwagon
Sunk-cost bias (Chapter 3)	Considering what has already been invested; leads to escalation of commitment: doubling down on a failing project (sometimes repeatedly)
The planning fallacy (Chapter 3)	Systematically underestimating complexity and risk, thereby underscoping resource requirements, especially capital

Why study biases? The essence of rationality is to know when you are being irrational, and how you are being irrational. The core of this chapter is then to recognize when System 1 may fail and when System 2 must be engaged. Because the error-causing biases and fallacies are systematic and predictable, a deeper understanding of them can lead to better decisions. As with a sharpshooter who corrects for wind velocity, an executive team who understands from the get-go the sorts of mistakes they will be prone to making in certain situations can attempt to correct for them. For example, a team member might say, "Our intuitive predictions and the data we have are very favorable, but conditions are ripe for overoptimism and the planning fallacy. Let us consider the strength of the evidence and moderate our expectations accordingly."

This chapter divides biases into perception biases, problem-solving biases, and solution-selection biases.

Perception Biases

"...where all the men are strong, all the women good looking, and all the children above average."

—Garrison Keillor

To solve problems accurately, and devise accurate solutions, leaders need to know where their biases lie and adjust appropriately—as the sharpshooter analogy suggests. Perhaps the most damaging of all cognitive biases are biases that tell you that you are right when you are wrong: the optimism biases. Physicist Niels Bohr (a contemporary and collaborator of Einstein) said, "Prediction is difficult, especially about the future." We are caught between hopes, fears, emotional attachments, self-justification, identity, psychological projection, and our limited cognitive abilities in areas such as planning, probability, judgment, and causal inference.

Confidence without Competence

"Only people blinded by ideology fall into the trap of believing in their own infallibility."

—Freeman Dyson, Physicist

In my Strategic Decision Making program at U.S. business schools, I ask executives to answer ten questions, some of which are:

- How many books are in the Old Testament?
- How long is the Nile River?
- How many neurons are in the human brain?
- How far is it from the Earth to the Moon?

Nobody but the truest nerd would get them all right, but I ask the business leaders to provide their answer as a range where they would be 90 percent certain of being correct, what statisticians call a 90 percent confidence interval. The most common score is 40 percent correct; that is, only four out of ten correct answers within the 90 percent confidence interval. My executives get over half wrong despite being 90 percent certain on all ten of them!

This phenomenon does not just apply to subjects where our knowledge is limited; experts are *more* dangerous than nonexperts in many cases. Berkeley Professor Philip Tetlock has spent a career studying tens of thousands of expert predictions. The experts that he studied came from every imaginable area of expertise and despite their credentials and reputation, fared little better than pure chance and worse than simplistic methods (such as merely averaging the election results in a precinct over the last few cycles). Fully 15 percent of events that had no chance, happened, and a whopping 25 percent of events they were *absolutely sure* of failed to happen.

Philosopher Isaiah Berlin, in a 1953 essay, categorized thinkers and writers as hedgehogs or foxes. Hedgehogs have a big idea, and are specialized and ideological one-trick ponies. They respond badly to challenge, deal badly with complexity, like straightforward solutions, and generally do not play well with foxes. Those are exactly the attributes that often get promotions, and are weakest leading complex, risky endeavors.[3]

Foxes know less but about lots of things, are self-critical, study the evidence, and are cautious and flexible. It sounds as if we want our world run by foxes, but quite the opposite is the case. We vote for hedgehogs, and employ them as CEOs—their self-confidence can be infectious and "strong leadership" is often confused with certainty. Are not leaders supposed to be sure of themselves, and have the answers? To demur, reflect, or to change ones views is seen as "flip-floppy" (more so in the political arena). Keynes, the quintessential fox, once accused of flip-flopping quipped, "When the facts change, I change my mind. What do you do, sir?" Al Dunlap built a lucrative business career as a master cost-cutter, earning him the moniker "Chainsaw Al." He slashed and burned his way through CEO roles with charisma

---

[3] Jim Collins in *Good to Great* advocated for hedgehog-like approaches to strategy, focusing on one big idea. This might be an excellent idea for start-ups, but is a poor idea for a complex multinational or for leaders in a complex environment.

and competence. It worked well when it was the correct strategy, and abysmally when it was the wrong strategy.

Hubris: The Dark Side of the Bright Side (Optimism)

> *"It ain't what you don't know that gets you into trouble. It's what you know for sure that just ain't so."*
> —Mark Twain

Scan the Internet for quotations and articles on optimism and you will find an overwhelmingly optimistic view of optimism. Yet optimism proves to be at the root of several other biases that doom change from the start, and sometimes destroy businesses. Optimism renders us "confident without competence" in our judgments, to analyze risk and probability badly, or to be Pollyannaish when planning change.

Lest it be thought that optimism is A Bad Thing, in general terms it is a Very Good Thing. An optimistic outlook means you live longer, are healthier, more emotionally resilient, earn more, attempt more, and succeed.[4] To be sure, when a new strategy or change program is contemplated, there is enormous value in full-throated commitment and enthusiasm. The challenge, therefore, for leaders, is not to stamp optimism out. It may be right to stoke it. Leaders must be conscious of when optimism becomes hubris, and when a positive outlook becomes self-delusion. Leaders must know whether to abandon, surge ahead, or proceed with caution.

Hubris and the Deepwater Horizon Trillion-Dollar Errors

> *"The fundamental cause of the trouble is that, in the modern world, the stupid are cocksure while the intelligent are full of doubt."*
> —Bertrand Russell

---

[4] As in most social science research, the arrow of causality could run either way, or both. Healthier, wealthier people are (understandably) more optimistic.

On April 20, 2010, the Deepwater Horizon oil rig exploded, immediately killing 11 people and injuring 17 others. That was just the beginning of the beginning. Thirty-six hours later, the $560 million burning rig sank. Fifty-six days later, hundreds of workers had succeeded in capping the well; while uncapped, 206 million gallons of oil (worth nearly $400 million dollars) gushed into the waters of the Gulf of Mexico.[5] Still, just the beginning.

One-quarter million jobs in fishing, tourism, and energy industries were lost and BP agreed to a $20 billion fund to compensate workers and municipalities that had been affected. Litigation will go on for decades and will exceed $100 billion. On the same 20-year timescale, *some* environmental damage caused by the oil, methane gas, and chemical dispersants will *only* take decades to undo. The rest of the environmental damage is permanent. Entire species are gone forever, coral reefs are destroyed, surviving species have mutated, dead baby dolphins washed up in unheard of numbers, and migratory birds carried toxins as far as Minnesota.

There were background conditions in the BP/Halliburton/Transocean consortium's partnership that set up the conditions for this failure:

- The rig was a month late, and leasing and contractor costs add up to real money: $1 million per day.
- The complex political environment among managers from the consortium partners, Transocean (the rig owners), BP (who lease and operate the rig), and Halliburton (the oil-services giant), gave rise to gaps in accountability.
- "Ultra-deep" wells (Horizon had previously drilled a deep-sea Everest to 35,000 feet in 4,000 feet of water) are novel and complex.
- The rig was nine years old and had never been to dry-dock. A 2009 audit had identified 390 necessary repairs.

---

[5] The factual material on the Deepwater Horizon case is excerpted from an MIT study entitled *BP and the Deepwater Horizon Disaster of 2010*, by Christina Ingersoll, Richard M. Locke, and Cate Reavis published in 2012 on MIT's LearningEdge, a "free learning resource for management educators and students."

- In 2007, BP's safety culture, incentive systems, and corporate values had come under scrutiny in the Baker Report on the Texas City disaster, which killed five workers.

Those background conditions provided dry kindling for disaster, but Congressional testimony focused on three fateful decisions that led directly to the explosion. Those three decisions, which are discussed in the following list, entailed an economic, human, and environmental calamity. Normally, leadership decision making is behind closed doors and we can only infer errors in decision making from outcomes. Even when a disaster can be pinned on a single decision, such as Lehman Brothers decision to "double-down" on its mortgage securities business as investors and banks were running for the hills, we can usually only guess at the psychological, cognitive, and group processes that led to the decision. Not so with Deepwater Horizon. Because of the scale of the disaster and subsequent investigations, the fateful email communications between BP managers and their Halliburton and Transocean counterparts are in the public record of the U.S. Congressional investigation. We have been awarded a ringside seat to the poor decision making. What were the three hubristic "I know better" decisions that caused the Deepwater Horizon calamity?

1. An internal British Petroleum report recommended against a "long-string casing," but engineers on the Horizon countered that using one, rather than the alternative, would "save at least 3 days, and $7–$10m dollars." Expedience won.

2. Halliburton modeling recommended using 21 "centralizers" to stabilize the casing. Some BP engineers agreed, "Having chosen the riskier casing, we need to honor the modeling." Other engineers argued, "It's a vertical hole so hopefully the pipe stays centralized due to gravity." Hope trumped expertise and policy again; BP used only six centralizers.

3. There were portents that the well had gas leak problems, and a test could have validated or disproven that, but other engineers argued that the test "was only a model" and could wait until full production began.

Here we see optimism's dark side: denial of expertise, antiscience thinking, mistrust of models, zero risk bias, "hope" versus prudence, and people "trusting their gut" where hundreds of billions of dollars and many lives are at stake. Any complex endeavor will produce competing signals: Some will suggest that all is well; some that disaster is around the corner. The task for leaders is to separate the signal from the noise. That requires superb judgment, but also superb awareness of the human frailties we present here—biases. A leader not only needs to be aware of his error-prone thinking, but also needs to detect it in subordinates. It takes great judgment to know when optimism has become denial, or hubris. Had things gone smoothly on April 20, the managers involved might have been applauded for their can-do practical attitudes. The world of risk means that very poor decisions can turn out well, or "perfect" decisions can fall prey to *force majeure.* In complex environments, feedback from the environment makes learning difficult because cause and effect are masked by the complexity.

Our Deepwater Horizon example illustrates not just cognitive biases, but also two themes picked up later in this chapter: (1) when to trust your gut, and when to trust a model, and (2) when are all of us smarter than one of us?

Green Light, STOP! The Halo Effect

Leaders have a great deal to worry about, so when all the lights are green on a project, division, or team, it is tempting to take one's eye off the ball. Leaders sometimes miss risks in successful areas of the business because they assume if results are okay, what is "under the hood" must be okay also. As our discussions of complexity and probability revealed, good decisions can produce bad results and *vice versa.*

This decreased vigilance may not be prudent. In my days as a risk management consultant, we had a well-known, but mostly ignored, dictum: *If you want to know where you are taking the most risk, look where you are making the most money.* This was the case at Baring Brothers, Long Term Capital, Bear Stearns, and Lehman Brothers: The department that brought the firm down had been the most profitable. Outside the banking sector, which firm was voted the U.S.'s most innovative company five years running, was named the U.S.'s best-managed company, was near the top of the "best companies to work for" list, was #25 on the most-admired companies in the world list, and had a P/E ratio far exceeding the rest of companies in their sector? Yes, Enron.

The *halo effect* (also covered in Chapter 9, "Leading with Science") is a bias that colors judgments rosy based on overall impressions, or a single example. If a company (or a person) excels at one thing, judgments about other (unrelated) categories will be positively skewed. When the news is overwhelmingly good in a complex endeavor, it may be an indication that the halo effect is working overtime. A leader's job is to peer through that rosy glow.

Honest and painstaking appraisal is also difficult when the going is very tough. In our coming example, past failure was too painful to look at, the opportunity to learn was missed, and the error was quickly repeated.

The Ostrich Effect

"Marriage is the triumph of imagination over intelligence; second marriage is the triumph of hope over experience."

—Samuel Johnson

In 2001, I was called into British Airways because they were struggling with an important change project, Project F. (An unfortunate choice of letter when things became difficult.) Within the first few hours, I was warned (in hushed tones) to "not talk about Project Phoenix." Project Phoenix, as far as I could tell from these snatched conversations, had been recently canceled after a two-year expensive change program had produced no results. Worse, staff were left demoralized and executives were humiliated. Phoenix was the elephant in the room, but in my desire not to rock the boat during these early conversations, and what proved to be a significant error on my own part, I acceded to British Airways' wishes, to not "pick at the scab" that was Phoenix.

A struggling project has *specific* causes, for example, bad planning or budgeting, but it also has *general,* systemic causes, which will dog every project the organization undertakes. For example, if a business has low trust, weak leadership, inexperience leading complex change, or a history of poor labor-management relations, it will not matter how well conceived an individual project may be. The business will "do what it always does, and get what it always got [sic]." Each project becomes a mirror of the core change capability, and project performance never exceeds that capability, but sometimes falls woefully short.

Before diving into the *specifics* of Project F, I should have gone deeply into what went wrong at Project Phoenix because these *systemic* factors were surely going to make my work more difficult. I chickened out, or *colluded* with British Airways to suppress a history that was making them uncomfortable.

Researchers call this the *ostrich effect*, averting one's gaze from painful, risky, or difficult situations. In bad markets, investors look up the value of their holdings up to 80 percent less often than in good markets. Hindsight allowed me to draw the following conclusion, which applies to change projects and equally to struggling marriages: The uncomfortable stuff is where the "juice" is—*what a business team least wants to discuss is what they will get the most value out of discussing*.

Indeed Project F repeated Project Phoenix's failures. There were teams of consultants doing analyses that the business didn't want and wouldn't use; business unit managers rejected project team authority; senior leadership pretended alignment, but behaved and operated as previousky; the executives did not have the skill to inspire, nor the will to enforce compliance with new behaviors.

Failure to learn from failure has team, cultural, structural, and emotional causes. In leadership teams, this is made easier by the blame game where others' faults can be magnified, and our own discomfort lessened.

Business culture often has norms such as "onto the next one." The structure of the business world also makes learning more difficult. Professional chess and poker players review each game intensively, but they have a hiatus between games where their "job" is to learn from mistakes. In business, it is very hard to make time to review each play because business leaders are frequently juggling so many initiatives that still-live ones press for their limited attention.

Countering these forces requires great leadership, courage, and discipline. Great leaders first ask "where did *I* go wrong?" and only then "where did *we* go wrong?" and then "where did *it* go wrong?" At PwC consulting, our Corporate Transformation team developed an AAR (After Action Review) process, which senior leadership made mandatory, just to combat the structural and cultural forces against honest postmortem analysis in the hyperbusy consulting culture.

Learning from failure is one place where a small amount spent on external advisors can yield vast dividends. Uninvolved in the setback, they can draw unemotional and unpartisan conclusions. Furthermore, they can see dimensions of the problem that those deeply involved are certain to miss (for if they had not missed them, perhaps the project might have been successful).

Perhaps the most difficult part of all this is adopting new practices and methods to prevent future failures. Say it is unearthed that key stakeholders were insufficiently engaged early enough. Just that knowledge, by itself, is useless unless the organization develops the know-how to do that well in the future. Developing and embedding new behaviors occupies Part III of this book, "Change Tactics."

To help leaders combat the perception biases, Table 5.2 provides killer questions that get to the root of which biases may be clouding judgment. We then turn to the problem-solving biases.

Table 5.2 Killer Questions to Combat Perception Biases

BIAS	DIAGNOSTIC (KILLER) QUESTIONS
Overconfidence bias	What is our confidence level in this decision? Will we be right 90% of the time?
Deterministic fallacy	This project estimate meets our criteria. How often will the estimate be wrong by 25%? 50%? 100%?
Halo effect	This company (or deal, or individual) looks perfect. Are we allowing ourselves to be swayed by the halo effect and being insufficiently diligent?
Ludic fallacy	How often will the project produce a fat-tail result? Is this an *extremistan situation*, where a single disaster could wipe out years of results?
Framing effect	Have we narrowed our options prematurely? Should be asking ourselves the bigger question?
Ostrich bias	Have we been sufficiently diligent in learning from what is an embarrassment to us all?
Zero-risk bias	I know the possibility is remote, but are we saying the risk is nil or negligible? If those small risks have great consequences, how can we protect against them?

Problem-Solving Biases

"If I had only one hour to save the world, I would spend fifty-five minutes defining the problem, and only five minutes finding the solution."

—Einstein

Businesspeople often skimp on assessing problems. The problems, they think, are obvious: "staff are unmotivated," "market share is slipping," "we lag the competition in innovation and time-to-market," or "our costs are too high." What they miss when they skimp is how they *see* the problem *is* the problem. The problems (as they see them) are really symptoms with a myriad of interrelated causes. To intervene accurately in a business with a performance issue, the leader and her team need an accurate view of cause and effect. As you saw in the previous chapter, cause and effect are very hard to identify (in fact, theoretically impossible to identify) in the complex system that is a business.

The Availability and Confirmation Biases

It is trivial to say, "we can only see what we can see," but the *availability bias* tells us that what we see is all that matters, and we discount factors we cannot see. The *confirmation bias* means we are more likely to see data that proves us right, than contradicts us.

Partners at PwC, having collaboratively sold a major job, used to have to weight their percentage contribution (and therefore reward) on a scale of 1–100 percent with 100 percent being "I did it all." This was done secretly, then the results tallied, and then differences arbitrated. The system was dropped because four partners would come up with a total contribution of 250 percent and persuading someone who self-assessed at 60 percent to accept 20 percent with gratitude and grace proved tricky. This was not greed; it was the availability bias. They were simply aware of how hard *they* had worked, how often *they* had stayed until midnight, how many stresses *they* faced, and how many times *they* met the client and, of course, they were much less aware of how much their colleagues had done.

When framing business problems, we can only evaluate what we can see. In a complex organization, that might not be much. The solution to the availability bias and the confirmation bias is a certain skepticism about our view of the world, "holding it lightly," but also in being on diverse teams. The leader's challenge, in a complex business, is helping his team gain perspective so that the team does not succumb to the availability bias. In the final section of this chapter, we look at under what conditions "all of us are smarter than one of us."

Getting Cause and Effect Wrong—The Narrative Fallacy

> "It is the only real truth: causality. Action, reaction. Cause and effect."
>
> —The Merovingian[6]

Cause and effect, as we saw in Chapter 4, "Decision Making in Complex and Ambiguous Environments," are hard to diagnose. Probabilities may further obscure relationships. What does it mean to say "an oil spill caused the accident" if it was only the 100th car that skidded? Furthermore, the arrow of causality can point both ways—are contented workers more productive, or are people who are productive more content? Such complications suggest, above all, that all the variables be considered before an expensive intervention to change just a single variable in the hope that we have identified the correct cause of the effect.

Late in the last millennium, I worked with the UK's largest utility to assess their reward system. A year earlier, call center workers had (after considerable wrangling with unions) agreed to a performance-related pay system. To management's amazement and frustration, performance had *decreased* despite increased monetary incentives.

To solve their incentives problem, they had benchmarked their call center rewards versus others in the industry, came up short, and

---

6 *The matrix reloaded* [Motion picture]. (2004). Warner Home Video.

got to work fixing it (paying a consultant nearly $200,000 in the process). Management had thus solved the incentives problem, but not the real problem called "how do we motivate workers?" or the real real problem "how do we increase performance (which had nothing to do with incentives or motivation)?"

Over my two decades as a consultant, I wish I had $10 for every time a management team called me to fix a problem with "them" that had nothing to do with "them." Quickly run through in your mind five of the factors that could produce a shortfall in call center performance (of which motivation and reward might be one). Here is my list: IT systems, product quality, product marketing, product pricing, working conditions, management skills, corporate strategy, corporate culture, after-sales service, corporate brand, new market entrants, and structural shifts (toward bundled energy, telecoms, cable packages). You will notice that everything on this list is a big problem that only senior leadership can fix—things that *they* are responsible for. How much easier it is to say "staff are unmotivated, let's motivate them" (with crop or with carrot) than to look at problems that they, the executives, have created? The egocentric bias locates the cause with people (other people) rather than the system, and oneself.

One solution to the problem-definition problem lies in deeper problem analysis for which there are a number of excellent tools. One such tool is McKinsey's "7-S" framework, shown in Figure 5.1. These models and surveys, of which there are dozens, allow management to take a hard and deep look at cause and effect, but they adhere to the GIGO rule (from information sciences): "garbage in, garbage out." Leaders need courage and self-honesty when the problem lies squarely at their door: "I think what we have here is a poor-quality, high-priced product" or "Most of our problems arise from lack of alignment on strategy in this team" is much more difficult to say than "Our workers are not performing."

Finally, one way to create a change strategy is to call in the cavalry, the consultants (or as one manufacturing client called us, the "cuff links"). With our extra brains attached to our hips, we can solve strategic problems with detailed analysis and recommendation. Or can we?

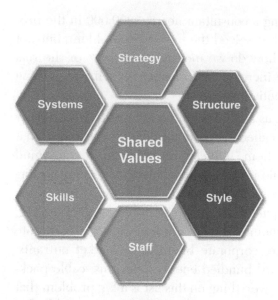

Figure 5.1 The McKinsey 7S model (circa 1980) helps analyze systemic causes especially when combined with "systems thinking."

Reports in Drawers and How "Passions" Drive Change

The "report in a drawer" phenomenon is well known to consultants around the world. We would like our analytical efforts to make a difference (despite the fact that we get paid anyway). Our report might analyze markets, products, channels, customers, geographies, pricing, and the competition in exquisite detail. It might also be based on very sophisticated data gathering and computer modeling. Despite what might be a superb analysis, it is unlikely that there is a consultant reading this who has not had a robust analysis and recommendations sincerely approved, and then tossed in a drawer.

Why might such excellent analyses be paid for, listened to, agreed with, and then not implemented? The best expression of the answer comes from eighteenth-century Scottish philosopher David Hume, whose *Treatise of Human Nature* remains one of the most important philosophy books ever written. Two ideas explain how this abstract, 300-year-old philosopher can help with twenty-first-century change:

1. From facts about the world ("is"), one can never derive norma-tive statements about the way the world should be ("ought"). (The "is-ought" fallacy.)

2. "Reason is, and ever ought to be, the slave of the passions."

Facts Do Not Drive Change; "Passions" and Values Do

The first of Hume's ideas suggests that facts (information) say nothing about what we *should* do. For example, someone with a body mass index (BMI) of 35 is obese, but unless they *value* being thin-ner (for whatever reason) the fact of their BMI is inert—it cannot propel action. A geological survey may discover oil under a pristine wildlife preserve; science only says the oil is there, not that we should drill. Whether to drill or not is a conversation about values, not about facts. Why these conversations go badly, in business and in society, is that people argue as though values were facts, and people who do not share their values are irrational. No facts in the world will persuade a naturalist to value oil over biodiversity, nor an oilman to value birds over oil.

Hume's second (most famous) statement says two things: Reason *is* the slave of the passions, and reason *ought* to be the slave of the passions. Our philosopher says that passion (emotion, commitments, drive, vision) dictates where we use our reason. He then says it ought to be so—what we care about provides our compass.

Many times in my career, I have seen a business commission some market analysis, benchmarking study, or feasibility study. Although they were obviously interested or curious enough to ask for the analy-sis, that initial curiosity proved utterly insufficient to drive change. Their team was not sufficiently committed to lead the harder work of implementation, and the facts in the report did nothing to build their "passions." (Sometimes, teams may even ask for more analysis as a defense mechanism to stop themselves from taking action they fear taking.)

Requesting further analysis of a problem, without a passion to act, can be a waste of time. However, with passion *first* in place, the data, analysis, and recommendations are "pulled toward" the problem as means for realizing the passion, rather than being "pushed toward" the executives in the hopes that information (facts, analysis) will persuade them to care and act upon them.

Although this is a book about science and change, science (reason) merely provides a better "how"—it does not tell us what is important. Recent science on emotions and cognition has underlined how important the emotions are. Emotions were once seen as an impediment to rationality; we now know that without emotions, human beings are directionless (a scientific validation of some of Hume's ideas a few hundred years after he proposed them).

Reports in drawers are full of facts, but unless the facts connect to the leaders' values and passions, they will remain inert.

Table 5.3 has five sample "killer questions" for combatting problem-solving biases.

Table 5.3 Five Killer Questions to Combat Problem-Solving Biases

BIAS	DIAGNOSTIC (KILLER) QUESTIONS
Egocentric bias/fundamental attribution error	We need individual accountability, but before assigning blame to individuals, let us ask, what systemic factors were important in getting us here?
"Is-ought" fallacy	This analysis is robust and suggests we should act, but how do we feel about this endeavor? Do we have the passion to see it through difficulties to the end?
Narrative fallacy	It looks as if we have a plausible story about the cause. Does the evidence back up that story, or are we creating a tidy narrative too quickly?
Hyperbolic discounting	This looks good in the immediate term, but have we paid sufficient attention to long-term costs? The immediate costs are steep; are we discounting the long-term value too much?
Availability/confirmation biases	Based upon what we can see, the decision seems clear. Are there any unknowns we should speculate upon? Are we only considering evidence that backs up our point of view?

Leaders must make sure that appropriate consideration is given to problem selection, problem finding, or problem definition before leaping into choosing a solution. There are biases that affect solution choice that lead to subrational, suboptimal strategies.

Solution-Selection Biases

Even excellent problem solving and reasoning skills are some-times short-circuited as leadership teams jump to solutions without doing the hard work of problem definition and problem solving. The three topics in this section discuss traps in choosing solutions: quick fixes, the herd effect, and the sunk cost fallacy.

Early research on decision making unearthed some fascinating discoveries about how humans make decisions. Although a solid formal process might create criteria, weight the criteria appropriately, select a wide range of alternatives, and evaluate each alternative against the criteria and select the best one. Researchers studied how people actually made choices, from choosing a college, to selecting a job, to business teams selecting a strategy. It looks nothing like that. Few of those steps are followed. Criteria are not defined, ill-defined, or inconsistent. The real process humans follow is chaotic. What usually happens is that a set of easily recognizable solutions is identified, and after informal evaluation, the first that appears "reasonable" or good enough is selected. This is called *satisficing*, or sometimes the "garbage can" model of decision making.[7] Research continues to show that people operate more like solutions looking for problems than problems looking for solutions. We decide, intuitively, and then retrofit criteria in order to make sense of the decision for ourselves and others.

Intuition is not the enemy of formal decision making, and the best studies of decision making include intuition as valid, often quicker, and sometimes superior to formal processes. However, the case is vastly overstated in popular literature such as Gladwell's *Blink*. The leadership challenge is to know when formality and structured processes should be followed, and when not. In short, when to trust models and analysis, and when to "go with the gut."

---

[7] Cohen, M. D., March, J. G., & Olsen, J. P. (1972, Mar.). A garbage can model of organizational choice. *Administrative Science Quarterly, 17*(1), pp. 1–25.

Trusting Guts, Trusting Models

You might wonder with our tour of human fallibility how humans built cathedrals, computers, and corporations given how wrong our judgments can be. Indeed, there is an alternative view, called naturalistic decision making (NDM), which celebrates the (alleged) ability of humans to make successful gut decisions in high-pressure, uncertain circumstances. Although the proponents have much to say that is of value, I believe the NDM research is weaker than the "biases and fallacies" research. The correct approach is the best of both worlds, and lies in knowing when "gut-level" decisions are likely to be right, and relying on more formal processes when they are likely to be wrong.

Two of the authors who have staked out positions contrary to the "biases and fallacies" approach taken in this chapter are Dr. Gary Klein, a U.S. consultant-researcher, and Professor Gird Gigerenzer of the Max Planck Institute. Klein has worked with firefighters, healthcare workers, and the military to understand the processes experts use in making tough decisions. He found that rather than systematically weighting criteria and reviewing options, the experts' experience allowed them to visualize, categorize, and select *one* option. Then this single-option is simulated, much like a chess player will examine how a choice will play out, and then modified if indicated.

There are two strands to Klein's thinking, one descriptive (how decisions are actually made), and one normative (how they ought to be made). To make the leap from one to the other, Klein has to assume that the experts who describe how they make decisions are actually successful, that they make the best decision possible—that a firefighter who "senses" (claiming a sixth sense) that a building is about to collapse and orders a life-saving retreat has made the right call. His research does not allow that. To conclude the decision was correct, you need to know how many false negatives and false positives the "sensing" generates—how many times does he/she order a retreat (thus prolonging a fire) when the situation was safe, and how many times the "sensing" missed a hazardous situation and lives were lost. Humans claim foresight, knowledge, and wisdom after the fact when they reconstruct events. Gamblers routinely claim they "knew" that an ace would come (poker) or that the next card would be a ten (blackjack) to justify actions that may or may not have been wise (usually not). People who persist in a traffic jam say, "I *knew* I should have taken the alternative route." When a business opportunity works out, people "had a hunch it would," and when it fails, they "never felt that sure about it in the first place." To recall an earlier theme, in a world where chance is everywhere, we can never be completely certain whether our good decision led to a good outcome or we just got lucky. Nor are we immune to, in the light of events, reconstructing a good-looking rationale that makes us look wise before the fact.

On the other hand, we should still take seriously the claim that humans are *ecologically rational,* that intuition can, through pattern recognition, fast-and-frugal decision processes, and situation-specific heuristics produce accurate judgments in many situations. To score a goal from a corner kick, the striker must judge the speed, trajectory, spin, wind, and position of the opposing team. To do that mathematically would require solving a complex system of differential equations—people can do it in split second. That means that we can solve *some* problems with those situation-specific heuristics that would take us hours by brute force calculation. In this respect, I concur with the esteemed researchers.

The vital question is: In *which* situations, contexts, and fields of endeavor is intuition a reliable guide? Klein and Kahneman (ostensibly at the poles of the debate) produced a joint paper in 2009 that they titled "Conditions for Intuitive Expertise: A Failure to Disagree."[8] Their combined summary of when and how intuition works is instructive for business leaders who often have to make gut decisions.[9] Their first point of agreement is to demystify intuition. They agree that intuition is a situation-specific, learned faculty, not a mystical "seeing" ability possessed by a few specially endowed individuals.

They then offer four guidelines for where formal decision making may be better than "gut feel." From my point of view, this list is a categorical condemnation of the "gut feel" school of decision making:

[8] Kahneman, D. & Klein, G. (2009). Conditions for intuitive expertise: A failure to disagree. *American Psychologist 64*(6), 515–526.

[9] Direct quotations are verbatim from the Kahneman and Klein paper. The interpretations of their findings for businesspeople are mine.

1. The success of Klein's model requires accurate pattern recognition, that is, a "family resemblance" that allows previous experience to provide a template. This is rarely the case, and never the case in complex systems (discussed in the previous chapter).

2. Learned intuition requires a high-validity environment, one where actions are quick and high-correlated with outcomes. Medicine and firefighting are two such environments. Business is not. Business problems may have multiple, interlinked causes, and interventions to solve business problems may take weeks or months for actions to bear fruit (or not).

3. "True experts know they do not know. However, nonexperts (whether or not they think they are) certainly do not know when they do not know. *Subjective confidence is therefore an unreliable indication of the validity of intuitive judgments and decisions."* When a businessperson says, "I always trust my gut in these situations," they may be deluded as to the previous success of that method.

4. "Although true skill cannot develop in irregular or unpredictable environments, individuals will sometimes make judgments or decisions that are successful by chance. These 'lucky' individuals will be susceptible to the illusion of skill and to overconfidence. The financial industry is a rich source of examples."

Intuition clearly has a role to play in business decision making, but, in my view, successful use of intuition depends on a familiar situation where normal rules will apply. Complex, volatile situations are not like that, and, in my view, reliance on individual intuition in those circumstances is hazardous.

The "trust your gut" notion has one further flaw: Intuition is very difficult to square with group decision making. Intuitive judgments are often based on environmental cues of which the decider is only dimly aware. The weighting of those cues, and which heuristics are used to generate a course of action, may be hard to articulate. For those reasons, it (1) is difficult to create an intuitive decision that is a product of more than one mind, and (2) risks lack of engagement with decisions arrived at by "gut" means.

Weighing "Bias-for-Action" and the Quick Fix

"Don't just do something, sit there."

—Unknown

In *In Search of Excellence,* Peters and Waterman highlighted "bias-for-action" as the first feature of high-performance cultures. Although there is no question that the opposite, analysis paralysis, can be a fault and lead to sluggishness, leaders often act in haste—sometimes in order to be seen to be doing something, particularly something perceived as favorable in the eyes of "the Street." New leaders may feel especially drawn to quick action, to exploit their "honeymoon period," and to be perceived as action-oriented and decisive.

This "do-something" mentality is, I conjecture, a source of quick fixes that fail and knee-jerk initiatives that produce more heat than light. The most common species of knee-jerk initiative is the reorganization.

Reorganizations

PricewaterhouseCoopers, 1999. If this is Tuesday, it must be Belgium, and we must be organized around product lines. It seemed like only yesterday we were organized around geographical lines, and the day before that around "markets" (Financial Services, Healthcare, Technology, and Government). Leadership could never stop fiddling with the organizational structure. To us consultants, it seemed as if *fashionistas* from Milan were running the show. We wondered how what was assuredly best practice and a critical priority one year became old-school so quickly a few months later.

A client, Jean, had just become Global Head of Learning. She discovered that each region had its own curriculum, its own set of suppliers and the same course was offered to small numbers of people on the same day in Indonesia, Canada, Germany, and Mexico because local Learning and Development departments had considerable autonomy. Naturally, her first job was to restructure—to centralize, to streamline, and to standardize—in order to eliminate redundant offerings in various regions and realize economies of scale. She began to prune local programs in favor of more cost-effective, centralized offerings. What she did not realize was that three years earlier her predecessor had decentralized for equally good reasons: widely varying regional management abilities, cultural differences, being closer to local "customer" learning needs, reducing air travel for suppliers, and using local suppliers who charge less than trainers from New York. Jean reorganized to undo the prior reorganization. Both moves had plenty of justification.

Because of the *potentially* powerful effect of structure on performance, the majority of CEOs launch a "reorg" during their first two years on the job. Yet one study found that most of those fall flat. A recent Bain & Company study of 57 "reorgs" between 2000 and 2006[10] found that fewer than one third produced any meaningful improvement in performance. Despite the poor record of knee-jerk reorganizations, the "new broom" CEO has to be seen to be decisive from Wall Street's point of view. There are good reasons for making big early moves. It is widely thought that during the first 100 days, newly elected officials and corporate leaders enjoy a honeymoon period where the organization (or country) grants them more license for major initiatives than it will later. In this way, Wall Street gets a seat at the table and Wall Street analysts, like the Roman public in the Coliseum, can vote thumbs up or down for major policy. The haste to undertake what "the Street" expects has costs when it is not the correct strategy, or it drains resources from strategies that might have produced bigger results.

Unnecessary reorganization is costly because every change produces disorder, or friction. Many research studies show that transitions into significant new roles are the most challenging times in the working lives of managers. As well as wasting capital, engagement, goodwill, and trust are also strained.

---

[10] Blenko, M., Mankins, M., & Rogers, P. (2010, July 30). The key to successful corporate reorganization. *Forbes.com*. Retrieved from http://www.forbes.com/2010/07/30/corporate-reorganization-abb-ford-leadership-managing-bain.html.

Professor Rob Briner defines quick fixes (of which reorganiza-tions can be an example) as a rapid implementation of a solution that has many of the following features:[11]

- Is not based on an objective initial assessment
- Is strongly influenced by fad and fashion
- Provides an answer to a political problem rather than a deeper or even presenting problem
- Is driven by the need to be seen to be doing something
- Is championed by an issue-seller or individual who stands to gain or avoid harm by its implementation
- Focuses on style and presentation not content or process
- Will not be evaluated
- Will never be as quick as had been hoped
- Will likely be followed by another quick fix
- Will likely become subject to organizational amnesia (as in Project Phoenix)

Briner's "checklist" of quick-fix attributes can be used by teams to explore whether the "bias-for-action" may be getting in the way of sufficient deliberation.

Copying the Herd, or Leading Like a Lemming

"A sound banker, alas, is not one who foresees danger and avoids it, but one who, when he is ruined, is ruined in a con-ventional and orthodox way along with his fellows, so that no one can really blame him."

—J. M. Keynes

If reorganization is sometimes a knee-jerk and unnecessary response, aping the competition is an equally seductive trap. Again, game theory suggests why. If we adopt a contrarian strategy, eschewing

---

[11] Briner, R. (2007, March). Is HRM evidence-based and does it matter? *Institute for Employment Studies.*

"market wisdom" we risk looking stupid, or behind the curve especially in the eyes of "the Street." If we follow the herd, we will have good company if things go awry.

No sector, in my opinion, does this more than banks.

In the late 1970s, hotel lobbies in Buenos Aires and Caracas were chocked full of SVPs from European, American, and Japanese banks falling over themselves to lend to Latin America, which was rapidly evolving from its third-world designation with soaring economies and large infrastructure projects. Then came the crisis.

When the cold winds of the late 1970s recession began to chill the Latin American economies, their creditworthiness fell, and suddenly bankers, still hungover from the lending binge, ran for the hills, triggering a massive economic slowdown and high unemployment, further compromising the countries' ability to pay, and thus triggering the lending disaster they were so keen to avoid. The lending bender ended abruptly and banks went cold turkey on Latin America: They went from being insensitive to risk and exposure to oversensitized, thus causing the disaster they were worried about—and economic meltdown in Latin America. Rinse and repeat: Japanese equities, Long-Term Capital, dot-coms, U.S. consumer/real-estate lending...

Herd behavior is not confined to banks and lending. Consultants are fad-peddlers par excellence (some would say by definition). A short list of fads would include: TQM (Total Quality Management), Six Sigma, BPR (Business Process Reengineering), Delayering, Learning Organizations, MBO (Management by Objectives), ERP (Enterprise Resource Planning), Emotional Intelligence, and Matrix Management.[12] Fads, like bubbles, are characterized by irrational exuberance and unthinking adoption. Some add valuable insight to the management canon, some add less, and some are consultant neologisms as they grasp for distinctiveness in highly competitive markets.

The answer to this question can be found in what some people believe to be a hardwired human attribute: herd behavior, which is the tendency for individuals to mimic the actions (rational or irrational)

---

[12] None of these are without value, in the right business, at the right time, to solve clearly articulated problems. See: Kellaway, L. (2013, April 9). Where others failed: Top 10 fads. *Financial Times*; and Miller, D., & Hartwick, J. (2002, October). Spotting management fads. *Harvard Business Review*.

of a larger group. Individually, however, most people would not make the same choice. Misery loves company. No business wants to miss the early mover advantage, but when contemplating a change that will take 18 months and costs tens of millions, the best way to *carpe diem* may be to seize the day for analysis and deliberation.

Escalation of Commitment and the Sunk Cost Fallacy

"The decision to invest additional resources in a losing account, when better investments are available, is known as the sunk-cost fallacy, a costly mistake that is observed in decisions large and small."

—Daniel Kahneman

While the ostrich effect makes leaders ignore difficult situations or failed projects at the cost of learning, and *increases* the chance that their mistakes will be repeated, another bias has the opposite effect: the sunk cost bias. The sunk cost bias causes leaders to *overweight* the past in deliberations rather than *underweight* it and leads to perhaps the most pernicious and costly change strategy error—the escalation of commitment.

To illustrate, suppose you and a friend have tickets to a sporting event a considerable distance away. You paid $75 dollars for yours and she was given hers for free. On the day of the event, the weather forecast is abysmal: cold and rainy. Who is more likely to skip the event? When Nobel Prize winner Amos Tversky (a pioneer in cognitive biases) consulted a new financial advisor, he was asked to provide a list of his stocks and what he had paid for them. He asked, "Why is what I paid for them important?" The financial advisor looked at our Nobel Prize winner as though he were crazy.[13]

Perhaps your gut response is similar. Of course what you paid for the ticket or the stocks matters! Yet such thinking is irrational. If stocks are down, the money is gone. What matters is whether the

---

[13] Purchase price and realizing losses and gains does matter when taxes are introduced, but Tversky's financial advisor was worried about sunk costs.

game will be a fulfilling use of your time despite the weather, or whether the stocks will rise or fall from here. If you have bought a lemon of a car, or a money pit of a house, or you are in a relationship or job that stinks, it may be profitable to invest more and escalate your commitment, or it might be right to fold. How much you have paid, or how long you have invested are (rationally) irrelevant.

The sunk cost bias, overweighting (or considering at all) past costs, leads to a pervasive and toxic phenomenon called "escalation of commitment": in everyday language, "throwing good money after bad," and, more formally, "redoubling commitment to a failing endeavor." Escalation of commitment happens because people do not like to feel like they have squandered resources or that past efforts have been in vain. Human beings self-justify, liking to feel that time and money have been well spent, and that past decisions were good (or not *that* bad). Another bias, the *confirmation bias,* seals the trap. Having invested, leaders seek out confirming evidence that things are going well. In executive teams, leaders do not want to lose face, so projects they have sponsored will continue to be endorsed long past what rationality would suggest. The program directors of the NHS ($15 billion overrun), facing government investigations, repeatedly pointed to all the little successes to avoid bigger questions and issues. Listening to the transcripts, one could conclude the project was 90 percent success, not 90 percent failure! U.S. President Lyndon Johnson faced substantial pressure to remain in Vietnam because to exit without victory would mean U.S. lives had been lost in vain.

Escalation of commitment costs a lot of money because when projects or investments turn sour, decision making typically gets *worse.* Baring Brothers bank was founded in 1762, but one trader, Nick Leeson, escalating his commitments to a losing arbitrage strategy, brought it down in 1995 when his losses that started small grew to $1.3 billion.

Escalation of commitment is not only costly, but it is commonplace: Escalation experts[14] suggest that 30 percent to 40 percent of all

---

[14] Professor Mark Keil of Georgia State University, personal communication, August 2013.

IT projects involve some degree of project escalation. Given the scale and breadth of the problem, what can a leader do?

Confronting Escalation

"Happy families are all alike; every unhappy family is unhappy in its own way."

—Tolstoy

Every unhappy project is unhappy in its own way; and many factors can lead to derailment. The escalation problem, with its complex psychological, cultural, social, and political causes, defies trivial answers. The very tough challenge for the leader is to balance the desirable virtue of persistence in the face of difficulty with the undesirable vice, one of stubbornness and throwing good money after bad. There are no panaceas, and no silver bullet that makes these calls easier, but there are five specific strategies that help:

- **Increase vigilance with troubled projects**—If there is one time to second-guess your gut, it is when a project or investment is failing, because of the psychological and cultural pressures to continue. Find an independent observer with no dog in the fight who can objectively assess the project. The ostrich effect will incline your team toward pretending things are fine, and the confirmation bias will mean they find the positive news they are looking for. Combat that confirmation bias by actively seeking out evidence that would contradict the decision to commit more money.

- **Create stopping rules**—If more resources are committed, create stopping rules now because the stakes will be higher, the losses will be greater, and the escalation force will be more extreme if, for example, six months from now, you face the same decision.

- **Adopt a trader's mentality**—Salomon Brothers famed CEO John Gutfreund used to berate traders daily: "Don't fall in love with your positions." We were trained from the beginning to constantly reevaluate trading positions in the light of new information sometimes abusing the Cat Stevens song "The First Cut Is the Cheapest" to make ditching loss-making positions less of a chore. When I ran a (smaller) trading desk, we used to use our morning meetings to criticize big holdings, especially those in trouble. Traders had to, in effect, provide a rational business case, and we were trained to sniff out self-justification behavior (not wanting to admit wrong or look bad).

Of course, two-year projects are different than trading positions that can be dumped with a phone call. One thing that can be learned from banks is when a position is "marked-to-market," the sunk costs are labeled as such and are already mentally written off. A leader can do the same, naming the sunk costs, and asking "the jury" (her fellow decision makers) to mentally write off the sunk costs and disregard what has already been lost as evidence.

- **Create imaginary scenarios**—Intel got into the memory business in 1969, and by 1981 was the market leader. During the early 1980s, Japanese competition and the scale of the computer industry had turned the memory business into a commodity business, which was becoming increasingly unprofitable for Intel. Memory was still over half of Intel's $1 billion revenue, but overall profitability had nose-dived from $198 million to just $2 million and the memory business was losing money. Andy Grove felt the writing was on the wall, but Intel's executives were focused on Intel's history, its identity as "the memory" company, and its legacy investment in technology and manufacturing capacity. They simply could not believe the mounting evidence that they were being outgunned in a market they had created and which was over half of their top line.

  In his book, *Only the Paranoid Survive,* Grove recounts a conversation with Gordon Moore (of Moore's Law fame and cofounder of Intel), "If we got kicked out and the board brought in a new CEO, what do you think he would do? Gordon answered without hesitation, 'He would get us out of memories.' I stared at him, numb, then said, 'Why shouldn't you and I walk out the door, come back, and do it ourselves?'"

And so they did. Thirty years later, Intel's revenue is greater than $50 billion, implying that their painful cut, getting out of a business they had founded, was correct.

- **Support emotional letting go**—For most of the last 20 years, Nokia has been the number-one manufacturer of mobile phones in the world (Samsung pipped it in 2012). The company traces its story to 1865 and the tiny Finnish town of Tampere. Over the next century, it grew into a multinational industrial conglomerate, with interests in rubber, wood, tire, telegraph, and electrical components. In the early 1980s, Nokia became a pioneer in the business that has made it famous today: mobile telephones. The legacy (nineteenth-century businesses) looked less than attractive in the digital era, so in 1992, the new CEO, Jorma Ollila, made a decision to concentrate solely on telecommunications and sell the legacy businesses that were part of Nokia's history.

  In an interview, shortly after the disposals, Nokia's CEO, Ollila, now Chairman of Shell, offered the following insight,[15] "selling our legacy businesses was a wise strategic decision, but also a gut wrenching one. We had to acknowledge that fact and support one another through the emotional process."

The solution to past-based biases is to look at the past analytically, to learn from failure, but detached from emotional, egotistical, nostalgic, or overoptimistic commitments to things going badly. Table 5.4 lists questions that decision-makers might ask themselves to guard against the biases in the previous section.

One of the most important questions is whether our biases counteract one another in groups, or whether they reinforce one another making group decision worse than individual decisions.

---

[15] Olilla, J. Personal communication, 1998.

Table 5.4 Four Killer Questions to Combat Solution-Selection Biases

BIAS	DIAGNOSTIC (KILLER) QUESTIONS
Action bias	It is tempting to quickly restructure (or to cut costs, or to acquire in this exciting area), but is our bias for action inclining us toward too much haste?
Institutional bias	All our competitors seem to be launching a product like this (or to be purchasing this kind of system, or to be captivated by this new idea). Are we being swayed by that? Should we be adopting a contrarian stance?
Sunk cost bias and escalation of commitment	If we had not sunk so much into this failing endeavor, would we invest what we propose to now if our judgment were not colored by those losses? If we do, how can we prevent this from happening repeatedly?
The planning fallacy	Is this plan EGAP or MLD? What could happen that is far worse than MLD? How confident are we that the worst case is really the worst case? How likely are "outliers" (50% or more overruns)?

The Wisdom (or Madness) of Crowds

In 1907, Francis Galton found that the mean of social group estimates could be more accurate than those of experts. Since then, 100 years of research has suggested that this can be the case in many kinds of prediction, in stock markets, in political elections, and in quiz shows. The idea that "all of us are smarter than one of us" has some research grounding, so does that mean that individual misjudgments (biases) can cancel each other out? On the other hand, the equally well-documented phenomenon of "groupthink" suggests that critical discussion can be suppressed in groups because of loyalty, conflict aversion, or other dysfunctions. Yale psychologist Irving Janis, who coined the term, maintained that: "The more amiability and *esprit de corps* there is among the members of a policy-making ingroup, the greater the danger that independent critical thinking will be replaced by groupthink..."

The question of which group features are necessary for the "all of us are smarter than one of us" is one of the hottest and most interesting areas of social psychological research.[16] The following features are among the most important factors:

---

[16] Lorenz, J., et al. (2011). How social influence can undermine the wisdom of crowd effect. *PNAS, 108*(22), 9020–9025.

- **Power differentials**—Social influence can mean that groups prematurely converge around a decision or prediction without an increase in accuracy.

- **Anchoring effect**—Once a credible estimate is lodged in decision-makers' minds, subsequent estimates tend to converge upon that estimate (good or bad).

- **Heterogeneity**—"Wisdom" is a function of heterogeneity. The greater the diversity of estimates, the more accurate their average tends to be.[17] Even in diverse-looking groups, diversity of opinion may be suppressed.

- **Group functioning**—To maximize use of distributed knowledge, groups must be high-functioning and have the conversational tools that make such knowledge "additive."

- **Overconfidence**—When a decision seems to be a product of group consensus, this increases confidence in the decision without necessarily improving decision quality.

By paying attention to these features, teams can move closer to the ideal that "all of us are smarter than one of us."

Conclusion and Implications for Change Experts

Research on individual decision making, cognitive biases and heuristics, and naturalistic decision making is still a relatively young area, and the jury remains out on many of the important issues. We have recently learned many of the sources of error, but we are still far less good at producing concrete prescriptive advice on personal and group decision making. Knowing when you can "trust your gut" or when "all of us are smarter than one of us" are, I think, two of the most important areas of applied psychology.

It is not too much of a generalization to say that biases are not typically part of change management knowledge today. That needs to change. Facilitation is one of the change expert's essential skills, but

---

17 There are many moral arguments for "diversity"; this is a purely functional one— your team will be smarter.

the facilitation we generally were taught and practice comes from the tradition of humanistic psychology, loosely based on the counseling principles of Carl Rogers. In that tradition, the client's interpretations and beliefs are only cautiously challenged. This is an empowering way of facilitating based on the assumption that learning and personal change happen best when the client draws their own conclusions. The understanding that clients (business executives) may be quite wrong in many of their interpretations opens the door for a more robust level of challenge—one that may be counter-cultural in some coaching/ facilitation schools. Thus, there is room for experts who help facilitate executive decision making to substantially increase their level of usefulness by understanding the world of biases to better point out these blind spots.

The vision of this chapter is that if we can "see ourselves seeing" and know where we as humans are likely to make systematic mistakes, we can course correct. This demands skepticism about the facts we perceive, and the automatic System 1 decisions we make. This skepticism applies even more in Part III, when we turn to change tactics and what science tells us about changing behaviors, hearts, and minds.

Part III
Change Tactics

"Victorious warriors win, then go to war; defeated warriors go to war and attempt to win."

—Sun Tzu

Sun Tzu might well have been talking about change; the standard approach is to launch a program, and then hope to win hearts, minds, and behaviors. I contend that the change "war" ought to be won before the project begins—sound change strategy in a change-agile business. No amount of masterful change tactics will fix a merger that is strategically doomed to fail. A change-agile organization will have fewer apathetic or recalcitrant stakeholders to manage.

Nevertheless, there will always be a role for supporting a change by aligning culture, behaviors, hearts, and minds with a change—what I call *change tactics* (because *change management* is too imprecise and means too many different things to different people).

How a few dozen people persuade a few hundred thousand to align with their will is the subject of the hundreds of books on change management. Each starts with a conceptual model, such as Kotter's eight steps, Booz-Allen's ten principles, or Prosci's five building blocks. Again, it is worth asking how these models and dozens like them should be evaluated side-by-side in science-free world. Are they all right? Is choosing one over another merely a matter of taste, or are some better validated? Each model's step or principle then has a series of tools that (in theory) deliver an aspect of the change, for instance for assessing stakeholders or culture. Each tool is based on a theory of human nature and how people change. It is a reasonable hypothesis that abysmal rates of success are related to the insufficiency of these models or our still modest understanding of people and how they change. However, change experts rarely question these conceptual models, or the tools beneath. When change fails, experts (stereotypically) say that the client didn't "get it" or failed to use their expertise correctly. That is often true, but time has come to stop giving the models a free pass and to begin to think critically about whether the eight steps are all correct and whether they are sufficient to handle every change implementation. We also need to begin to question the underlying science of human behavior upon which these are based. For example, when many models talk about "aligning reward systems," they are endorsing a behaviorist view of human nature that is much more false than true.

The Road Ahead

Misunderstanding of how people learn and change at work has many causes, but chief among them is the newness of psychology as a scientific discipline and the misrepresentation or exaggeration of its findings by the media. This section, in three chapters, debunks some psychological myths and introduces competing, new theories of human nature. For example, traditional methods of stakeholder communication during change focus on providing information. However, when faced with ideological resistance, research suggests that providing more facts may induce more resistance, not lessen it. Most models of personal change focus on changing attitudes first to change behaviors—"think your way into a new way of acting." Research suggests that, just as often, people "act their way into a new way of thinking."

The first chapter in this section, Chapter 6, "Misunderstanding Human Behavior," first looks at the myths, the gurus, and the hype that masquerade as psychological knowledge. This leads us to the most destructive phenomenon in the leadership world—pop leadership. Psychological science should counter this, but psychology's status as a science is debated, and in the hands of the media and pop psychology writers, there is sometimes more truth than fiction.

Chapter 7, "The Science of Changing Behaviors," begins with the dark legacy of behaviorist psychology—the attempt to control our fellows with punishment and reward. Neobehaviorism, on the other hand contains approaches that focus on changing behaviors without coercion—and averts the negative effects of coercion on engagement, trust, and relationships.

Chapter 8, "The Science of Changing Hearts and Minds," takes a fresh look at new ideas on influencing and what those mean for change communication. Those include a new model of resistance, a new way of thinking about emotional responses to change, multistakeholder engagement and dialogue, and the potential role of mindfulness practices in personal change and change leader development, the *sine qua non* of organizational change.

6

Misunderstanding Human Behavior

"The difficulty lies, not in the new ideas, but in escaping from the old ones, which ramify...into every corner of our minds."

—J. M. Keynes

Change fails at the tactical level when even sound strategic decisions fail to engage layers of affected staff. The skills and tools of those change leaders depend on notions of human behavior, how people learn and change, and how and why they act in response to what a leader does. When change implementation gets stuck, it is often because those notions are formed of bad ideas about people, which lead to bad ideas about how to produce engagement, commitment, and passion, or fail to combat resistance, cynicism, and apathy.

This chapter covers where those bad ideas about human nature come from; the next two chapters suggest good new ideas for changing behaviors, hearts, and minds.

How to Not Get Invited Back to Dinner Parties

To label something a myth is pejorative, and because many myths are deeply cherished, when the myths are challenged, people react badly. When fellow parents say, "Sugar makes kids hyper," and I respond by saying that controlled studies show it categorically does not, they are more annoyed than thankful for the illumination. The argument then proceeds, "But I have seen sugar make my kids hyper!" To which I reply, "The confirmation bias means you observe what you believe rather than believe what you observe." Telling people they do not "really" see what they see lands you in a world of trouble. Their single observation has more "proof" than would a study of a few thousand kids under carefully controlled conditions.

This happens in business as well. In 1995, I was asked to advise PwC's Mergers and Acquisitions practice leader on how to build engagement and culture change into the firm's methodology for making mergers work. Within ten minutes, he was apoplectic with rage as I disputed his notion that paying people more (who were already very well paid) was the best, most effective, or even a necessary method of producing engagement, behavioral, and cultural change. There is zero evidence for, and plenty of evidence against, the assertion that you can buy long-term compliance or change culture this way. However, my colleague was philosophically a "carrot and stick" guy and would rather have thrown money at the problem of engagement than try touchy-feely engagement techniques. His intuitions and assumptions about human nature trumped whatever research evidence and expertise I could furnish.

This chapter is, like that, irritating, because it takes aim at a dozen shibboleths. We need, I think, great humility and skepticism about our knowledge of human behavior because our knowledge of the mind and of what makes people tick are far from certain. To frame this chapter in terms of our initial framework (Figure 1 in the introduction, repeated here in Figure 6.1), we try to move a great number of practices from the lower right (widely used, little validity) to the lower left (no evidence and limited usefulness). While this is a book on business, pseudoscience myths about people (often fueled by the media) harm parenting practices, public health debates, and public policy.

Some of the conclusions of this chapter are still hotly debated. My hope is to open up a dialogue that does not currently exist about which widely known ideas about people are true and which are false, and which are helpful in leading people at work, and which are useless (or worse).

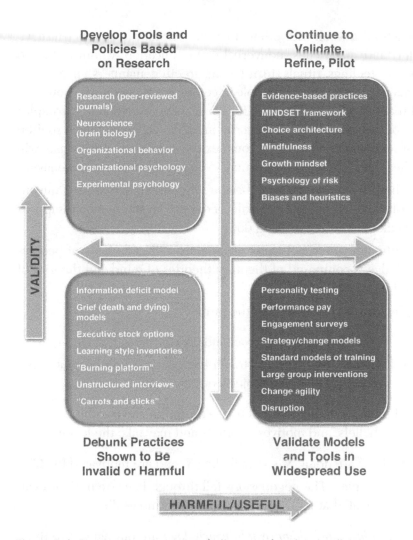

Figure 6.1 Change management and other people-related policies must move toward increased validity and accountability.

Folk Psychology

The first, and most practically robust, source of knowledge about people, and what makes them tick, comes from growing up—on the playground so to speak. We learn about mind and behavior by watching, mimicking, and learning experientially, that is, by trial and error. Reflect for a second on the magic of this—each of us has hundreds of interactions a week with others that pass without a hitch because we understand social cues, nonverbal communication, whom to talk to and how, feelings, rituals (turn-taking, greeting, manners), nuances in language, what motivates people in common situations, and how they will react to what we say and do. These are the myriad and complex rules of the social game. This social intelligence, about which so little is formally understood, is so complex that while computers may win at Chess and Jeopardy, they cannot even approximate social behavior.

These savantlike abilities become ingrained: We are so "unconsciously competent" that the skills of day-to-day interaction disappear much like the skill of walking does.

Although we do not think of them as such, this body of people-knowledge is composed of theories: theories of mind and theories of behavior.

Theories of behavior take the form:

- "If I do X, people will react and do Y."
- Example: "If I give Joe tough feedback, he will become more motivated and finish projects on time."

Theories of mind allow us to see an action and ascribe thoughts, feelings, beliefs, and motives to others and may take the form:

- "They are doing X, so are feeling Y, and are motivated by Z."
- Example: "The negotiations fell through because of their cynicism; all that motivates these people is money."

Everyday psychology or *folk psychology* are our aggregate theories of what makes people tick, and we were expert at that sort of psychology millennia before Pavlov and his drooling dogs, or Freud and his cigars.

Folk psychology gets a lot done. Few people formally study psychology, yet our complex social and linguistic tools, and our ability to understand others, allow us to collaborate in war, art, enterprise, politics, and science. That understanding of people has allowed the building of cathedrals, corporations, and computers.

Limitations of Folk Psychology

Powerful though it is, folk psychology is prescientific—that is to say the theories become common sense, and not really tested and revised because "everybody knows" (for example, that sugar makes kids hyper). Folk psychology gets us into trouble in just some of the following ways:

- We do not know our theories are theories. They are, for us, just the way people are, or common sense, or "facts" about the social world, and thus are not revised.

- When what others do conflicts with a theory, we probably conclude something is wrong with the person, not the theory. (Example: We gave Joe a salary increase, what is wrong with him that he hasn't taken more initiative?)

- We think our theories are vastly better than they are. People wildly overestimate how "good they are with people." This bias is called illusory superiority. (Example: 96 percent of Americans think they are above-average drivers.)

- Our theories, right or wrong, become normative ("shoulds"): "If X happens, people *should* do Y." (Example: Jane hasn't been the same since her loss; she should find a way to let out the emotions she is holding back.)

- Our theories of *attribution*—what is inside peoples' heads driving their behavior—are very inaccurate. (Example: She hasn't spoken up at the last three meetings, she must be angry about not being promoted.)

- Theories derive from just a few experiences, and may not apply in richer, more varied contexts (such as other cultures). (Example: Amusingly, I was an "American barbarian" in France for ordering a cup of coffee, to combat exhaustion, *with* my dinner instead of *after* it. *Quel paysan!*[1])

Exquisite though folk psychology may be, our theories fall down in everyday situations because, after a time, we stop revising them.

---

[1] What a peasant!

Worse, from our point of view, leading major change is *not* an every-day situation. These folk psychological theories, cemented by adult-hood, mostly work for smaller groups, in familiar contexts. Leading change, especially big change, introduces scale, complexity, conflict, and volatility. This higher-stakes game, steering a ship with hundreds of thousands of workers, leading people through change, cannot be learned "on the playground" (through college and early career) because the psychology of groups and the behavior of complex sys-tems comes into play. Change requires much greater levels of coor-dination and communication because old, habitual, second-nature patterns are disrupted. At the same time, our everyday psychological theories may break down because people are typically no longer at their best: Change disrupts the status quo, threatens interests, pro-vokes anxieties, and evokes conflict and competition. (Who has not been baffled at the behavior of people under stress? "Are you kidding me? Don't they get it? How can they think that?")

A business example of how a folk psychology belief gets us into big trouble is the fundamental attribution error (FAE). The FAE describes the persistent, theoretical error of blaming people in a complex system. Recall in the previous chapter, a management team thought their call center workers lacked motivation. They tried to motivate them with carrots and sticks and produced the opposite effect (because the workers knew it was a lousy product and their computer systems were poor). In the change context, the effect of the FAE can be toxic: Blaming people when they are largely power-less annihilates morale. The more you try to motivate the people you blame—with workshops, inspirational talk, communications, rewards, and so on—when they are not the cause of the problem, the more cynical they will become. This is just one example of when a faulty theory about people means our efforts to effect positive change pro-duce the opposite effect,

In short, folk psychology means we perform as if *virtuosi* in com-monplace situations, but are error-prone, do *not* hold our theories skeptically enough, and are out of our depth when the stakes get high. Folk psychology and common sense are of limited use in complex organizations and during high-stakes change.

From Folk Psychology to Folk Management

When I managed my first team a long while ago, the only education I had in managing people had been gained in my first job, from watching my first manager. I learned a few things to say and do, but management in banks was largely informal then—we made things up as we went along using folk psychology and common sense to manage our teams. (I find it worrying today that my team of eight managed assets of several hundred million dollars—we were not playing with chicken feed. Was common sense really enough?) Research suggests that 70 percent of people management is learned by watching others and imitating them, through trial and error (learning on the job), or through "oral tradition" (getting guidance from an early boss). The question we must ask is: "From whom did the boss learn?" and "How do we know that the boss knows what she is doing?" People are promoted for many reasons and sometimes for the wrong ones.

In many ways, this method of knowledge transfer mimics preliterate societies! Contrast this kind of evidence with organic chemistry, naval architecture, or medicine. In those more formal disciplines, centuries of accumulated knowledge is codified so that if I wanted to, for example, manufacture a synthetic polymer, I could do so based on replicating the tested ideas of science rather than flying by the seat of my pants.

Like the folk psychology learned on the playground, *folk management* may get us a long way. Some folk management is supplanted by formal training—which *if transferred to the job* will correct aberrant practices. However, how we relate to and manage people is deeply ingrained, and training programs, as you'll see in the next chapter, are limited in their ability to effect deep changes in work behavior.

Gurus and Pop Psychology

"Don't let Deepak Chopra manage your change program."
—Paul Gibbons

Folk psychology makes psychologists of us all. Yet imagine a non-engineer making a proclamation about the required load-bearing structure of a bridge, or a nondoctor prescribing a risky medication, or a nonarchitect commenting on the optimal structural design for a building. Because we are all folk psychologists, anyone can claim authority on human behavior in a way that would be ignored if attempted in other disciplines.

The pop psychology world has some authors/experts with 50 years' research experience sharing that experience in distilled format (such as in *Thinking Fast and Slow* by Nobel laureate Daniel Kahneman, or *Authentic Happiness* by Martin Seligman). From there it goes downhill. There are authors who grab a few tentative research findings and craft a well-told, half-true (or even untrue) story simplifying and cherry-picking research along the way to make their case. It is hard to judge expertise in the world of "human sciences" because some nonexperts are very good at self-promotion and we use *popularity* as a proxy for expertise. If you sell a million books, you gain an expert reputation, which is not the same thing as expertise. This bizarre happenstance means that the popularizers of psychological science are seen as greater authorities than the scientists themselves. Both Dan Pink and Malcolm Gladwell are on lists of "top-100 thinkers." This may be understandable because reading original research can be dull, but we therefore depend a great deal on the accuracy of their interpretations of research.

Malcom Gladwell puts the pop in pop psychology and his (intensely readable) books are replete with examples from psychological (and sociological) research. His books (*Blink, Outliers, David and Goliath,* and *The Tipping Point*) have all reached number one on the *New York Times* best-seller lists. If you google "top popular psychology books," his occupy three of the top five slots. Yet Gladwell draws intense criticism from researchers, even those who he makes famous through his citations. According to Professor Christopher Chabris, "He excels at telling just-so stories, and cherry-picking science to back them up."[2] Chabris criticizes "Gladwell's manipulative

---

[2] Chabris, C. (2013, Sep. 29). Book Review: *David and Goliath* by Malcolm Gladwell. *Wall Street Journal*. Retrieved from http://www.wsj.com/articles/SB10001424052702304713704579093090254007968.

logic—namely, the writer's penchant for reporting correlations as causations—a move he uses so often, he has made it iconic."[3] Elsewhere, Harvard's Stephen Pinker challenges, "Gladwell is apt to offer generalizations that are banal, obtuse, or flat wrong...."[4] Daniel Kahneman, when asked for his views on *Blink,* said, "Malcolm Gladwell definitely created in the public arena the impression that intuition is magical.... That belief is false."[5]

I will not weigh in on whether Gladwell's critics are right, that he sometimes misuses psychological science to tell a good story. (Indeed, this book picks and chooses research in some highly contested areas also—although I do not claim that any of these matters are established truths.) I can say that his work passes for gospel in the change community despite the surrounding controversy. For example, Gladwell's "10,000 hour rule" is treated as fact, whereas the most recent study I have unearthed suggests that merely 12 percent of the variation in performance is due to practice time.[6] Where there is substantial controversy among experts, there is almost no controversy in lay circles.

Experienced researchers, such as Kahneman, and the best writers, such as Gladwell, are still the quality end of pop psychology. It goes quickly downhill from there. There are highly paid people masquerading as "business psychologists" who pay much less attention to science than does Gladwell, and there are thousands of books written by coaches and self-help gurus who pay no attention to science at all. I once had occasion to share a platform with a "business psychologist," author of a dozen books on leadership and change, and a self-styled "professor" (prominently titled as such on all his many

---

[3] Fitts, A. (2013, Oct. 10). The Gladwellian 'debate': Why are we still listening to Malcolm Gladwell's cherry-picked gospel? *Columbia Journalism Review.* Retrieved from http://www.cjr.org/the_observatory/the_gladwellian_debate.php.

[4] Pinker, S. (2009, Nov. 7). Malcolm Gladwell, eclectic detective. *New York Times.* Retrieved from http://www.nytimes.com/2009/11/15/books/review/Pinker-t.html?pagewanted=all&_r=0.

[5] *Charlie Rose Show.* Broadcast February 28, 2012. Retrieved October 2014.

[6] Macnamara, B. N., Hambrick, D. Z., & Oswald, F. L. (2014, August). Deliberate practice and performance in music, games, sports, education, and professions: A meta-analysis. *Psychological Science, 25*(8), 1608–1618.

books and publicity) who dropped out of college never to return. His education, as such, was under the tutelage of new-age guru Wayne Dyer. Our hero spoke about psychology and leadership for an hour at a world-famous, five-star hotel, to 200 senior partners of a big-four audit/consultancy firm for a fee of $25,000. His fees were not a one-off. We then shared a cab to British Airways, where he again was advising senior leaders (again for very large fees) in one part of the business.

The world, for sure, has a place for motivational speakers, perhaps even when the truth-value is zero. In my view, we must not confuse inspiration with information, nor confuse something that sounds good, with something that is true.

This phenomenon is particularly acute in the leadership world.

From Pop Psychology to Pop Leadership

Leadership is a serious business: Senior business leaders are stewards of enterprises in which they only have a small moral stake (compared with thousands or millions of others) and vast power. They are the custodians of people's livelihoods and when they screw up, people lose those livelihoods. Great leaders can make working lives a joy; bad leaders can make lives unbearable. Leaders make or break countries, corporations, and communities. They must serve shareholders, staff, and customers, and their judgments affect the economy, the jobs of millions, and the environment.

Developing leaders matters. Leadership can be learned, but it takes considerable skill, hard work, significant character development, great foresight, and the right context or opportunity. At the very least, it includes an attitude of care (stewardship) toward stakeholders; a solid foundation of expert knowledge and dedication to keeping up to date; substantial skills in influencing and other people-related skills; the ability to deal with stress and conflict; alignment in thought, word, and deed; a strong moral code; great motivation and drive; an ethical/values stance; and a clear sense of purpose.

Pop psychology abuts what I call "pop leadership," which, I will argue, is among the most destructive forces in the business world, spreading misinformation and half-truths, and drowning out serious attempts to understand an important subject. Because anything goes in pop psychology, anything goes in pop leadership.

Here are two titles of pop leadership articles, from one of the most auspicious business journals. "Leadership Wisdom Tells Us Not to Think Too Much." Is that true? Or could it be that the most costly leadership errors come from thinking too little, leaping to conclusions, or being too confident in biased thinking? "Leadership Is about Emotion." In leadership, nothing is as important as relationships, and, yes, emotion is central in those. Yet, leadership is also about strategy, self-development, decision making, planning, envisioning, coordinating, negotiating, and influencing.

In no other domain of human performance, being a virtuoso musician, a famous athlete, or an innovative scientist, do we distill success down to such half-truths (1 percent truths sometimes) and trivialities (for example, "golf is all about accuracy" or "playing the piano is about feeling the keys").

I worry that thoughtful, scholarly, reflective, humble, insightful, and wise leadership education, so vital to communities, corporations, and governments, is trivialized. If a book full of pop leadership articles were devoured in its entirety, would it create an excellent business leader? Would it have prevented Enron? The most intriguing (and worrying) feature of pop leadership is the lack of critique. Ask yourself how often you have seen a critique of the ideas of Drucker, Kotter, Christensen, or Bennis. No scientific idea, nor any scientist— not even Hawking, Turing, or Einstein—gets a free pass the way management thinkers do. When a statement about leadership is preceded by "according to Drucker," it is taken as axiomatic—like the angles of a triangle adding up to 180 degrees.

Our folk psychology, folk management, pop psychology, and pop leadership provide a bad set of answers to leading complex change. We are still looking for sources of systematic knowledge about what makes people tick, and even if we inoculate ourselves against guru hype, we are surrounded by psychological myths that have a veneer of science to them.

Psychology: Science in Its Infancy

"What a piece of work is a man! How noble in reason, how infinite in faculties! In form and moving, how express and admirable! In action how like an angel! In apprehension, how like a god! The beauty of the world! The paragon of animals!"

—Hamlet, II, 2

The human's fascination with humankind extends back before Shakespeare and ancient Greece, but the great philosophers of 2,500 years ago handed down the first well-recorded answers to big questions:

- What constitutes the good life, just happiness, or more?
- Does happiness matter? What makes humans happy?
- Are abilities innate or learned?
- Why do we act contrary to reason, or against our best interests?
- What drives and motivates people?
- What are reason and rationality? What are their limits?
- Are we, by nature, good or evil? Collaborative or competitive?
- What is knowledge and how do we acquire it?
- What are excellence and virtue, and how are they attained?
- Can one's basic character be changed?
- How do you persuade someone to change their mind?

Some Greek answers have not been surpassed. What survives from their writings on these topics is far richer than almost anything you will find on a pop-psychology bookshelf today. The Epicurean concept of pleasure is one example: a counterpoint to modern consumerism, emphasizing developing one's mind, learning about the world, simple pleasures, moderating ones desires, and leading a virtuous life. The Stoics (circa 300 BCE) theorized emotional intelligence a little before Daniel Goleman. (I am unsure whether contemporary accounts add much to the Stoics ideas.) Plato spelled out the famous

Theory X/Theory management theory[7] a few millennia before pioneer leadership thinker Douglas McGregor "invented" it for a management audience. Greek notions of ethics (virtue ethics) still compete with nineteenth-century ideas such as utilitarianism ("the greatest good for the greatest number"); Greek ideas on rhetoric, logical argument, and influence are foundational, even today.

Despite how well many of those questions were answered long ago, most of the Greek answers do not find their way into contemporary writing. When I began to study psychology formally a few decades ago, it was as if the first crack at those questions was in the twentieth century, and no mention was ever made of the long intellectual history of grappling with them.[8]

Nineteenth-Century Psychology and Its Legacy

Psychology and the physical sciences made little progress for a few thousand years, but then in the 1800s, psychology, unlike the physical sciences, went downhill. Three psychological trends whose offspring persist today seized the academic and public imaginations, mesmerism, phrenology, and graphology. Franz Mesmer persuaded the world of an energetic transference that occurred between animated and inanimate objects, mesmerism. Franz Joseph Gall "proved" that personality and ability could be predicted by reading bumps on the skull, phrenology. (When experts criticize fMRI[9] brain imaging, or psychometric testing, they frequently refer to such things as "the new phrenology.")

A third invention of the 1800s was graphology—the notion that handwriting analysis could determine the psychology of the writer. Alfred Binet, the psychologist best known for the invention of intelligence testing, called graphology "the science of the future." Despite the fact that graphology has the same predictive power as tarot cards

---

[7] Douglas McGregor coined Theory X and Theory Y, and Plato's parable, "The Ring of Gyges," wondered whether invisibility would reveal an essentially good nature, or an essentially evil one.

[8] Some very good contemporary academic writers are beginning to incorporate older texts, such as Jonathan Haidt in *The Happiness Hypothesis*.

[9] Functional Magnetic Resonance Imaging

and astrology, this "future science" was still in use in the 1990s (!) in some (otherwise) excellent companies. In 1981, while interviewing for a position as a securities analyst at the most prestigious investment bank of that era, I had to submit a handwriting sample for "scientific analysis."

Psychological pseudoscience dies hard, especially when people have commercial interests in its continued existence.

Psychology Turns to Science in the Twentieth Century

The revolutions in the natural sciences, physics, biology, and chemistry began about the time of Newton and Gallileo; within 200 years, alchemists had turned into chemists, and we went from knowing nothing about the chemical structure of matter to having it nailed by 1910 or so. One hundred years ago, we had no idea at all how genetic information was transmitted between generations (we had no idea that it was DNA, and the chromosomes were thought to support cell structure), but now we have sequenced the human genome.

This is not the case with psychology. Experimental psychology was late to the Scientific Revolution party and was not born until nearly the dawn of the twentieth century, Harvard's William James proclaimed it "The Science of Mental Life." The problem with a "science of mental life" is that mental phenomena cannot be measured, so objectively studying the contents of a person's mind is impossible. Asking people what is inside their heads (thoughts, feelings, beliefs, desires) produces variable results because we are not accurate observers of our mental life, and even when we are, social desirability may influence us to skew what we report.

Because of this, psychology's status as a science is hotly contested (as far as academics ever get hot). Measurement problems mean snooty physical scientists would deny psychology (and economics, and definitely sociology) a place alongside "real science" because they lack "clearly defined terminology, quantifiability, highly controlled experimental conditions, reproducibility and, finally, predictability and testability."[10]

---

[10] Berezow, A. (2012, Jul. 13). Why psychology isn't science. *Los Angeles Times.* Retrieved from http://articles.latimes.com/2012/jul/13/news/la-ol-blowback-pscyhology-science-20120713.

This scientific fuzziness leads in two directions and creates two problems in business psychology: (1) the tendency to measure nothing, and (2) measure what you easily can and devalue everything that cannot be measured.

Measuring nothing means abandoning the scientific ship, that is, to not worry too much about which things measurably work. This is the rule with almost every people-related intervention, OD workshops, training, HRM practices, offsite learning/strategy conferences, and change communication. This ends up being very useful for practitioners (like me) who sell such things for a living. Value-for-money is hard to measure, so why bother?

One multinational CEO confided in me, "We don't know within $20 million what we spend globally on training and organization development, and we have no idea whether any, some, or none of that money spent produces organizational value. That we keep doing it is a matter of faith, not science." For example, in business learning and development (training), participants' reactions are easily measured by "happy sheets." Sadly, happy sheets are like applause at the end of the concert. Everybody applauds whether or not they thought it any good. Those instant postprogram reactions are almost uncorrelated with learning transfer to the job. It is much more difficult to measure real learning,[11] so few businesses bother.[12]

The alternative path is to try to measure what can be easily quantified, and ignore the rest. There is a raging debate in health care on doctors being measured, evaluated, and paid by "relative-value-units"—broadly speaking, patient throughput. The downside is that

---

[11] Little things like what concepts we're learning, did they sustainably stick, what behavioral changes were made, and what business results were produced?

[12] Some research suggests that as many as half of all companies go beyond participant reactions and measure other outcomes (Twitchell, Holton, & Trott, 2008). It depends what you mean by measure. In my, anecdotal, view, what businesses report they do here and what they actually do are miles apart. Having run programs for more than three dozen organizations, only once was any serious attempt made to capture more than participant reactions, yet all would claim to be interested in training-ROI. L&D specialists know this is poor practice, and I suspect the research reflects their discomfort. I should also say that one emerging trend in learning and development is to arrest this lack of measurement and accountability.

this drives physician behavior, away from spending extra time with chronic conditions, away from harder-to-measure outcomes, such as disease prevention and patient satisfaction, and away from patient long-term value and risk management behaviors.[13] Outcomes are skewed toward the measurable, which creates unwanted, unintended consequences.

What can be done to solve the problem of measurement (and sometimes unmeasurability) of people-related outcomes? This is one of the areas where the gap between leading and trailing organizations may be the largest, and one of the most important transformational trends in business. (Recall IBM's finding that some organizations claim 80 percent success implementing change and some as little as 8 percent.) These general prescriptions are already being enacted by a few organizations.

HR analytics is a potential new dawn in this area, and although very new, leading organizations are beginning to note analytics' applicability in what is now a black hole of accountability in the area of HRM/OD—lots of expenditure and faith that it does something. Beyond the recommendation to "get on the HR analytics bus," here are some general recommendations, including some of the pitfalls of early HR analytics implementations:

1. **Use more science**—Begin to measure (even if qualitatively) and to test causal hypotheses as a way of holding HRM/OD interventions accountable for results. Do you use personality surveys in recruitment? A trait that performs well in one culture may not perform well in a different one. Begin gathering data on how different traits succeed in *your* business (rather than rely on what survey firms tell you *generally* about how certain traits perform in certain roles). Evaluate whether the predictions these instruments make about performance are true. Do you use OD type interventions for strategic planning or to engage people in change? Agree what (qualitative and quantitative) measures define success of the workshop, and evaluate

---

[13] Baltic, S. (2013, Oct. 7). Liked or loathed, RUC wields broad influence. *Modern Medicine.* Retrieved from http://www.modernmedicine.com/content/ modernmedicine/modern-medicine-feature-articles/liked-or-loathed-ruc-wields-broad-influence.

changes in behaviors, attitudes, values, and skills[14] *and* the business results those changes are intended to produce.

2. **Combine qualitative and quantitative measures, and long-term and short-term measures, in a single dashboard**—Even if performance items cannot now be measured, they should appear on the dashboard as placeholders until processes and systems can be implemented that deliver the data. If there is a quantitative-only performance dashboard and then "other stuff" not on the dashboard, only dashboard measures will be managed.

3. **Treat early HR analytics implementations as experimental**—All such analytics suffer from the GIGO rule ("garbage in, garbage out"). All of their findings are highly algorithm/model dependent.

4. **Be cautious about HR analytics driving outcomes and behaviors toward the easily measurable**—The risk is as with physicians measured and paid by RVUs—behavior is driven in directions that destroy long-term value.

"We cannot easily measure it now, so why bother" is a costly cop-out. Some scientific theories take decades to validate (such as Einstein's), but we must start somewhere. It may take five years or a decade to get it right, but the idea of a business spending money it cannot count, on outcomes it cannot measure, is worrisome.

Psychological Myths

"Science must begin with myths and with the criticism of myths."

—Karl Popper

---

14 I have probably designed and facilitated over 100 such OD (strategic planning, engagement) type workshops in 20 years. Not once has a client insisted that we measure long-term value of those interventions.

When I began training as a change expert in 1995, I took change management masterclasses from Daryl Conner, then among the best-known change experts in the world who had sold his methods and tools to my employer (PwC) and at least three of the biggest five consulting firms for millions a pop. In 1994, he had a tidy corner of the market.

Table 6.1 lays out nine of the myths, since dismantled by research, which I learned as "truth" in those early days and that are still taught.

Table 6.1 Psychological Myths Propagated by the Media[15]

MYTH	TRUTH
When confronting death or experiencing loss, people must pass through five stages of grief. (And change in organizations is like this also.)	This lovely piece of storytelling was never validated by research. People experience and adjust to death and loss in widely varying ways.
Intelligence and personality are stable and unchangeable.	This view is not only false, but is correlated with worse performance and mood outcomes.
Happiness is mostly related to external circumstances—one's environments or life's happenings.	In the long run, happiness is largely unrelated to external circumstances. It is partly genetic.
It is better to express ("work through") anger (and strong emotions) to others than hold it in. (People may need to "vent" emotions during change.)	This "catharsis" hypothesis is unproven, and research suggests the opposite is true.
Effective treatments for psychological discomfort rely on exploring roots in childhood.	Research shows that treatments that place little or no emphasis on the past are equally or more effective.
Some people are left-brained; some are right-brained. Right-brained people are more creative and artistic and less analytical.	There is no such thing as a right-brained person. The two hemispheres have slightly different capabilities, but they can fill in for each other. There is no relationship between brain dominance and creativity.
People have different learning styles to which teaching styles should be matched.	There is no agreement on what a learning style is, and no relation between tested learning style and how fast or much people learn.
There is a hierarchy of psychological needs (Maslow), and they are met from the bottom up with self-actualization dependent upon meeting the lower needs.	Maslow's hierarchy looks sensible enough but no aspect of it (despite much effort) has been validated. Maslow created a way of thinking about human flourishing, rather than scientifically describing it.
Ninety-three percent of communication is nonverbal.	The original researcher, Mehrabian, has spent decades trying to dispel this misrepresentation of his research that said 93 percent of the *emotional content* comes from nonverbal communication, not 93 percent of the communication. Unsurprisingly, words matter more than 7 percent.

---

[15] Taken from *50 Great Myths of Popular Psychology: Shattering Widespread Misconceptions About Human Behavior,* by Lillienfeld, et al. The book weighs the evidence for and against many of these myths, and is an excellent resource for the curious.

These myths are downright damaging to human flourishing and to organizational change. The quick witted satirical newspaper *The Onion* fronted the following headline in response to the learning style notion: "Parents of Nasal Learners Demand Odor-Based Curriculum." The parents were tired of school teaching methods that discriminated against their nasal-learning kids. The theory (now myth) of learning styles, that people have visual, kinesthetic, or auditory styles (or one of the many other models) and that they learn better and quicker if information is presented in that style, allowed a generation of people to resist learning and change. "I can't really learn that way, I'm a 'K'." Naturally, this is an example of a self-fulfilling statement. Having been fed the learning style dogma, you decide you cannot learn in a particular way and then (in a most human way) set out to prove yourself right.

How many of that list of myths have you heard presented as "fact," avowedly supported by research? Even my expert friends believe such things as "right-brained" people are more creative. This is a worrisome situation because not only do we have folk psychology, gurus, and the media propagating mistruths, but we also have an expert community who are insufficiently skeptical, allowing the persistence of these myths. How is a nonexpert executive, concerned with leading change, to separate fact from fiction?

Neuroscience

On the face of it, neuroscience is psychology's great white hope: Rather than rely on what people tell us is inside their heads, we can have a look-see. Can neuromarketing, for example, use imaging to see what people *really* think and feel, and *really* like and dislike, and improve upon traditional methods such as focus groups? Neuroscience promises to provide facts where before we had something more slippery.

Neuroscience also raises the possibility of linking biology, mind, and behavior—of understanding how biochemistry, physiology, and the structure of the nervous system give rise to consciousness, and explain why we do what we do. Can we change the biology of our nervous systems? Or, do changes in biology help us understand how to change minds?

No wonder the buzz. Neuroscience is the new black when it comes to understanding people—at work or otherwise. As author Jonah Lehrer said, "If Warhol were around today, he'd have a series of silkscreens dedicated to the cortex; the amygdala would hang alongside Marilyn Monroe."[16] I meet consultants/coaches who call themselves "neuroplasticians." The media is on the bandwagon: "God spot discovered in brain." The neurohypers tell us that neuroimaging can tell us whether you are guilty of a crime, how you will vote, or what you will buy at Whole Foods.

Perhaps this fascination is understandable. In addition to a narcissistic fascination with ourselves, we have in our heads a biological entity more complex that anything we have created, seen, or even anything that we can imagine. A single human brain has more switches than all the computers and routers and Internet connections on Earth. Add to this little factoids that if our neurons were laid end-to-end, they would stretch around the planet four times, or the fact that the brain performs millions of times more operations per second than the fastest computer and we have a (intellectually anyhow) fascinating subject.

Why I Am a Neuroskeptic

"If the brain were so simple we could understand it, we would be so simple that we could not."

—Lyall Watson

In discussing this book with colleagues and friends, coaches, and consultants, they generally assume that neuroscience and business, or neuroleadership will take several chapters. When I say that there is not that much neuroscience that I think can be usefully applied to

---

[16] Thornton, D. (2011, Sep. 11). The rhetoric of neuroscience. *Wired Magazine.* Retrieved from http://www.wired.com/2011/08/the-rhetoric-of-neuroscience/.

business, they are astonished. There are three reasons that I am a neuroskeptic.

The first reason is that "neuroscience says..." has become a popular way of justifying many claims that have nothing to do with neuroscience. Today, it is a scientific trump card, and because so few people understand neuroscience, it is an argument stopper. It depends on what you call neuroscience. A reasonable definition is "any or all of the sciences, such as neurochemistry and experimental psychology, which deal with the structure or function of the nervous system and brain."[17] The most notable feature is that *neuroscience links mind and behavior to the biology of the brain*. Brain images are very science-y, and so is talking about neurotransmitters. This leads to the "great neuro land-grab," where old-fashioned psychological findings (or myths) are labeled neuroscience to give them a face-lift. For example, the finding that working memory can hold seven or so items is frequently called a "neuroscientific" finding—except it comes from the 1950s, and has nothing to do with the biology of the brain. It was good old-fashioned cognitive psychology. I believe it is wise to be very cautious when a claim is prefaced today by "neuroscience says...."

The second reason is that the science of brain imaging is much less conclusive than the media (or business coaches) portray. Neuroscience has a scientific look to it (brain scans are pretty cool), and the "science end" (not the applied neurobusiness and neuroleadership end) is published in peer-reviewed prestigious journals, based on rigorous scientific method, with proper caveats around careful conclusions. However, in addition to overhyping of results by the media, there are major technical and philosophical flaws with neuroimaging (one of the most popular techniques, and the one that produces those gorgeous pictures of lit-up brains). The "fish in a brain scanner" controversy is one, and there are weaknesses in the statistical methods used to generate the images. This is not to say that neuroimaging is bad science, but merely a young science.

As Professor Scott Lilienfeld and Sally Satel say in *Brainwashed: The Subjective Appeal of Mindless Neuroscience*, "These mappings

---

[17] Neurochemistry (2015). OED Online. Retrieved from http://dictionary.oed. com/.

are oversimplifications. Most of the brain is zoned for mixed use."[18] When the media refers to the amygdala is the fear center, they are telling two white lies: Many brain areas are involved in the fear response, and the amygdala is involved in many different emotions, not just fear. Professor William Uttal, author of *The New Phrenology: On the Localization of Cognitive Processes in the Brain*, summed it up as follows: "fMRI [one technique that produces brain scans] is as distant as the galvanic skin response or pulse rate is from cognitive processes."[19]

The third reason is that neuroscientific talk may sometimes be a useful metaphor, but sometimes it is harmful or counterproductive. Although there are interesting findings from cognitive affective neuroscience, we are a very long way from being able to make huge claims such as: *"By understanding the brain science behind commitment, coaches and managers can then develop interventions that target the left frontal cortex."* Structures perform multiple functions so when you "target the left prefrontal cortex," it is like telling a fisherman to "target the Mediterranean." How exactly a coach may, as the author suggests, "target" neuroanatomical structures such as the "ACC[20] in order to reach the amygdala" is beyond the ken of this coach/neuroscientist.[21]

How useful is it to discuss the biology of the brain in business? The reaction of octane with oxygen is fundamental to the internal combustion engine, yet no book on becoming a successful Formula One driver would include it nor the structure of the internal combustion engine. Knowing where the camshaft resides and what it does is unlikely to help you through the *chicanes* at 250 kph. Does knowing the *amygdala* has a role in emotion management, or that *oxytocin* produces feelings of closeness, help with leadership (as many popularizers would have us believe)?

---

[18] Satel, S. & Lilienthal S. (2013). *Brainwashed: The subjective appeal of mindless neuroscience*. New York: Basic Books, p 12.

[19] Uttal, W., (2003) *The new phrenology: The limits of localizing cognitive processes in the brain*. Cambridge: MIT Press, p 18.

[20] Anterior Cingulate Cortex

[21] I studied neuroscience at undergraduate and graduate levels, stopping before completing a PhD dissertation. Perhaps a doctorate in neuroscience is necessary to perform such surgically precise coaching?

My fear is that this neurotalk may actually be a distraction from the real work of developing leaders. Does introducing such abstractions (dorsolateral prefrontal cortex, GABA receptors) *prevent* leaders from dealing with disengaged workers, or damaged trust? Imagine a couple in marriage counseling discussing brain structures and neurotransmitters for an hour. Has the discussion brought them closer? "Dearest, my 5HT-1 receptor is saturated when you criticize me, and my *nucleus accumbens* is unable to help regulate my reward centers."

Take another neuroscience insight: "Effectively, by remembering that the amygdala is connected to the DLPFC, the mPFC, and the ACC, coaches can inform leaders that short-term memory, risk-benefit assessment, and attention are also disrupted by anxiety."[22] This sounds supersmart, but does the half of that statement before "coaches..." add anything *useful* to the sentence? (And, as we have seen, the truth-value is very limited.)

Attempts to localize psychological processes in the brain are, from a businessperson's point of view, practically useless. As philosopher Jerry Fodor says, "If the mind happens in space at all, it happens somewhere north of the neck. What exactly turns on knowing how far north?"[23]

On the positive side, many of the books that are written have interesting and useful tools. I do not want to discount the efforts to apply cognitive psychology to business. For example, David Rock's SCARF (Status, Certainty, Autonomy, Relatedness, and Fairness) is an extremely useful way of understanding responses to threats and rewards at work. However, SCARF is not really very neuroscientific (grounded in the biology of the brain), *and its usefulness is completely independent of that neurobiological grounding.* You can use Rock's good ideas, SCARF, or AGES (Attention, Generation, Emotion, and Spacing), or most other supposedly neuroscientific models without reference to brain anatomy or physiology. In that way, Rock's books are exceptional contributions to coaching and leadership.

---

[22] Pillay, S. (2014). *Your brain and business: The neuroscience of great leaders*. New York: FT Press, p. 193.

[23] Fodor, J. (2009, Sep. 30). Diary. *London Review of Books*, 21(19), pp. 68–69.

There is excellent work, both applied and research, being done by people who append a "neuro" to what they do (neurocoaches, neurofacilitators). I, for the sake of appearing "leading-edge," have been tempted to rebrand much of my earlier education as "neurochemistry" (from biochemistry), and "neuropharmacology" from (pharmacological chemistry)—after all, I was working on the brain. For businesspeople, roughly speaking, the more "neuro" a finding is (the more biology of the brain), the less useful, and the more useful something is, the less likely it is to be grounded in the biology of the brain. The science is simply not far enough along.

Despite that, I am a neuro-optimist. The twenty-first century may well be the century of the brain, where our knowledge multiplies the way knowledge of the genome did after the 1944 discovery that DNA was the carrier of genetic information. (Think where we have come in just 70 years!) I suspect in 50 years that the tragedy of degenerative diseases of the brain and spinal cord injury may leave us the way that killer diseases Polio and Smallpox did a few decades ago.

The Century Where Brain, Mind, and Behavior Come Together?

"Financial economics, as a discipline, is where chemistry was in the sixteenth century: a messy compendium of proven know-how, misty folk wisdom, unexamined assumptions, and grandiose speculations."
—Benoit Mandelbrot

The views I have expressed on the human sciences echo those of Mandelbrot's on financial economics, a discipline with a veneer of rigor. Yet, psychology is becoming more rigorous and more empirical in every decade. It is also becoming more useful because academic psychology increasingly tackles not just the Greek questions, but also today's big messy questions of living well, for example, growth, career, loss, parenting, leadership, relationships, achievement, happiness, and meaning. Those subjects were, until recently, more speculative and less empirical (for example, Maslow's work). However, both academic psychology and organizational psychology suffer from the "theory-practice" gap. However useful a top-ranked paper such as "Unpacking the Cross-Level Effects of Tenure Diversity, Explicit Knowledge, and Knowledge Sharing on Individual Creativity"[24] may be, translating it into language and tools that help people lead better lives takes considerable effort. (Even with my voracious appetite for academic writing, titles like that one make me want to run for cover.) Using the model of this book, most of the rigorous research has to move from the upper-left box (valid, not much used), to the upper-right box (valid, and useful/used). There are encouraging trends for the adolescent science:

- **Focus on human flourishing**—Movements such as "positive psychology" are a return to Greek psychology of 2,500 years ago, and are a turn away from the psychology of mental illness, or dysfunction, toward how to promote human flourishing and peak performance. The best ideas on flourishing combine happiness with engagement, meaning, and contribution (service) making flourishing a more robust concept than happiness. Furthermore, such topics are increasingly being studied experimentally and not just as the objects of philosophical speculation. This is a move (using our model) from the lower-right box to the upper-right box, asking psychologists to devote increased energy to studying phenomena about which humans care and validating tools they use.

- **Evidence-based**—We need to push charlatans off the bookshelves and out of the TED talks, and promote more evidence based ideas that are practically adaptable. We need an end to psychobabble and pop leadership. In our model, this involves moving a considerable number of ideas from the lower right to the lower left and then letting history wash them away (as it did with mesmerism).

---

[24] Gilson, L., Lim, H., Luciano, M. & Choi, J. (2013). Unpacking the cross-level effects of tenure diversity, explicit knowledge, and knowledge sharing on individual creativity. *Journal of Occupational and Organizational Psychology* 86(2), pp. 203–222.

- **Link to biology**—Neuroscience is among the most promising areas for the twenty-first century and also currently the most hyped. Eventually, we may be able to "see inside peoples' heads," but while imaging science today provides many medical applications, the notion that a businessperson should know where in the brain risk and reward are localized (if they are) is wrongheaded. Does discussing their amygdalas and dorsolateral prefrontal cortices help a leader to engage her team? It is far too early for commercialization of neuroscience ideas, but in a few decades, neurobiology may have practical applications beyond just medicine.

- **Neobehaviorism**—The gap between thought and action, between belief and will prevents solving our most pressing individual and societal problems. Just a few years ago, 93 percent of people said they take environmental factors into account when choosing a car, but only 7 percent actually did so. Less than 5 percent of heart attack survivors change their behavior. Diet books make little dent on obesity and eating behavior (perhaps making it worse). No progress will be made on climate, obesity, population, AIDS, or any other global issue without individual behavior change. As you will see in the next chapter, the backlash against behaviorism went too far because what matters a great deal is not just what people think and feel, but what actions they take. Yet disregarding what people think and feel is callous and destroys long-term relationships, and coercion compromises autonomy. How can we square that circle?

- **Integration with other disciplines**—The biggest task for twenty-first-century psychology, and applied business psychology, is to integrate with other disciplines. The next two chapters, on behaviors, and hearts and minds, look at research from nonpsychology areas that are academically grounded findings from law, public policy, public health, medicine, economics, religion, finance, anthropology, philosophy, and neurobiology that provide foundational insights into people at work.

Conclusion

"It may turn out, years hence, that a solid discipline of human science will have come into existence, hard as quantum physics, filled with deep insights, plagued as physics still is by ambiguities..."

—Lewis Thomas

In business, as in other domains, we have to make policy decisions based on theories about people. Leaders not trained in psychology (or a related field) often rely on hunches, folk psychology, or theories circulated by the media, sources that are riddled with error. Close to those hunches about people are folk management and pop leadership. The former is management ideas conveyed by oral tradition, the kind I learned early in my career, from people who had received the same kind of informal training as I was about to. Pop leadership is the body of well-intended leadership sayings, mistruths, truisms, feel-good aphorisms, and oversimplifications that circulate uncritically in the leadership world.

As psychologists and change practitioners in business, we need to have hard conversations, about what is valid and to think critically about leadership aphorisms, whether "targeting the ACC" is useful, or whether learning styles really predict learning.

Science should help, but psychology is a very young science, and the mind is complex entity. We do not yet have the tools to produce the perfect answers and will have to live with some uncertainty. Given the immaturity of psychology, there should be much more debate and critique than exists among practitioners who rely upon it. Instead, there is little. However, if the "science of mind" enjoys the kind of progress in the twenty-first century that chemistry did in the nineteenth and twentieth centuries, we have a lot to look forward to.

Now, having endured a long chapter on what is probably *not* true, and probably *not* useful, the next two chapters focus exclusively on new ideas that seem both true and useful for changing human hearts, minds, and behaviors.

7

The Science of Changing Behaviors

Major change requires behavioral change. This spectacular statement of the obvious is oft forgotten in practice. When the new CRM system fails, it is often because staff fail to use it rather than because of some technical fault. When a reorganization fails, it is more often because behaviors do not follow the redrawn boxes. Our aim is to explore new ways of changing behavior, but first, what is wrong with the old ways?

From the "Science of Mind" to the "Science of Behavior"

The first revolution in psychology, the "science of mind," was called behaviorism. Appearing on the scene in the 1920s, behaviorism proposed that psychology focus only on observable behavior. Environmental stimuli (for example, rewards and punishments) were used to reinforce correct behaviors and discourage incorrect ones. Behaviorism was a change methodology that applied psychologists recommended in spheres as distinct as child-rearing, public policy, education, and workplaces. In the twenty-first century, when people talk about carrots and sticks, or rewards and sanctions, or bonuses, incentives, and punishment, they are using behaviorist language.

The behaviorist view of the world is depicted by the "black box" diagram shown in Figure 7.1.

Inside the box are things you cannot observe, such as feelings, motives, drives, goals, and beliefs. Those are, according to J. B. Watson, *explanatory fictions,* stories we make up to explain why we do what we do that do not correspond to any physical reality. Those fictions, according to behaviorists, have no place in an account of human behavior. The change leader's job in this world is to organize appropriate rewards and sanctions that drive behavior in desired directions.

Figure 7.1 Behaviorism and the black box.

The great advantage of behaviorism is that it lends itself easily to measurement—therefore, it looks scientific. The frequency, intensity, and kind of stimulus are easily quantifiable, and the behavioral responses can similarly be measured.

Behaviorism's legacy lives on in thinking in ideas such as executive incentive schemes (stock options), time-outs for children, and punishment for offenders. If behaviorism were right about human behavior, these encouragements would work. Largely, the evidence says that they do not.

Bad Behaviorism—Not So Good in Theory

Behaviorist science, for all its veneer of precision, did not produce precise results. The black box did not explain much. The "response" in the black-box (stimulus-response) model is mediated by our beliefs, preferences, and feelings. A science that wants to predict how a human will respond cannot ignore what is in the black box and produce accuracy. Contrast the different behaviors of a skier, a house owner, and a commuter when the stimulus "heavy snow" arrives—the same stimulus causes very different behaviors.

We do not respond to incentives as did the behaviorist's rats, nor, as economists might like, do we just seek to maximize our "utility" (wealth). Imagine a neighbor asks you to help move a few things. Most people will gladly help. Now imagine the neighbor offers you 5 dollars, or 10, or even 50 in exchange for your help. You might possibly take offense and probably refuse. Incentives are a disincentive. Other less-than-rational features of incentive behavior are that sometimes small incentives work better than medium-sized ones or large ones, and sporadic incentives are sometimes more effective than predictable ones.[1]

Behaviorism also suffers from two ethical challenges. The first concerns our goals in studying psychology: We care a lot how others and how we feel, and not just about how they behave. The black box matters (deeply) to us, as it ought. There is a certain brutality in treating as irrelevant people's thoughts, feelings, beliefs, and concerns. This kind of thinking can be costly: The Qantas CFO's riposte to engineers' wishes to be consulted on a new system (of which they were the principal users) was, "We wouldn't ask the engineers what their views on our software systems were. We'll put in what we think is the appropriate for us."[2] The engineers refused to use the system.

Second, behaviorism in workplaces is always coercive, using power to manipulate rewards and sanctions. Direct punishment always risks relationships, but even rewards can have bad long-term effects: Because people get used to them, they feel like they are being punished if and when the rewards stop. In fact, loss aversion, a cognitive bias, suggests that losing a reward can be more emotionally punishing than some direct punishment.

Bad Behaviorism—Both Ineffective and Coercive

"People do not resist change, they resist being changed."

—Peter Senge

---

[1] See Gneezy, U., et al. (2011). When and why incentives (don't) work to modify behavior. *Journal of Economic Perspectives,* 25(4): 191–210.

[2] Why do projects fail?: Qantas (2008). Retrieved from http://calleam.com/WTPF/?p=2347.

The behaviorist mythology persists in the way we run not just businesses, but also society. Setting aside any ethical questions about coercing behavioral change, what are the practical failures of behaviorism?

To summarize a complex area in one sentence: Punishment may alter short-term behavior, but does not work in the long run and, in many cases, produces the behavior it is trying to punish, or produces harmful side effects. We incarcerate people (partly) to change criminal behavior (and partly just to get them off the streets). The people we jail have a *greater* chance of committing a crime than before they enter prison. Not only does prison *not* seem to act as a deterrent,[3] longer sentences (more severe punishment) *increase* recidivism.[4] We discipline kids using corporal punishment. It does not work and more severe forms produce deleterious long-term effects. There has been a dramatic reduction in its use over the past two generations— an unprecedented change in a pattern that had likely been fixed for millennia. In the United States, for example, 94 percent of parents endorsed hitting kids in 1968, but only one half approved by 1999. Today, corporal punishment is covered by UN Convention on Rights of the Child and signed by nearly 200 countries.

Other forms of punishment, likewise, show little effect on long-term behavior. But what about rewards?

How Rewards Can Be Harmful and Punitive

Today's dedicated behaviorist leaps in and asserts that focusing on the positive works—when we observe good behavior, we use rewards and praise to reinforce the behavior. In a landmark book, *Punished by Rewards: The Trouble with Gold Stars, Incentive Plans, A's, Praise, and Other Bribes,* Alfie Kohn differs saying that, "There are at least

---

[3] Lee, D., & McCrary, J. (2006). Crime, punishment, and myopia. *National Bureau of Economic Research.* Retrieved from www.hber.org/papers/w11491.

[4] Przybylski, R. (2008). What works? Effective recidivism reduction and risk-focused prevention programs—A compendium of evidence-based options for preventing new and persistent criminal behavior. Colorado Dept. of Criminal Justice. Retrieved from www.colorado.gov/ccjjdir/Resources/Ref/WhatWorks.pdf.

70 studies showing that extrinsic motivators including A's, sometimes praise, and other rewards—are not merely ineffective over the long haul but are counterproductive with respect to the things that concern us most."[5] Those "things that concern us most" include the desire to learn, commitment to good values, creativity, commitment, quality, relationships, and motivation.

Kohn's work, a summary of 60 or so years of research on rewards, is a shocking indictment of a behaviorist change theory still in widespread use which can be paraphrased as, "Catch them doing something good and praise them to reinforce the behavior." The reward story is perhaps more nuanced than Kohn's work suggests, but nevertheless the deep belief of our culture, that rewards—effectively, always, and without negative consequences—change behavior is mostly false.

The most famous study showing the harmfulness of rewards involves giving young children markers to play with. They naturally enjoy markers and need no further encouragement. Then, with one group as a control, the other group is offered rewards for using markers. They use them more. So far, so good. Yet when the reward is taken away, the group that at first naturally enjoyed markers now uses them much less than the control group. The theory is that *rewards kill internal motivation* by replacing it with external motivation (a reward). If this is correct, as subsequent research confirmed, then every time we use a carrot to nudge behavior in a direction that we want, we make the task a little more about the reward and less about the joy of doing it.

So why spend time on behaviorism, a hundred year-old paradigm? Behaviorism was coercive, did not explain much scientifically, ignored things that we care about (such as feelings), and did not work. This historical division is important, first because it is part of a default series of theories about people still considered "commonsense." The principal culprits are the ideas that humans maximize utility (economics) and that carrots and sticks change behavior (psychology). Second, it is important to study and remember just how wrong a body of theory can be and still be widely accepted in the professional and lay

---

[5] Kohn, A., (1993) *Punished by rewards: The trouble with gold stars, incentive plans, A's, praise, and other bribes.* Boston: Houghton Mifflin. Ebook edition.

communities. Uncritical acceptance of orthodoxy is the enemy of real progress, both in the sciences and in business.

By the 1960s, it was time for a change, and (being the sixties) that change was utterly radical.

The Cognitive Backlash Throws the Behavioral Baby Out with the Behaviorist Bathwater

In the 1960s and 1970s, psychological theory, practice, and popular culture began a massive U-turn away from behaviorism toward cognitivism and humanism. Compared with the harshness of behaviorism, cognitivism and humanism were much more cuddly kinds of psychology and are the dominant paradigms today.

Humanism[6] (in psychology) focuses on the whole person, on his or her experiences, the meanings that person attaches to those experiences, identity, personal growth, and self-image. Humanistic psychology took an ideological stance against dehumanizing people through objective study, and against the doctor-patient model of psychoanalysis, where an expert told you how you were sick and what you had to do. This new trend emphasized self-expression, creativity, unconditional positive regard, and self-actualization. The idea that every individual has potential and can reach that potential through discovering its nature and then developing it is accepted as something of a universal truth about humankind today. If you pause and think critically about this belief, you might find it is more inspirational than true. Today, almost all of the counseling (and coaching) training is based on the values and approaches of humanistic psychology. Coaches do not prescribe that a client change careers, leave a spouse, and buy a Harley—instead they mostly ask good questions to help clients discover their own insights.

Cognitivism in psychology returned attention to what behaviorists had shunned: the black box, bringing psychology back to its roots, as the "science of mind." To see how far we have come from behaviorism

---

[6] Humanism is also an unrelated philosophical notion and a political movement. As used here, it means "humanistic psychology."

that once completely dominated psychology, consider the contents of a typical psychology bookshelf. Most of the topics are cognitive topics such as motivation, goals, emotional intelligence, trust, happiness, creativity, attitudes, culture, beliefs, and values. "Change the insides to change the outsides" is the cognitivist's change mantra. How might that be limiting?

The Limitations of Strictly Cognitive Approaches

Today, when we think about changing behaviors in organizations, we think first about persuasion or influencing. When we work on internal mental states to change behavior (communications, influencing), we endorse a two-step process, relying on successfully changing hearts and minds, then on the relationship between changed hearts and minds and changed behaviors (actions). Both steps of this process are fraught with difficulty.

As you shall see in the next chapter, persuading someone, particularly someone negatively affected, or ideologically opposed, of the rightness of a certain course is extraordinarily difficult. A cursory glance over the political landscape should persuade most people that "facts never won an argument." Even when the facts are the same, values and needs vary, and what may make eminent sense to a VP with stock options (increase shareholder value), may look misguided at the shop floor level where behaviors need to change.

Even once hearts and minds are changed, there is a gap between new beliefs, intentions, and commitments and what people do. The second step of the process is just as challenging because you may create sincere good intentions to change, but people might not know how, or might have hard-to-change habits, or prevailing culture might counter their intentions. The fantasy that changing beliefs necessarily leads to changed behaviors is pervasive.

I recall one of the top global gurus on culture and values telling me that to change behavior, "you have to measure then change beliefs and values." When I countered that measuring values was fraught with error, beliefs and behavior do not always line up, changing values was not that easy, and (ethically) who gets to say which values are "right," he looked at me as if I were from Mars. And now we know. Research suggests that when there is cognitive dissonance between beliefs and behavior, it is the beliefs that give way, not the behaviors. Smokers are less likely to believe evidence on smoking-related deaths, and people who drive huge cars and trucks are much more likely to dispute climate change findings than to go out and get a Prius.

Rather than completely ignoring mental states, as behaviorists would have suggested, I believe that (today) the pendulum has swung too far and that we are out of balance in the other direction. That is, we are too focused on internal states to change behavior: motivation, what people think and feel. We pay far too little attention, in business and society, on whether influence, motivation, persuasion, inspiration, participation, involvement, or any other methods that appeal to the black box really change behaviors.

Lest this sound callous, those internal states (for example, happiness, fulfillment, and meaning) matter a great deal. However, we ought to care what people think and feel not for its *instrumental value* (so they do what we want them to do), but because of their *essential dignity as humans*—people are "ends in themselves" and not tools to be used instrumentally. We want people engaged and inspired because engagement and inspiration are human goods in their own right, not because it will make our enterprise more efficient or profitable. If we examine relationships within other communities—say, within families—this is an obvious standard: We want our kids to be happy because we want our kids to be happy, not because we want them to work harder. In workplaces, it may be different, or seem different to employees, that efforts to engage are just manipulations to get people to work harder, or to stay longer. Where that pretense is detected, employee cynicism and disengagement will be extreme.

Here is the problem that this and the next chapter tackle. We need behavioral change, but coercion, including rewards, destroys intrinsic motivation, damages trust, is ethically worrisome, and does not work well (if at all). On the other hand, if we limit ourselves to purely cognitivist methods of influence, we rely too heavily on alignment of intention and action. When we use cognitive methods to inspire and engage, they ought to be motivated by inspiration and engagement being human goods in their own right.

Are there methods of changing behavior that allow people choice, dignity and autonomy, and that work better than just influencing, yet are not coercive or paternalistic?

Neobehaviorism[7]

The good news is that the twenty-first century has seen a resurgence of a form of behaviorism that retains some of the good features but that actually works and is much less coercive.

I define neobehaviorism as the twenty-first-century school of applied research that emphasizes changing behaviors without first changing hearts and minds. The good features of these neobehaviorist approaches are:

- We can measure behaviors accurately, and hence can assess cause and effect scientifically, and know whether policies or interventions really work.
- We can care what people think and feel, but sincerely, and not just so they do what we want them to do.
- Behavior never lies. Phenomena such as engagement and commitment can be defined in behavioral terms, not just by self-report surveys—that is, by what people actually do, rather than by what they think.
- Some neobehaviorist methods are well studied, and so provide evidence-based guidance for managers.
- The methods produce real-world change, and not just change inside people's heads.

The neobehaviorist recognizes that sometimes hearts and minds change once action is undertaken. Consider your own experience. How often have you not felt like doing something, but after having done it feel really pleased? Feeling good about something can

---

[7] Strictly speaking, the term *new behaviorism* was coined in the 1950s to describe new trends in behaviorism that attempted to shore up behaviorism's methodological and conceptual shortfalls. That was behaviorism with a Band-Aid; this is different.

be caused by, and not simply cause, the chosen behavior. The neo-behaviorist mantra is: You can act your way into a new way of thinking, rather than think your way into a new way of acting.

There are five very promising areas of neobehaviorist practices that are slowly infiltrating business: behavioral specificity, behavioral safety, choice architecture, changing habits, and changing behavior through training and development.

Behavioral Specificity—Checklists

Where I have seen behavioral change fail and thereby cripple a major program, there has been one standout cause.[8] The change was not specified in detailed behavioral terms. For example, during the British Airways restructuring described in Chapter 5, "Cognitive Biases and Failed Strategies," part of the resistance resulted from people not knowing what to do. Financial analysts, and clients they served, had to follow new routines for the program to work. They did not, so it did not. In their confusion, from lack of clarity, they reverted to old, comfortable behaviors.

The precise specification of new behaviors provides clarity, but also a means of measuring progress and giving feedback. Without clarity, it is difficult to criticize or sanction someone who is off-piste behaviorally.

In the current organizational change paradigm, practitioners and authors spend considerable time on vision, engagement, inspiration, and communications. In my view, this is out of balance—they need to spend more time talking about behaviors, telling people what is expected of them.

This is not a call for return to command and control—attempts by senior leaders to specify and dictate the value-producing activities of their direct reports. The *only* sensible way to design new behaviors is to ask the people expected to behave in a certain way what the behaviors should be. This calls for much *more* extensive involvement than is commonly practiced, not less.

---

[8] Culture is critical too. As you'll see later, culture is mostly defined by behaviors.

This brings what started as an abstract historical discussion to two practical tools which facilitate alignment of behaviors with a change: the checklist, and the VSC (visualize, specify, commit) coaching tool.

Behaviors are critical everywhere but in professions where there is great risk, such as aviation and medicine. There is a tool used by both that helps with behavioral specificity: the lowly checklist.

In one striking example, Dr. Peter Pronovost of Johns Hopkins studied *line infections* in hospital ICUs. Improperly inserted, the *central line*[9] can become infected, which can result in death for someone critically ill. Pronovost developed a five-part checklist of non-rocket-science behaviors, which included hand washing and sterilizing the insertion area. This was scientifically tested (with control groups), and in one 18-month study, the method saved $100 million, and 1,500 lives.[10]

Checklists, despite their astounding simplicity, have considerable benefits:

- Introduce behavioral specificity into the change process
- Help learning of new behavioral routines
- Release cognitive resources for more creative work
- Make delegation easier
- Streamline routine work
- Reduce human error
- Improve task performance

In today's workplace culture, just telling people what to do will not fly. Behavioral checklists need to be combined with two standard change tactics tools, vision and involvement. Vision gives people the big emotional "why" and the business rationale. Involvement works on two levels: (1) New behaviors will be more accurately specified by people who actually do the job, and (2) having developed the behaviors themselves, engagement and compliance are much more likely.

---

[9] A central venous catheter, used to deliver fluids, nutrients, or medicines over longer times.

[10] Gawande, A. (2009). *The checklist manifesto: How to get things right.* New York: Metropolitan Books. Ebook edition.

We borrow the second behavioral specificity tool, not from medicine, but from the coaching profession. The tool is "visualize-specify-commit" (VSC), and it helps create accountability structures that deliver results. Using the tool, a leader may hear an intention from a follower: "Yes, I'd like to..." or "I need to..." The three questions for VSC are:

- **Visualize**—What does it look like when you are doing it?
- **Specify**—What specific behaviors will be different?
- **Commit**—When will you use them?

Dr. Pronovost claimed checklists were more relevant to highly complex, stressful, fast-paced environments saying, "Levels of cognitive function are often compromised with increasing levels of stress and fatigue, as is often the norm in certain complex, high-intensity fields of work."[11]

Few workplaces are as dangerous as offshore drilling platforms, and our next example comes from that arena.

Safety Behaviors HSE—Environmental Behaviorism

A decade ago, I visited Shell's Corporate Center, which overlooks the Thames River. The meeting was with a friend and client, John Holt, who was then head of Health, Safety, and Environment for one of Shell's three divisions, Gas and Power. This dreary London morning, we stayed in, rather than brave the trip to Starbucks, and headed to the canteen for our meeting. Taking the escalator, I faced downward chatting to John while clutching my briefcase and gesticulating Italian-style with my free hand. His rebuke was stern: "At Shell, we always hold handrails." Feeling somewhat like a bad six-year-old, I blushed, and grabbed the handrail wondering where this new control-freakery had come from. After grabbing a coffee, I headed over to add the usual condiments and John once again upbraided me: "At Shell, we cover all liquids always."

---

[11] Ibid.

Never very fond of being told what to do, this micromanaging of my conduct irritated me but made me curious enough that I sought insight elsewhere. The answer is Behavioral Safety (BS), an approach to safety management that has deep intellectual and practical roots in behaviorism.

When it comes to safety, we just don't care about the black box—whether a worker "feels like" wearing their PPE (Personal Protection Equipment)—we just want them to do it. We want our policies to be exceptionless because where exceptions exist, they will be stretched. We also want to bypass the cognitive complexities of reasoning and justification that might impede compliance. True to its roots in behaviorism, BS requires detailed specification of safety behavior, strict rules about which behaviors are pro-safety, observation of the behaviors in action, and consequences for compliance or not. Behavioral safety has its limits. In more complex situations, we do need people to reason their way to the right choices. The most advanced organizations, such as Shell, use a holistic approach that includes the behavioral rigidity, but which also pays attention to safety attitudes, beliefs, and values.

What was my friend John doing that morning? Spilling coffee down my shirt or tripping on the stairs only risked personal dignity—was he concerned with that? On an offshore platform, or in a lab, the consequences and frequency of mishaps with spilled liquids and falls are much higher—while the rules are not designed for "suits" at the head office, workers watch how suits behave when they visit the rigs. But John was doing more than that. Shell's safety program is holistic and includes "cognitive stuff" (their program is called "Hearts and Minds") as well as behavioral.

Shell's holistic program also operates at the level of culture—and John was a cultural change leader—modeling the behavior and insisting that others do so. The most important cultural dimension is less the ritual of holding the handrail, but more the culture of speaking up, that it is okay to challenge behaviors. In Shell's view, if you cannot challenge behaviors on the stairs, then how can you be expected to challenge them on a rig?

Shell wants a culture of people who follow basic rules of conduct unconditionally, and a culture of people who catch people not following rules and tell them immediately (an antithesis of the Wall Street culture in which my early career was spent). In addition, they want people who are passionate about safety, and who can think safety in complex situations, but first comes the rote learning of safety behaviors characterized by behavioral safety.

The Deepwater Horizon disaster was very complex, yet, in all of the three fatal decisions that Congressional testimony unearthed, had best-practice and written policy been slavishly followed, it is possible that 11 people would be alive, the environment spared substantial trauma, and the trillion-dollar disaster perhaps averted. The flawed decisions were made by senior people who felt free to use their guts, when strict behavioral adherence would have worked better.

Behavioral safety has been around for several decades, but the neobehaviorist practice we turn to next is perhaps the newest, most-exciting, practical behavioral change method on the market.

From Change Agent to Choice Architect

One problem with strictly behaviorist approaches, where behaviors are specified, monitored, and incentivized without involving the black box, through persuasion or education, is paternalism, or nanny-statism by those who despise it most.

People do not like to be bludgeoned into new behavior, even in cases (like helmets and seat belts) when it is unarguably in their best interests. Most people find regulating heroin or seatbelt use unproblematic, but may draw the line at removing Coca-Cola from schools, or at New York City's attempts to control sugar consumption by limiting the size of carbonated beverages that can be sold in restaurants to 16oz (550ml), or at discouraging fossil fuel consumption, or at vaccination. Depending on their political philosophy, some people have trouble with all of those restrictions, and some with none. Where one draws the line, and where public safety and larger social and environmental issues ought to trump personal liberty, is one of the great debates of the beginning of this century.

Neobehaviorists achieve behavioral change in much more subtle ways that get around many of the problems with influence-based models, and some of the ethical problems with direct behaviorism. In the book *Nudge*, Richard Thaler and Cass Sunstein describe ways of shaping choices that leave full autonomy with the chooser. In an everyday example, supermarkets place most shopped-for items (such as milk and bread) far at the back so that shoppers have to pass through aisles of cookies and Doritos along the way. They can buy what they like, but profitable, yet unhealthy decisions are made easier by item placement. We do not, as a rule, find such commercial manipulations troublesome (we expect that retailers will try to shape our needs, preferences, and behavior), yet there are people who see "nudging" by the state as the thin end of a paternalistic wedge.

Nudgers (sometimes called choice architects) use a few different strategies. The first is manipulating the default settings (to use computer-speak). Unscrupulous e-commerce sites set the default to auto-renew your payments (telling you in very small print that your purchase is not a one-time charge). More legitimately, some countries (and U.S. states) are shifting to opt-out for organ donation, rather than opt-in. Although, logically, the choices are identical, states and countries that use opt-out rather than opt-in donation may achieve higher rates (99 percent of Austrians are registered organ donors, compared with 43 percent of Americans). This might be the status quo bias in action, or it might be old-fashioned laziness, but it works.

The second nudge strategy is to restrict the number of options (or attributes) on view. Consumer choice, so much revered, can actually confuse and prevent action (such as buying). In the U.S. health insurance market where policies have more than 20 different attributes (for example, co-pay, prescription charges, deductible, maternity, and mental health), they are "helpfully" arrayed in an 8×20 matrix for "easy" digestion. (I do not consider myself dim, but once spent two hours with a broker trying to understand the myriad of options available to my family!) Now brokers simplify these bewildering choices into bronze, silver, and gold, leaving many of the details under the hood. Why? Too many choices confuse and prevent buying.

Thaler and Sunstein open their landmark book with the third generic strategy, an example of a school cafeteria manager who, through choice architecture (knowing that items at eye level and at the beginning and end sell more), can guide kids' purchases toward the most nutritious and healthful. As with the grocery store example, you make it easy for kids to do the right thing.

All three strategies—default settings, choice removal, and choice architecture—perform an end run around the black box, to steer behavior without giving the brain too much to think about and without direct coercion.

Nudging in Society and Business

Use of nudging has produced auspicious results in the UK where a specific cabinet body, The Behavioural Insights Team (also known as the Nudge Team), has used research on behavioral change to effect policy change in areas as wide as tax payment compliance, car registration, community safety, public health behaviors, consumer financial health, post-hospital self-care planning, and organ donation.

How does this apply to businesses and more particularly to change tacticians (change managers)? Because of the novelty of the approaches, there are many fewer examples of nudge usage in corporations. The "how-to" book has yet to be written. Few change agents are talking and writing about it, and in my view, this misses an opportunity to learn from what is working well in other disciplines. Yet there are a few business examples. One choice architecture tool used by an increasing number of businesses is helping take-up of 401(k) membership and benefits. Because of tax breaks and other employer incentives, signing up is free money for the employee, yet as many as 30 percent to 40 percent do not take up the benefits.

All three of our above strategies have been tested on the savings problem. Switching to opt-out, from opt-in, increased take-up by 50 percent(!); removing choices almost quadrupled sign-ups(!); and Thaler and Sunstein devised a Save More Tomorrow program that uses choice architecture to promote long-term positive financial choices. By comparison, standard education and influencing methods increased 401(k) sign-ups to a meagre 14 percent. This appalling result should lend credence to the view that changing insides (the black box) to change behavior is a tricky business and that neobehaviorism has something to teach us.

People are more productive when they are alone, but more collaborative and innovative when they are in groups, claims Marissa Mayer, Yahoo!'s CEO. To shift Yahoo!'s culture toward one that emphasizes collaboration and innovation, Mayer controversially ended Yahoo!'s WFH (work from home) policy within the first few months of her tenure. Mayer changed the environment to change behaviors and culture, a neobehaviorist philosophy. Similarly, Google and Microsoft are famous for their innovative use of space to promote certain kinds of behaviors, and to discourage others. Given this, it is surprising how few companies deploy their creativity in office design. Do rows of grey cubicles inspire creativity in anyone? Although innovation was a focus for PwC in the 1990s, nobody thought to redesign the rows of cubicles sending a symbolic contradictory message to staff. Whole systems change, as touched upon in Chapter 2, "From Change Fragility to Change-Agility," including changing the physical working environment.

Many standard change management methodologies use communication, involvement, or education of some kind, but in our 401(k) example we see a clear-cut example of a neobehaviorist approach getting the job done where standard communication approaches do not.

In my opinion, nudging is a new idea for effecting behavioral change in business that we need to explore further. I believe that it may have much broader potential for shifting behaviors during many types of change: strategic, or during a merger, or with a new IT system. However, it will require inventiveness on the part of the change leader. That is the price of novelty; the toolkit is not yet fully assembled.

The Mastery of Habit

Humans are uniquely gifted in their ability to reflect, envision, set goals, and plan. Such faculties have allowed us to transcend our basic needs and narrow self-interest and to erect monuments of art, science, and commerce. This astonishing gift relies upon the ability to *embody*: to translate those goals and plans into behavior, getting our hands to do what our head would like.

This sometimes requires translating extremely complex tasks into tightly scripted routines. Consider a tennis pro returning a serve hit at 120 miles per hour that will be upon him in one third of a second. Should the player have to solve the physics with differential equations, and think through the correct pace and direction to run, all the while adjusting for spin, wind, and other factors, it would be impossible. They make it look easy because the calculations and movements happen as if on autopilot—without the need for thought.

By the time we are adults, so many complex tasks are automatic, the conscious oversight is not necessary. Our life is a collection of these routines. This is both a blessing and a curse. The beauty is that we can groove complex tasks and excel at them. The trouble comes when we try to change the groove, that is, our habits.

A typical morning routine may involve the usual hygiene habits, then eating, dressing, and hustling out the door. We may decide we want to add 15 minutes of exercise, or yoga, or connecting properly with a spouse, or meditation to that. (Few people disagree that something like one of those would add a great deal to their lives.)

Now the collection of habits we have had since our teenage years becomes the enemy of our intentions for ourselves. It used to be known (another myth) that 21 repetitions was enough to groove a new habit. In a UK study,[12] participants chose an everyday behavior they wanted to turn into a habit: some chose fruit with lunch, some chose running, and some chose walking for ten minutes after breakfast. On average, 66 days were required for these to become automatic, although some were grooved after 20, and some never made it at all.

Office habits are similarly hard to change. Most people have the habit of coming into the office, and instantly checking email. Best-practice email management calls for postponing email until high-value tasks, such as planning your day or putting a dent in the most important strategic task of the day, are done. Yet after 20 years with email at my disposal, I can often not resist a peek. This "peek" can turn into an hour or two if I get sucked in to long correspondence (almost all of which can wait a few hours or a few days). Most productivity

---

[12] Lally, P., et al. (2010). How are habits formed: Modelling habit formation in the real world. *European Journal of Social Psychology, 40*(6), pp. 998–1009.

specialists assert that if you have to peek, the peek needs to be a disciplined ten minutes, just in case there is something really urgent, but many people fall into the email trap until a meeting pulls them away. Strategic thinking and planning fall by the wayside.

The interesting thing is that the habits of today create the life we have tomorrow. A running habit creates a certain life; the habit of disciplined time management creates another; the habit of coaching staff regularly creates yet another. Some people do "not have time" to keep up with professional reading. Yet, ten minutes on each of the 200 working days per year means one million words per year. That is ten very chunky books. Over a few years, this can make the difference between someone knowledgeable and well-read in their area, and a pretender. Fifteen minutes walking will burn around 100 calories (a quarter of a blueberry muffin). Yet just doing this for a year, unless you walk to the patisserie, will burn about 7 pounds. By adding a constructive habit, the life trajectory we are on becomes just that little bit steeper.

In the world of organizational change, we are concerned with resistance, yet resistance may not be willful, it may just be habitual. Staff may well appreciate the need to change, but just be stuck—the way anyone who has tried to change one of the habits described above will understand. If change leaders deal with this kind of resistance the way they deal with people who disagree, or are threatened, results will be hard to come by.

Reason, influence, and inspiration will not change employees' habits—in the neobehaviorist tradition, we need to work directly with behaviors.

Indeed habits are even *harder* to shift in groups (and businesses) because shared group habits become cultural regularities and rituals. Social mimicry means pressure to relapse, or one's earnest efforts at habit change may be perceived as weird. One coaching client decided, after promotion, to be more proactive and strategic. This included the excellent practices of using the early morning for strategy and planning. However, her desk was mobbed by 10:00 a.m. by people demanding answers to emails sent earlier that day. The email culture was (dysfunctionally) used to 15-minute response times. Her new habits were at war with cultural norms.

Creating Good Habits

Habits are yet another area where circumventing the black box may be useful. In the world of habits, we either do things today for benefits far in the future, or stop doing things to prevent future dis-benefits. There are usually costs in immediate pleasure to not smoking (if you smoke), or passing on the jelly donut, but the benefit/pain is far in the future. Our brain discounts these future benefits/pains making short-term sacrifices less attractive.

In finance, most people would rather have 95 dollars today, than 100 in a year's time. The future cash is discounted. Avoidance of distant loss and pain, or creation of long-term well-being years in the future may be very heavily discounted—what we call *hyperbolic discounting*. In our cash example, that would mean preferring 50 dollars today to 200 in a year's time. When we weigh, "Should I do X right now" versus a far-future gain, the reward center in our brains is no ally because of hyperbolic discounting.

We need to circumvent—that is, put in place automaticity with regard to positive new habits (in ourselves or our followers), but how do you do that?

First, you need to recognize that *motivation is mercurial and thus not your friend*. Motivation is important, but only *before* embarking upon habit change, to create the context and to have that clear emotional *why* and rationale. Thereafter, the up-and-down nature of motivation (sometimes you are "feeling it," and sometimes not) can get in the way of the kind of automaticity that a new habit requires. When I lived in Wisconsin, I used to admire in awe runners out on –10 degree mornings (14 Fahrenheit) in near-blizzard conditions. I wondered, "What *are* they thinking?" The point is that they were not thinking, they were out running.

Then, there are two research-based habit-mastery tricks you can use, *implementation intentions* and *minihabits*. Implementation intentions (usefully called *action triggers* in the excellent book *Switch* by Heath and Heath) are the opposite of vague, "I will go running everyday" type intentions—they are specific behaviors linked to specific events in "when-then" statements. For example,

- "*When* I arrive at work, before turning on my computer, *then* I will take ten minutes and think strategically about the highest leverage things I can achieve today."
- "*When*, in a conflict situation, I feel anger rising, *then* I will remember to breathe deeply and consider the importance of the long-term relationship."
- "*When* I feel that my team is being overoptimistic, and under-estimating risks, *then* I will speak up and inquire about assumptions that might be leading us astray."

Smokers, or former smokers, will recognize the power of action triggers ("When I finish a meal, I have a smoke") and the power of tightly linking actions so that one happens after the other without thought. (As in "Immediately, when I arrive home, I will put on my running shoes and go for a run.") By linking actions in this way, and creating triggers, you pass control of your behavior to the environment, thus short-circuiting the vicissitudes of motivation and thought.

"When-then" statements can also be created in anticipation of motivational obstacles: "*When* my little voice says 'you deserve a pepperoni pizza,' *then* I will instantly reach for a healthy, filling alternative." The mind, like the body, can be habituated in useful ways.

The second habit-mastery trick is to start very, very small. In an exceptional e book, *Mini-habits*, Stephen Guise describes the battle between motivation and willpower. His clients frequently struggle with exercise motivation until he tells them to just do a single push-up. This seems absurd, but once on the floor, they might do more than one. His theory is that committing to just one push-up per day until this habit becomes so grooved that they cannot not do it is a way of building new habits.

The major insight is: *Forming the habit is more important than achieving any number of "reps."* To start a new habit, especially one at which you have failed, is hard. Your self-efficacy, confidence in your own ability, has been diminished, making the first instance the most difficult. In physics, there is static friction (sometimes called "stiction") between nonmoving objects, and there is dynamic friction, when the objects are moving. The first is greater than the second is, as anyone who has tried to open a stuck jam jar knows.

If, like me, you sport more than a few extra pounds, you might chortle cynically at the idea of one push-up. Here is the two-part theoretical rationale. First, doing a little is better than doing nothing, and those littles may add up. Recall our example where 10 minutes of reading a day produced 12–15 hefty books a year.

Second, according to Guise, "When you're trying to establish a good habit, size doesn't matter as much as consistency."[13] For example, say you want to get in shape and decide you are going to do 100 push-ups a day. That is a lot of push-ups each day, so the chances you will stick with that regime are very slim.

Paradoxically, seven 10-minute workouts might be quite a lot better than one 2-hour workout. How can I make a claim that defies arithmetic in this way? One 2-hour workout per week is hard to start and hard to sustain. It does you no good if the first three Saturdays in January, you hit the gym for two hours, and then take 49 weeks off. However, by learning to repeat the 10-minute workouts, you build the habit of working out.

Success of the one 2-hour workout strategy may depend on motivation, muscles, weather, tiredness, family commitments, or other. The habit depends on none of those.

Minihabits get you in the game doing something rather than on the sidelines waiting for motivation. When you are in it, you can win it.

Breaking Bad

"The problem with immediate gratification is that it isn't soon enough."

—Unknown

In creating habits, we want to make certain areas of our life automatic so that motivation and excuses do not sidetrack from healthy practices. Breaking bad habits is the opposite; we want to undo that automaticity and to return more of our life to conscious control.

---

[13] Guise, S. (2013). *Mini habits: Smaller habits, bigger results*. San Bernadino: CreateSpace, p. 20

There are four generic strategies for doing so. The first, *absti-nence,* deserves a mention although its applications are limited in the business world. This is a favorite strategy in the world of addictions, although the evidence base for its success and as the *only* solution to addictions is questionable.[14]

The second generic strategy is replacing bad habits with good ones, the idea being that a life full of good habits will leave little room for the bad ones. I once coached a very high-flying executive who had a gaming addiction. The obsession with gaming meant other aspects of life (marriage, job performance) deteriorated, making the gaming world more relatively attractive. The strategy was to replace gaming, bit-by-bit, with more life-affirming behaviors. Those areas became more fulfilling; gaming was crowded out, and receded to a few hours a week.

This strategy, replacing bad habits with good habits, is particularly relevant to business life. For example, meetings are a costly, yet necessary ritual in business, and they run on autopilot. The average manager has 61.8 meetings per month, and surveys say fewer than 50 percent add corporate value. Perhaps they start late, without an agenda, or an agenda of "topics" not decisions, or disciplines around facilitation, note-taking, clear actions and accountability, review of the meeting are missing. They frequently overrun and infrequently produce desired results. Research suggests that this is the case more often than not.

One of the most powerful ways to begin a change in corporate culture is to disrupt the conduct of this critical ritual. Different strategies include limiting meetings to 15 minutes, holding them standing up, assigning a "chair" accountable for executing decisions, or nominating a facilitator with license to challenge unhelpful behavior to strict reviews of agreed-upon actions. Good meeting habits are well known, but rarely used. Replacing each bad habit, one-by-one, with good habits can turn a sometimes wasteful ritual into a productive one.

---

[14] See Lillienfeld, S., et al. (2010). *50 great myths of popular psychology: Shattering widespread misconceptions about human behavior.* Oxford: Wiley-Blackwell, p. 232.

The third habit-breaking strategy means returning behavior to conscious control. This is much more nuanced and difficult because operating on autopilot takes less effort than engaging the brain's executive function. Take the habit of better listening, fewer interruptions, closer attention, and more empathy. We have been listening since childhood, and how we listen is deeply grooved. It takes considerable effort not to just do as practiced for decades, and to consciously try to create a new listening habit. Mindfulness practice, as you will see in the next chapter, is a way of developing the brain's executive function so that greater awareness is brought to every situation.

Finally, the fourth strategy is choice architecture, passing control to the environment. When writing, I am easily distracted. The more browser windows and programs that are open, the more likely that one is to "wink" at me somehow and I might find myself spending 25 minutes reading about the upcoming elections in Malaysia or cat pictures on Facebook, which, although gripping, do not get books written. Closing all programs and browser windows and disabling all alerts and reminders is an effective way of limiting my choices.

Choice architecture also works to break dieters' poor habits. Portion control is one of the many struggles of people who are trying to lose weight. Research has shown that simply buying smaller dinnerware reduces portion consumption drastically—much more than weighing or measuring, which (of course) requires motivation and willpower.

Habit mastery is critical for personal and cultural change. One way of looking at life is as a sum of previous habits. If you have practiced yoga daily, you are flexible; if you have been in the office since 6:30 a.m. daily, you have achieved more than others have; if you have really practiced listening hard, you will have an empathetic presence that builds trust. Leadership development is many things, but new practices (habits) can have a profound effect on long-term performance.

Recall from Chapter 1, "Failed Change: The Greatest Preventable Cost to Business?" that culture change programs seem to succeed 19 percent of the time. Part of the reason for that is habit mastery. One way of looking at a business culture is a collection of habits, routines, and rituals performed more or less unconsciously because that is "how we do things." Changing culture, as you'll see in Chapter 8,

"The Science of Changing Hearts and Minds," is a function of collective changing of those habits.

Without habit mastery, there can be no culture mastery.

Changing Behaviors through Training and Development

Business is an applied discipline. The notion that a business idea "works in theory, but..." is nonsensical. By implication, business knowledge, for the practitioner, is principally applied knowledge and not conceptual knowledge.

These two different understandings of *knowledge,* which we get from the Greeks, are today referred to as propositional knowledge (*know-about*) and practical knowledge (*know-how*). *Know-how* can depend on *know-about,* for example, a maxillofacial surgeon needs to know the locations of the twelve cranial nerves. Nevertheless, in applied disciplines, know-about is never sufficient. By the know-about definition, my knowledge of biochemistry and exercise physiology make me knowledgeable about nutrition and weight loss. Knowledge equals gaining information. By the know-how definition, someone who struggles with weight loss still has a lot to learn. You cannot "know," by the know-how definition and fail to do.

Know-how knowledge takes into account the things that get in the way in the real world: habits, personalities, conflicting priorities, politics, interpersonal conflict, culture, and failures of motivation and will. Know-how is knowledge that works in context, not in the abstract, and it is the kind of knowledge that we are interested in when we talk about change—what will work in the context of our business, with our stakeholders, in our culture. Problems in business are never as easy as they are on paper.

All leadership and change models are conceptually trivial (four boxes, eight steps, three stages). Applying those trivial concepts is not easy. In this respect, business is more like golf than calculus. It would be absurd to say "I know about hitting a golf ball, you generate torque and angular momentum by accelerating the club on an elliptical path. Let's play!"

If Business Is Practical, Why Is Business Education Mostly Theoretical?

This realization, that most business learning is applied, and is therefore learned on the job, is codified in descriptive research finding called the 70-20-10 model: 70 percent of business learning is working on tough problems, 20 percent from peers, and only 10 percent through courses and books. The research is descriptive because it says only how things *are*, not how they *should be*. Despite the fact that the research is only descriptive, I often hear it quoted as if it were an ideal (prescriptive) rather than descriptive. I do not think that it is ideal.

Looked at another way, is 70-20-10 a function of the nature of business, or should we be disappointed that business education only furnishes 10 percent of what (descriptively) people use on the job? An MBA is typically two years in length; what percentage does a typical leader use day in, day out? Many MBA friends claim most of what they learned is never used, and the most useful aspect of the degree was developing a network. This may be because a traditional business education focuses on theory, and business is simple theoretically, but extremely challenging in practice.

For a moment, let us consider what professional education looks like in other areas. Take a typical U.S. medical education. A 4-year premed education in basic science with almost no reference to the human body is the ante. Then 4 years of medical school, in which only the last 2 involve work with sick people. Even after these 8 years, the physician is far from qualified. Most locales require a residency of another 4 years, and some specialisms require a fellowship, a further 4 years. It takes 12 to 16 years before a doctor can be certified in certain specialisms. Consider architecture: Qualifying as an architect takes between 10 and 17 years. Is it much more difficult, or much more important to build good buildings than to build good businesses?

Are medicine and architecture too technical and too unlike business for this comparison to be fair? Both are part craft, part science, and in Chapter 9, "Leading with Science," I ask whether the idea of leadership as a science-based craft could be a useful one.

Today, the challenges are twofold:

- The people dimensions of business are based on social sciences that are much more immature than the physical sciences. The theory that is taught in these areas is not yet strong.
- At the same time, much business education focuses on theory rather than practice.

Getting Hard Results from Soft-Skills Education

If MBA degrees teach very little about real-world business problems that involve people, personalities, conflict, politics, and culture, where do people turn to learn those things? We saw some of where the theory comes from in Chapter 6, "Misunderstanding Human Behavior." Executive education programs at business schools, and soft-skills programs delivered by consulting/training firms are one answer. During the last fifteen years, this has been a large percentage of my professional activity. I offer the following critique from "inside" that profession, as it were.

Definitive research on how well soft-skills management programs work is hard to find because so few organizations have mastered evaluating the behavioral and business effect of training. However, some research suggests that they work very badly and deliver little value. Surveys suggest that only 25 percent of business managers think that soft-skills training and development contribute measurably to business performance.[15] Experts estimate that the transfer of leadership development education to the job ranges between 10 percent and 30 percent.[16] As you have seen, businesses measure participant reactions

---

[15] Cermak, J., & McGurk, M. (2010, July). Putting a value on training. *McKinsey Quarterly*. Retrieved from http://www.mckinsey.com/insights/organization/putting_a_value_on_training.

[16] This is a controversial area. The most commonly quoted percentage is 10 percent, but that is a misrepresentation of what the author (Georgensen), who was researching something else, said. Other studies place it somewhat higher. It depends a great deal on how you define *transfer*. Whatever the precise number, and I think it nearer 10% than 30% for conventionally structured programs, it is very poor.

to programs ("happy sheets") that are almost uncorrelated with business benefit.

Given a $50 billion training industry (in the United States alone), that is a lot of potential waste.

We need a revolution in business education, and a new paradigm of accountability for training results. This applies particularly in the skills development/leadership development/executive education areas where we care about *know-about* (behavioral learning). Did they attend project management 101? Let us measure excellent project management behaviors using self-report and peer review. Let us furthermore look at project results, comparing people who attended and those who did not, and let us see how much our investment in project management training may be saving us. Did leaders attend "Coaching for Managers"? Let us assess the frequency of coaching and the value that staff derive from being coached. Did they attend negotiation? Let us at least gather, anecdotally, how much of those skills they were able to use, and how much they might have been able to save through better negotiation. These sorts of evaluations are very low tech; much more can be done, and, perhaps, with the advent of HR analytics, more will be done.

Change in the leadership/business education world will take decades because there are many institutions and lots of capital invested in the current model. The institutions that deliver education today are part of a system that pays them very (very) well to deliver happy sheets and checked boxes on development plans. Despite the sincerest of intentions, and the highest professional standards, habits and culture will impede progress.

There are two cultural norms (at least) in the way. Businesspeople are used to the idea that a two-day course will teach them everything they need, underestimating how much they need to learn in areas they do not know. Then, they set a very low bar for training providers. They expect good content and charismatic speakers, but do not demand being able to use a high percentage of what they learn—who is holding them to account for changed behaviors? (Again, it is as if a course on surgery were evaluated purely on how well surgeons could identify anatomical structures, and tell a scalpel from a forceps, and not how successfully they can perform operations.) HRD (Human

Resources Development) professionals who buy soft-skills training set a similarly low bar; they have to keep their (executive) customers happy, and those executives include people whose expectations are for one-and-done type programs. Budgets are also skewed toward program structures that do not deliver value. For example, adding coaching support to a soft-skills program and spreading the multiday program over many months is best practice because people can practice what they have learned before trying to learn something new, and coaches can help with real-world implementation problems. Yet despite the fact that training take-up rates may be as low as 10 percent for the one-and-done type program, businesses would rather pay $1 million and achieve what everybody knows will be abysmal transfer rates, than $2 million and quadruple (or more) the amount of skills businesspeople can apply on the job.

Getting More Behavioral Change and Greater Accountability from Soft-Skills Programs

Having run these sorts of programs for nearly 25 years, I have experimented with a few interesting ways of adding behavioral teeth to soft-skills training. Some promising[17] innovations are:

- Programs with behavioral change at the core should last one to two years or so, and be structured so that participants learn a little, apply a little, learn a little more, and apply some more, rather than a huge five-day dump of "learning" that is impossible to apply. A two-to-four week summer "intensive" program at a prestigious business school will cost five figures. What percentage of the many theories, tools, and case studies will be easy to *remember, let alone apply*, back at work?

- Similarly, a whole day can furnish too much content to reliably and sustainably deploy. Shorter, bite-sized sessions are better because trying to change too many behaviors at once is

---

[17] These were experiments, and not done with control groups; hence, it is too much (given our interest here in science and evidence) to claim "they work."

impossible. Consider how a would-be professional ice skater will practice just a single technique many hundreds of times.

- Just-in-time training means delivering the program only when skills are urgently required. For example, a change leadership program should only contain people who are leading complex change day in, day out. They will be hungrier for the learning, and able to practice it as soon as they return to work. By contrast, I once delivered a course on how to conduct performance appraisals for new managers only to find out at the end that it was to be eleven(!) months until they would get a chance to practice it! What percentage could they realistically be expected to remember?

- Structure program objectives so that they deliver financial value. In one program that focused on selling and client relationship management, the metrics were individual revenue, team revenue, deal size, and "pipeline size."

- Project-based learning programs require participants to actually deliver some financial value. In one program, the bank's chairman personally reviewed the projects to assess how much value the participants were *delivering*, not just *getting* from the program. Jack Welch's Work-Out program at GE was a pioneering attempt at this learning structure, but few have followed this example.

- Link application of learning to performance management processes. When someone attends a program, deployment of the skills, behaviors, attitudes, and concepts is part of how they are evaluated.

- Involve the participant's manager in preprogram goal setting and postprogram review. As with the above, this generates "skin in the game" for the participant and the manager.

- Do not invest in one-and-done programs; there should always be follow-up events to support know-how knowledge transfer. Follow-ups can include online top-ups, coaching support, peer group "action-learning" type support, and managerial review. (This is sometimes called blended learning and is now the rule in the best firms.)

- Linking program structure and objectives to strategy provides a bigger context for learning. This can be achieved by spending the first 20 percent (or so) of a program on the "why am I here, why are we here" question, providing context and motivation to learn.
- Pay educators only for results. Amazingly, I have offered fees for business education programs linked to financial performance of the business to clients, but only one client has ever said yes. Even when I offer to put some personal, financial skin in the game, no business says yes.

The poor results delivered by business education are a function of the adolescence of the field—the lack of focus on behavior, emphasis on concepts (which themselves are not well proven), and the low bar set by buyers of business education. The brief suggestions here do not exhaust possibilities, but have the potential to augment results a great deal.

Conclusion

There are two traditional ways to think about changing behavior. The first is changing hearts and minds, which is a cognitivist model. The second (behaviorist) involves coercion, rewards, and sanctions. Neobehaviorism returns the focus to behaviors but avoids coercion. With habit change, behavioral safety, and choice architecture, the neobehaviorist changes the context (environment) to influence behavioral choices without first changing hearts and minds. This second approach takes into account human foibles, the fact that we do not always act rationally, and is still neglected in literature on change management. Even though business is an applied discipline, education in business focuses insufficiently on application of theoretical knowledge and changed behaviors—both executives and people who commission soft-skills training have to set more exacting standards of success.

The next chapter looks at new research on changing hearts and minds. During change, we need passion, commitment, and motivation, as well as clear thinking and good problem-solving skills.

Although neobehaviorist approaches work at changing some work-place behaviors, they depend on knowing which behaviors we want to promote. In complex systems, behaviors cannot be specified by a central authority, and we want to maximize the capacity for self-organization that people possess—so we need hearts and minds, and not just hands.

8

The Science of Changing Hearts and Minds

The Craft of Changing Minds

"Let not princes complain of the faults committed by the people subjected to their authority, for they result entirely from their own negligence or bad example."

—Machiavelli

Greek rhetoric, Roman oratory, prophets, polemicists, and politicians—human history is the history of leaders changing people's minds. Business history is likewise the story of triumphal influence such as Bill Gates persuading IBM to use an obscure operating system called DOS, or failed influence such as Alexander Bell failing to persuade Western Union of the value of his little invention, the telephone. "What use could this company make of an electrical toy?"[1]

Machiavelli's idea suggests that when change goes badly, the leader must look first to his own negligence or bad example. Who has not seen leadership teams tearing their hair out as one group, irrationally it seems, opposes the change. It is certainly easy to make monsters out of a stakeholder's irrationality. In Machiavelli's view, if they are not doing as they ought, it is your fault.

Influence and persuasion, as seminal leadership skills, are the subject of hundreds of books. In recent times, the emotional dimensions

---

[1] Attributed to William Orton, President of Western Union

of influence have dominated the discourse. (I cannot think of a popular book on rhetoric or influencing with facts; it is so out of fashion.) This is understandable. Results where we Sheldon Cooper types generate lengthy tomes in the hope of producing change, only to scratch our heads bewildered when change does not happen, are commonplace.

This chapter does not try to add weight to an already substantial body of popular literature on emotions and influencing, but rather focuses more on research on the power of facts to influence people. After all, if the facts are on our side, we would like them to work!

There are four topics in this chapter on how to change a mind. The first is redefining and reconceiving *resistance* to change. The second topic is *high-engagement* techniques for dealing with social complexity. The third is how to effectively use *facts* to influence people, and the fourth is on the phenomena of metacognition and *mindfulness* and how they are useful to personal and leadership development.

Resistance to Change

"Resistance... is means times will."

—von Clausewitz

Adult human minds are never blank slates, nor sponges waiting to soak up what we have to offer—if only. To every situation where the change leader must change hearts and minds, humans bring their beliefs, prejudices, emotions, ideas, and values. The influencing job is as much undoing what is already there, as instilling something new. But we are fond of our own ideas, and are attached to our irrational habits. Economists call the first the *status quo bias;* the Greeks called the second *akrasia.*

Change practitioners describe this as *resistance to change,* a phenomenon that is exacerbated in twenty-first-century organizations because of two factors. First, volatility means business has to change faster, and dealing with resistance typically takes time nobody has. Second, people are less securely attached to an organization than they were 25 or 50 years ago. There is much greater career and geographic mobility and competitor organizations are much more aggressive in "winning the war for talent." If people do not like the direction a company takes, or feel coerced into a change, they just leave.

At the same time, one day, resistance might be a thing of the past. How? In an agile organization, with high trust between levels and parts of the organization, with dynamic structures (project-based businesses), with a culture that is eager for innovation, and with processes that support learning and change, I can imagine (can you?) resistance to change being something that only dysfunctional organizations have to deal with. In Chapter 2, "From Change Fragility to Change-Agility," you learned about the growth mindset, a mindset that is antithetical to the idea of resistance. The possibility is that the growth mindset can be extended to great "growth cultures."

The notion of resistance is based on old models of organization, where change is the exception, not the rule, where command-and-control is the *modus operandi,* and where change is a threat, not an opportunity to grow and learn. Senior leaders often forget that *resistance is engagement,* just not yet the kind of engagement we want.

In effect, I offer two contradictory perspectives on resistance: the first that it ought to be a thing of the past, and (given it will not be for some time) a better way of working with it.

Spotting Resistance to Change

Before examining some more apt models of resistance, in order to better manage it, you need to be able to detect it. Unfortunately, people rarely say, "I'm uncomfortable (or unhappy, or I disagree, or other) with this change, I'm going to make it difficult for you." Sometimes consciously, but often unconsciously, they begin to behave in unhelpful, frustrating, and dysfunctional ways. These behaviors can be called the four Ds—the four categories of resistance behavior: destruction, delays, dissent, and distancing. As you survey the list, think of a change project and mentally check off the ones you observed.

Destruction and sabotage might seem ridiculously extreme words. *Sabotage* comes from the French word for *clogs* (*sabots*), which disgruntled early Industrial Revolution workers tossed into machinery to protest the mechanization of their workplaces and loss of jobs. Fewer and fewer workplaces have actual machines and tasseled loafers would not have the same effect on a database server as heavy wooden sabots. Today's "machinery" is information and it is very easy to sabotage information. It can be withheld, it can be deliberately biased (to either make things look much better or much worse), and it can be delayed.

Delays happen all the time and are hard to challenge. In today's businesses, people are always juggling priorities. It is hard, if someone says "I will get this to you in two weeks because I'm busy," to know whether he is really busy, or would prefer anything other than to support the change project.

Overt *dissent* is good. All progress through conflict comes through conversation. When people are dissenting, they are talking, which gets the change leader in the game. In fact, when you see nonovert resistance behaviors, the *best thing you can do* is get them to label their disagreement and discomfort. You then have something to work with. The next time you are leading a change and someone dissents publicly, before giving them the corporate "red card," remember how much worse it is if they "go covert" with their dissent.

In an age of distraction, *distancing* behaviors (sometimes called "checking out") are hard to challenge. People run late, do not return messages, appear distracted, and forget to do stuff all the time. The best you can do is form a hypothesis that it is related to the change, and see if you can surface what is going on without starting a war. "I notice you have been under pressure lately, running late, and not your usual self. Could it be related to...?" The idea, as with delays, is to start a conversation about how they are feeling, what they think, and what they are committed to doing.

Once you are sensitized to the various manifestations of resistance, you are ready to tackle it. First, let us take a deeper look at how resistance is viewed incorrectly, to help us become more effective in dealing with it.

Managing Resistance

The biggest errors I see leaders make in dealing with resistance are, first, to assume it is lack of information, "if only people had the facts, as I do, they would see things clearly and come along." The second is to psychologize and to use labels such as "cathartic" or "denial" that put people with particular responses in a (dysfunctional) psychological box.

Many models are either rational or emotional, and ignore research from the last 20 years that suggests:

- We are tribal; social influences are supremely important. (Research from the public health arena suggests that if you want to get thin, find some thin friends.)

- Network effects mean nonlinear uptake of ideas, and certain actors have a thousandfold (or much more) influence on uptake.

- When beliefs and facts contradict each other, facts often lose. (We are ideological in the negative sense of that word.)

- We are creatures of habit, and resistance to change can be an example of an "intention-action" gap. People may sincerely want to change, and still fall afoul of existing habits.

- We are cultural and political creatures—we create meaning out of events, group norms matter, and political allegiances frequently trump the rational.

In short, there is much more to resistance to change than just reason and emotion. Recall that less than 5 percent of heart attack survivors manage to change their smoking, diet, and exercise behaviors. Facts about mortality are not enough, nor is the prospect of an early demise sufficiently emotional.

The holistic model of resistance (shown in Table 8.1) shows a much broader way to examine the problem and the model is a practical tool for assessing the sources of resistance, a sort of rational backdoor to empathy if you will.

This list is far from exhaustive of human concerns at work, but it provides another way of looking at the sources of resistance, and thereby being better able to understand and to shift it.

At PwC, we used this framework to turn around a billion-dollar change program at the UK's Department of Work and Pensions (comparable to the U.S. Social Security Administration). This seven-year program involved large IT spending, but also centralization of key functions, redesigning processes, and eventually headcount reduction. The project had been misfiring for a year with senior staff almost unwilling to collaborate with the project team. This led to great difficulties in getting access to the business information required for process and system design. When our change team arrived on the scene, industrial action was a real possibility. We used the model to unearth the sources of resistance, and shifted the communication strategy to a high-involvement one that dealt with the ideological, social, and political issues. We stopped treating staff as if all they needed was information to see the matter clearly (that is, that they were being irrational), and we stopped psychologizing them and treating legitimate concerns as if they were part of some (emotional) grieving process. Using the resistance model and the Large Group Intervention methods (described in the next section), we were able to have adult-adult[2] conversations, transform their level of engagement, expedite program decision making and collaboration, and harvest their energy for solving problems with the change.

Table 8.1 A Holistic Model of Resistance to Change

CAUSE	THEY RESIST BECAUSE...
Rational	...they possess insufficient or wrong facts, or disagree with reasoning based on those facts (agree with premises, dispute the conclusion)
Habitual	...they have a will to change, but habitual behaviors produce lack of adoption or relapse
Emotional	...they are angry at or afraid by a proposed change ("Will I be able to do this?" "Will I lose my job?" "How dare they?")
Identity	...they see change as a threat to "who I am" or how they see themselves (e.g., getting physicians to adopt antiseptic practices required them seeing themselves as disease carriers)
Ideological	...the change is contrary to values, a philosophical stance, or morals (e.g., religious pharmacists selling contraception, or increased petrochemical use for an environmentalist)
Social	...there are social disruptions to important relationships or loyalty to others harmed by the change (e.g., survivor effects), nonlinear network effects on information transmission (virality, influencers)
Cultural	...organizational norms, meaning social mimicry, rituals, language, and values that reinforce old (undesirable) patterns of individual thinking and behaving
Political	...political allegiances, change in power structures, or loss of perceived power, influence, control, or autonomy

---

[2] From Transactional Analysis (TA)—adult-adult, as compared with adult-child, parent-child. Treating resistance as if it were some kind of dysfunctional emotional response is, in my view, "parental" and evokes "child" reactions.

Psychologizing Change and Transitions

Change expert William Bridges, author of *Transitions*,[3] claims that the biggest error change managers make is confusing the *change* with the *transition*. By transition, Bridges means the psychological process of letting go of old familiar ideas and behaviors. Because transitions are fundamentally about loss (says Bridges), all change processes involve dealing with that loss. Bridges' model, from Gestalt psychotherapy, is a model for dealing with the grieving process of "endings," the groundlessness of the "neutral zone," and the energy of "new beginnings."

Although the notion of a psychological transition to accompany an organizational (or personal) change is valuable in some instances, Bridges makes a psychological mountain out of a molehill. Yes, post "change" comes "transition," but there need not be an experience of loss (involving grieving) as Bridges suggests. Yes, there are new skills to learn, patterns to unlearn, new things to try—but many people leap at such change. Yes, there may be a period of not-knowing, but unless that not-knowing is cataclysmic (the possibility of losing one's job), even the ambiguity can produce a sense of excitement (Christmas morning for grown-ups). Yes, even positive change means leaving some things behind (an overseas promotion and leaving treasured colleagues), but the resilient take such things entirely in stride. Their process and scheme of responses look nothing like Bridges' process.

Some people relish change and novelty, even if the challenge is a difficult one brought on by a difficult situation. Learning new skills, innovating, climbing new professional mountains, and finding new friends in new colleagues are all part of what makes work interesting, not dull. The personal transitions do not necessarily entail negative emotions. There may *sometimes* be emotional letting go, but treating people and change as if this were normal is to misjudge the diversity of people's experience as they go through change. As you saw in Chapter 6, "Misunderstanding Human Behavior," the grief cycle (Elizabeth Kubler-Ross) is one of those canonical change models that

---

[3] Still, after 20 years, one of the top-five books on change (despite the criticism that follows).

is complete myth. *The grief cycle, for some people, in some situations, may be excitement, enthusiasm, engagement, effort, and excellence.*

Panta rhei, "everything flows," said Heraclitus. It is stability that is an illusion. To add a dash of Buddhism to my Greek, attachment (to the illusion of stability) is the source of all suffering. To add some biology to that, change defines life and what makes us different than a rock. The mindset that working life is other than dealing every day, every minute, with change contributes to the false notion that things ought to be stable, and is part of the cause of change suffering.[4]

This "change is other than the stuff of life itself, and must be hard" is a reality that we *create*, rather than *observe*. In this author's view, this psychologizing in the arena of change is misguided, and psychologically trained people often project their psychological mental models onto situations (for example, this is how grief ought to look, this is how authentic looks, this is how anger looks).[5]

Worse, if someone does not follow an "approved" psychological response, it is (astonishingly) labeled "denial" or "repression" (terms picked up from Freudian counseling that have found their way into everyday use).

There are many people whose attitude to change is "bring it on!" and there are corporate (agile) cultures whose collective attitude is similar. Transitions for these people and businesses are the threads from which joy is spun.

Canonical change teaching suggests that (1) change is the exception, (2) it always provokes resistance, and (3) it must always be emotionally challenging. These notions of change are ones we need to leave behind in the twentieth century.

We now turn to the mother of all change management problems, social complexity.

---

[4] Again, from the Buddhist teaching that once something is truly accepted, the associated suffering disappears.

[5] Again, organization development has deep roots in 1960s "human potential" movements, in the psychodynamics of groups (National Training Laboratories and the Tavistock Institute), and in Rogerian and Gestalt psychotherapies.

From Change Management 101 to "Wicked Messes"

In Chapter 3, "Governance and the Psychology of Risk," you saw that technical, dynamic *complexity* meant multiple moving parts interacting in nonlinear ways that produced emergent outcomes. Those "parts" are sometimes people and groups whom, being essential to our goals, we must align with our strategy.

Some of the problems Change Management 101 tries to solve include:[6]

- How to deal with resistance
- How to resolve conflict
- How to develop change leaders at every level
- How to engage the workforce
- How to build skills and capability
- How to analyze and influence stakeholders
- How to communicate optimally
- How to develop a network of influencers and change leaders

To solve those problems, Change Management 101 uses a well-established set of tools, for example, change risk and readiness assessments, mapping stakeholders, analyzing stakeholders' power, developing sponsorship, and creating a communications strategy.[7] There are hundreds of books, methods, courses, and tools that tell you how to do that. Change Management 101 works extremely well in situations with low social and technical complexity, that is where stakeholder diversity is slight,[8] when the dynamics of the system are

---

[6] Not by any means an exhaustive list.

[7] In a change management practitioner's toolbox, there will be 100 or so different tools of this kind.

[8] I do not mean visible diversity or ethnic diversity. Human beings are also trivially diverse. Ideological diversity is closest to what I mean. Strongly diverse stakeholders might, for example, be Native Americans, suburban communities, oil industry executives, and environmentalists talking about fracking on Native land.

only complicated or simple (not complex or chaotic[9]), and where the purpose is clear and shared. The biggest problem in many organizations (those that IBM called Change Novices in Chapter 1, "Failed Change: The Greatest Preventable Cost to Business?") is either lack of in-house expertise in using Change Management 101, or that they skimp on the change management on major projects.

Most businesses would profit enormously from just using Change Management 101 well.

The Core of Change Management 101—Participation and Involvement

In a series of groundbreaking experiments in the 1940s, it was discovered that behavioral change in groups was substantially enabled through involvement (sometimes called participation) in decision making. This notion is, today, a cornerstone of change management, and how much to involve people in decision making is one of the most important trade-offs in management (between the speediness of the boss making the decision and telling people what to do, and the high-engagement, but potential rabble of starting with a blank sheet of paper). In the *Fifth Discipline Fieldbook*, Peter Senge offers what I often refer to as the most useful model in the change tactics canon (see Figure 8.1).

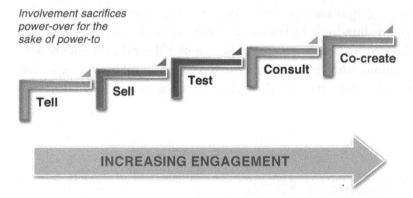

Figure 8.1 The most useful change-tactics model. Which involvement/ engagement style should we pursue?

---

[9] From Snowden's categorization in Chapter 3.

Telling is the lowest level of involvement: "This is what you are going to do." *Selling* is, "This is what you are going to do, and here is why I think it is a good idea." *Testing* allows still more involvement, challenge and input, "Here is what I think we should do; how can we improve upon it?" *Consulting* provides even more involvement, "Here are some broad parameters; where do you think we should go?" Finally, *cocreating* starts with a blank canvas, "What basic principles should guide where we go, and how do we get there?"

There are many factors that a leader should consider in selecting an approach, and leaders make three big mistakes in involvement decisions. The first is, obviously, not involving people enough thence achieving poor compliance, or worse active dissent. Recall Qantas Airlines' $40 million write-off when engineers refused to use the "Smartjet" system (calling it "Dumbjet") is an example of insufficient involvement with extreme consequences. Senior leaders thought (and said), "Why would we ask an engineer?"

The second mistake, much less often seen, is for a leader to be insufficiently directive (too little telling and selling), and too much involvement. There are contexts when people welcome directive leadership, such as in a time of crisis.

The third I call an involvement pretense. Frequently, in organizational change, we just want behavioral compliance and we want to do a lot of telling/selling—the parameters are clear and the path is narrow. Yet sometimes, leaders decide to run a high-involvement event ostensibly to solicit input (but input they do not really want). This is a commonplace situation because senior leaders are (rightly) taught that involvement in the decision-making process is a way to gain long-term acceptance of a change. However, involvement includes being able to disagree and to shape matters. Senior leaders do not always want that! A physician and participant in one of these involvement workshops, sensing the disconnect, muttered to me in confidence, "I wish they would just tell us what they want rather than going through this *charade*." By pretending to solicit input when they really want compliance, they lower trust and compliance rather than increasing it. Nothing breeds cynicism as quickly as asking people for their opinion and then ignoring it. This pitfall can be avoided by making it clear which aspects of a change are up for debate, and which are not.

Deciding how much, and in which matters, to involve particular groups is part of the art of change tactics. Involvement can be time consuming. On the other hand, strong resistance to change can consume even more time and resources. Senior leaders need to clarify, authentically, how much input they really want and then be straightforward with the business about that—being prepared to say (if indicated), "We need to make progress quickly, and need your trust and complete compliance on this one even though there are aspects you may not understand or like."

Recall also that in the change strategy section, I drew attention to the need for continuous involvement—that is, a constant flow of insight, information, and ideas—not through set pieces, so that strategists understand the real world of the workers, and staff constantly feel they are part of the big picture. The "involvement staircase," excellent though it is, remains a legacy of historical organizational structures and ways of thinking about change.

Wicked (Social) Messes

The problems Change Management 101 was *not* designed to solve are problems where social complexity meets technical complexity—so-called "wicked messes" or "social messes." Those problems require solutions on the far right of the involvement scale, that is *cocreation*.

Social messes have the following intractable features:

- There is no central authority that can muscle the change through without high levels of acceptance and engagement. (This is *always* the case with extraorganizational stakeholders who have power, and is *often* the case inside businesses.)
- No unique (correct) view of the problem exists, perhaps caused by battling ideologies and values. (U.S. health care and Middle Eastern politics are extreme examples, as are issues where business, community, and environment intersect, and in mergers of equal-sized companies.)
- There are multiple problem solvers, problem experts, and problem owners creating an intractable influence problem.

- There is no clear agreement on facts, or even that facts are what is most important (compared with values, history, human rights, feelings).
- Outside experts are of limited value (what counts as expertise is contested).
- Problems are interconnected and that layering of problems (such as education, poverty, housing, health) makes solving one in isolation impossible.
- Layering of problems leads to contradictory, mutually exclusive, competing solutions.
- Implementation defies rational planning and process-driven approaches (for example, "winning the peace" in Iraq post 2003).
- Between stakeholders, there can be substantial mistrust, very high emotions, and deep resistance to deployment of power.

These "social messes" are the rule in social/development problems, and all the paradigmatic cases have a political element. They also *always* apply to businesses especially where they intersect with diverse communities. For example, in major infrastructure projects, there can be a difficult multiplicity of stakeholders, such as contractors, shareholders, vendors, unions, engineers, project managers, government bodies, NGOs, communities, multiple joint venture partners, customers, and project teams. To this complexity, you can often add a global dimension when these stakeholders come from different countries and cultures.

Extractive industries routinely face these social (wicked) messes. Hydraulic-fracturing (fracking) polarizes communities that vehemently disagree on priorities and values; should they focus on jobs, profit, tax base, and energy independence, or, in contrast, safety, environment, renewables, health, climate, and environment?

Although the political contexts are the messiest messes, no change leader looking over the characteristics of social messes will find them entirely alien. In the biggest change programs with which I have been involved, there have been as many as four different consulting firms each with eight-figure commercial interests in the project, dozens of subcontractors, multiple labor unions, cabinet oversight, and massive organizations to align. One of the factors in the Boeing Dreamliner overrun ($12 billion price tag) was the number of (nonaligned) consortium partners and suppliers each with a small piece of a very complex puzzle.

In all change, stakeholder engagement separates the sheep from the goats. Businesses can learn how to handle social complexity on a lesser scale by mimicking the methodologies used to align diverse, antagonistic stakeholders. In other words, the same methodologies that have been used in those paradigmatic (political) situations, to take antagonistic stakeholders and have them work together, can be used to take modest levels of engagement and cooperation to enthusiasm and passion in traditional business contexts.

Moreover, the methodologies we are about to suggest are the way to get parts of a complex system to engage and talk to each other, thus improving information flows that can lead to a better understanding of the dynamic complexity we saw in Chapter 3.

These tools are social technologies that practitioners call collectively Large Group Interventions (LGIs). At PwC, we based our methodology for dealing with social complexity upon the pioneering work of Marvin Weisbord,[10] calling it the strategy café. Others call theirs multistakeholder dialogue, conference model, future search, open space technology, world café, or transformative scenario planning. Specialist practitioners and communities of practice exist who work hard on problems as wide-ranging as the political integration of South Africa post-Apartheid, to dialogue with indigenous communities over planned economic development, to solving malnutrition.[11] In business, they have been used to generate high engagement in redesign, restructuring, strategic planning, process improvement, and alignment of joint ventures and partnerships. Even though these contexts may be alien to the work-a-day manager, there is much to be learned from how they achieve the results they do.

---

[10] Weisbord, M. (2012). *Productive workplaces: Dignity, meaning, and community in the 21st century*. New York: Pfeiffer.

[11] Kahane, A. (2012). *Transformative scenario planning: Working together to change the future*. San Francisco: Berrett-Kohler.

Benefits and Characteristics

One way of summarizing the philosophy of interventions such as this is leaders sacrifice "power over" for the sake of "power to." Even the notion of resistance is misguided in socially complex situations because that implies a power difference and a right-wrong way of thinking about the problem.

At PwC, we developed a simple rubric imported from Newton's second law of motion, F = MA (Force equals Mass times Acceleration), $O = E^2$ (Output equals Excellence times Engagement). An "excellent" solution with zero engagement produces zero output. Consequently, LGIs focus pragmatically on a solution that creates optimal engagement because expert solutions with which people are disengaged are useless. Some benefits are:

- **Technical**—Solutions are developed by people closest to the problem, and who have multiple perspectives on it, such as customers, consumers, communities, or other key stakeholders.

- **Trust**—People are handed back autonomy and control over what happens (loss of autonomy and control is an important contributor to stress at work). They go from being "done-to" to "doers."

- **Emotional**—Engagement, enthusiasm, and passion are unlocked, and there can be an outpouring of new ideas.

- **Social**—Groups that were once polarized in opposition have a common view of the problem and a sense of shared purpose in solving it.

LGIs handle social complexity by bringing the whole system into the room. Each group/individual has a piece of the puzzle and a piece of the solution. In a business, this can be relatively straightforward; however, we have seen instances where conveners want to exclude "problem stakeholders," for example, unions. This is always an error.

LGIs are another example of a tool that 100% of change experts have heard of (yet use all too infrequently), but that almost no non-experts have heard of (despite their power to resolve conflict and effect change). Part of the problem is that to use them you have to release power—and sometimes, it seems, people would rather retain power and remain at an impasse, than release power and solve problems. The ethos of LGIs is: "People engage when they talk, less when they are being talked at." The process varies tremendously depending on which variant of this family of interventions is selected. LGIs are high-engagement methods and never used at all for one-way communication; PowerPoint projectors are rare; there are very few sessions where an authority figure is speaking with lots of people listening (but, participants frequently ask for expert input; the difference is that they are pulling it rather than it being pushed at them). Agendas are sometimes structured, but features such as who attends, what is on the agenda, and what is the purpose can be deeply contested in some situations. In those situations, a blank sheet of paper functions excellently as an agenda.

LGIs in Action

We began to use these types of interventions in businesses in the early 1990s, in situations of varying complexity such as (in order of decreasing difficulty and complexity):

- Improving health and safety performance in developing-world mining operations by engaging local community leaders, health and safety experts, local business leadership, workers, unions, and head-office leadership
- Aligning four consortium partners, unions, and antagonistic internal groups with a leadership team's strategy
- Creating a transformation strategy for a global bank that required passionate engagement from middle management
- Redesigning an organization (processes) from the ground up, listening to suppliers, customers, and workers for efficient design ideas
- Engaging the most senior 1000 people of a business with a complex and deeply unpopular change and reconciling two warring factions

For standard, multistakeholder engagement within a business, an intervention may take as little as two days [12] In a business redesign, or strategic refocusing, conferences might be every six weeks, with prototype project delivery between conferences.

When finished, one CFO of a major airline, who had brought together frontline staff, unions, and middle and senior management to develop a new policy, said, "I have never seen so many antagonistic groups in this business so fully engaged with a problem and so committed to finding a solution." These methods can turn the most conflicted situations, replete with despair and mistrust, into energetic, engaged communities of action.

On the other end of the influencing scale lies expert communication. We want people to react rationally, and when the facts are on our side, we would like them to shift minds. However, shifting minds with facts proves harder to do than we would mostly like.

Influencing with Facts

"You are entitled to your own opinion, but you are not entitled to your own facts."

—Daniel Moynihan, U.S. Senator and Ambassador

Fact-based influencing strategies may work as long as the target does not care too much about the matter. By "care," I mean not too much emotional/cognitive attachment, nor behaviors that are ingrained (habits). Habit change, as you saw in the last chapter, requires behavioral strategies, not simply cognitive ones. That situation is an unfortunate one—facts fail most when the stakes are highest. Fortunately, in the last decade, much more has been learned about influencing from research in human sciences areas as diverse as public health and political science.

---

[12] In the political sphere, or in work on development issues, multiple weeklong events might take place periodically over many years.

When Facts Fail

The notion that views can be changed by further provision of facts is called the *information deficit model*: If only people had enough of the right information, they would see the problem clearly and be on our side.

It is clear that the information deficit model fails in the public sphere. No data on CO_2 concentrations and Arctic ice melting (or the dozens of other supportive analyses) will change a climate skeptic's view. No Carbon-14 dating (proving a fossil is 50 million years old) will change the mind of a "young earth" creationist who thinks it all began 6,400 years ago. Worse, on emotive subjects, there may be an *inverse* correlation between possession of facts and strength of belief. Professor James Kuklinski, at the University of Illinois, found that research subjects held varied and highly inaccurate views about welfare[13] (how much is spent, on whom, and what percentage of the federal budget), but the more *uninformed* that they were, the more strongly they held their beliefs.

Kuklinski's work suggests two things. In a communication vacuum, during change, people may fill the vacuum with stronger adversarial positions. Therefore, we might hope that provision of information would help bring them alongside.

Unfortunately not. Providing facts may not be just ineffective, facts may actually *strengthen* opposition to an idea!

The Backfire Effect

In his research shifting political opinion in the United States, Brendan Nyhan, Professor at University of Michigan's School of Public Health, found that, when presented with unwelcome facts, people may not simply resist changing their views, but they may support their original opinion more strongly. This backfire effect was found among political conservatives who held the view that the Bush tax cuts (of 2001) *increased* government tax revenue (a tenet of supply-side economics). When presented with hard numbers that showed an actual

---

[13] What the United States calls social assistance programs for the poor, disabled, elderly, or unemployed.

fall in tax revenue, they perversely *strengthened* their beliefs that tax cuts increased government revenue (and were ergo good for the deficit and the economy). The backfire effect has been shown in other, similarly, emotive and ideological issues, such as climate change and whether Iraq had weapons of mass destruction (WMDs) prior to the 2003 invasion.[14]

Facts backfire in two ways. First, facts fail when we try to use them to influence a disagreement that is not factual in nature, that is, when we ignore the other seven dimensions of the resistance model and treat people as if a bit more knowledge would bring them around. Second, Nyhan's research suggests that when the disagreement is ideological, facts may actually strengthen resistance and demands we rethink how we use facts. This kind of thinking is called *motivated reasoning,* which is not really reasoning at all because it is impervious to reasons.

Using Facts Effectively

We need to be careful how we use facts when faced with strong opinions. By using the resistance model, we can gain insight into the nonrational sources of dissent. When we do use facts, recent research has pointed toward four concrete strategies that a change tactician should take note of when designing communication to change twenty-first-century minds:

- **Facts first**—Although facts will not alone win the day, they are more effective if placed first in the communication, rather than later. In *The Debunking Handbook,* John Cook and Stephan Lewandowsky present evidence that mentioning the myth first reinforces it. The communication structure "here is what you believe and here is why you are wrong" *increases resistance.* For example, to dispel the myth "the sun is warming and that explains the rise in global temperature...," first show a graph of declining sun temperature over the last 40 years. Once that factual premise is accepted, we can work on the reasoning that followed from it.

---

[14] Nyhan's findings did not just apply to one side of the political spectrum. He found some fact-resistant ideologues on the left also.

- **Less is more**—Contrary to intuition, more facts can be worse than fewer. Cook and Lewandowsky's finding show that too many facts overwhelm and that the bare minimum should be used. Hitting a climate skeptic with CO_2 concentration, global temperature, desalination, sea-level data, ice-sheet thickness, satellite images, ecosystem changes, and weather anomalies at the same time may just leave someone feeling bludgeoned and confused.

- **Use pictures**—Nyhan also compared the effect of graphical data with textual data. Few will be surprised that the infographics were much more persuasive than text and numbers.

- **Self-esteem matters**—For those of us who sometimes, wrong-headedly, seek to reinform people with snark, sarcasm, and derision, there is bad news. Self-esteem of the influencee seems to matter a great deal and people whose identity is threatened strengthen their resistance to new information. Nyhan tested a way of correcting this by asking subjects a simple question about their values (called a self-affirmation) and compared the extent of belief change with people who did not receive the self-affirmation question. He found this strategy had a measureable effect on people's revising of their views on emotive and ideological issues. It seems Mary Poppins was right about that spoonful of sugar.

Some insights into how to better change hearts and minds come not from traditional writing on change management, but rather *inside businesses* from the marketing department and research on consumer behavior whose focus is on changing minds outside businesses.

Linking Influencing to Changing Behaviors

In the classic work on influencing, *Influence: The Psychology of Persuasion,* Professor Robert Cialdini sets out six principles. These principles are excellent examples of evidence-based prescription and, although written in 1984, have stood up to the challenges of further research and field-testing by practitioners. Cialdini's principles are reciprocity, commitment and consistency, social proof, liking, authority, and scarcity. I rarely see Cialdini's principles taught in change management circles, perhaps because of their roots in consumer behavior and marketing. The "behavioral insights team" (of the UK's cabinet office) has combined Cialdini's insights with neobehaviorist research to produce an elegant framework for changing hearts, minds, and behaviors. The MINDSPACE framework is shown in Table 8.2 Its elements are based on considerable research (as are Cialdini's), and they have been field-tested and have shown great promise on very thorny social problems.

Table 8.2 The MINDSPACE Framework

MINDSPACE Element	CHANGE COMMUNICATION IMPLICATIONS
Messenger: Who communicates information matters a great deal.	This, and Cialdini's "liking" and "authority" suggest that both senior leaders and closely connected others should communicate change.
Incentives: Incentives shape behavioral responses in unpredictable ways; humans avoid losses.	The most powerful effect of incentives may be their symbolic communication effect.
Norms: Social, cultural, and network effects have extremely powerful effects on behavior.	Modeling of new behaviors creates a virtuous cycle; consider who are disproportionately important influencers and get them modeling.
Defaults: People "go with the flow" of preset options.	Eliminate unhelpful options, and have people opt-out rather than opt-in.
Salience: We pay attention to novelty and personal relevance.	Specific, targeted change communications are more effective than generic ones.
Priming: Our acts are often influenced by unconscious clues.	Offer stakeholders "when-then" scenarios so that the environment triggers the right behavior. (When I arrive at the site, I instantly put on PPE.)
Affect: Emotional associations powerfully shape our actions.	Create an emotional relationship with the status quo and with the desired outcomes.
Commitments: We seek to be consistent with public promises and reciprocate acts.	Encourage behavioral commitment, and ask people to make commitments publicly.
Ego (identity): We act in ways that make us feel better about ourselves.	Help groups and individuals to create new identities— we are the kind of people who..."

MINDSPACE summarizes some of the best current research on changing behaviors, hearts, and minds. It is an excellent summary of both cognitive and neobehaviorist ideas on engagement, and makes an excellent checklist for change communicators.

Allied Signal CEO Larry Bossidy once said, "I can only change this company as quickly as I can change myself." He implied a now widely accepted link between personal development, leadership development, and change success. Our next topic, mindfulness, not only produces desirable outcomes, but it strengthens the leader's personal capacity for change, and improves resilience and agility.

The Mindful Leader

"If you just sit and observe, you will see how restless your mind is. If you try to calm it, it only makes it worse, but over time it does calm, and when it does, there's room to hear more subtle things—that's when your intuition starts to blossom and you start to see things more clearly..."

—Steve Jobs

As someone fascinated by peak human mental performance,[15] I have often wondered whether minds can be trained like muscles. Athletes who desire peak muscular, physical performance work on endurance, stamina, strength, agility, and flexibility, as well as the specific skills of their discipline. This was not always the case. Tiger Woods, anecdotally, was the first golfer to practice yoga and weight-lifting to develop those general faculties alongside his (ample) specific skills. Even in the physical domain, this is a relatively new thing—there were few gyms in the 1960s either for athletes or for common folk.

Is it possible, in the twenty-first century, we will learn better how to train those foundational **mental** skills for knowledge workers the way endurance, stamina, strength, agility, and flexibility are developed for athletes? Those fundamental skills include attentional control, situational awareness, cognitive flexibility, emotion regulation, processing speed, working memory, purposeful control of reasoning, and impulse inhibition.[16]

With the focus on this book on thinking more clearly, are there push-ups for the mind?

There are. Mindfulness practices are mental training techniques that come to us not from twenty-first-century cognitive psychology, but from much older contemplative traditions. *Despite their ancient origins, there is much more scientific evidence for the value*

---

[15] My hobbies include chess, backgammon, bridge, and poker and I have competed at an international level in three of these.

[16] Adapted from Jurado, M. B., & Rosselli, M. (2007). The elusive nature of executive functions: A review of our current understanding. *Neuropsychological Review, 17*(3), pp. 213–233.

of mindfulness practice than there is for any other method of personal change found in the psychology section of your local bookstore, or on commercial brain training sites.[17]

What do we mean by mindfulness practices?

Defining Mindfulness[18]

"Meditation is essentially training our attention so that we can be more aware—not only of our own inner workings but also of what is happening around us in the here and now."

—Sharon Salzberg

According to two researchers, mindfulness is "a family of self-regulation practices that aim to bring mental processes under voluntary control through focusing attention and awareness."[19] Mindfulness practices develop and habituate metacognitive processes that control mental life so that they are readily available from day to day.

The most common mindfulness practice is meditation, and the most common form of meditation is just to sit quietly and observe the breath, an automatic, subtle process that requires intense concentration to follow for any length of time. When attention wanders, as it more or less instantly does in the unpracticed, the object is to notice the wandering, and to return your attention to the breath. The astonishing thing, from my point of view, is what happens when you

---

[17] The evidence for "brain-training Web sites" is skimpy. Although performance on the onsite exercises improves, few of those enhanced skills transfer to real-life situations. See Owen, A., et al. (2010). Putting brain training to the test. *Nature, 465*(7299), pp. 755–778.

[18] Despite its roots in mystical traditions, we can use the term *mindfulness* in completely secular ways: Our discussion will be purely of its benefits of thinking and the control of emotion, and not on spiritual or ethical components. Mystical practitioners assert that these descriptions miss a vital trick and that there are aspects that cannot be described in secular, psychological, or cognitive terms.

[19] Walsh, R. & Shapiro, S. (2006). The meeting of meditative disciplines and western psychology: A mutually enriching dialogue. *American Psychologist, 61*(3), pp. 227–239.

try to do that in any sustained way. First, it is incredibly difficult. My attempts to focus on the breath unleash a stream of thoughts like sitting trackside at the Monaco Grand Prix. Second, things "come up." In my case, boredom, restlessness, irritation, rumination, and dreaming, all part of my default (hidden) cognitive makeup, are now front and center in all their ugliness. The plethora of benefits described in the upcoming paragraphs follows from seeing those more clearly, and from practicing setting them aside. Over time, rare glimpses of what it is like to have a "mind like a still pond" become more frequent and longer. The promise of mindfulness practices is that the "still pond" state can be trained, so that it becomes a habit.

Anecdotal Benefits of Mindfulness Practices

Before delving into the evidence for those benefits, let us review the anecdotal, descriptive evidence that gives a flavor on how that simple exercise produces such immense psychological benefit.

Mindfulness practices *strengthen control of attention and concentration*. In paying full attention to the present during practice, and by returning to the object of concentration repeatedly, the practice enhances the faculty of paying attention to just one thing. With time, the wanderings become shorter because the practitioner develops a meta-attentional faculty that quickly notes distraction. In a world full of distractions and competing demands, being able to concentrate hard, and at length, on just one thing is an asset.

This thinking about thinking, or metacognitive faculty, "sits above" thinking and feeling processes, and monitors and regulates those. This permits the practitioner to "step outside her thinking," to interrogate assumptions, and to gain perspective. Are the thoughts ruminating about the past, incessantly planning the future, engaging in fantasy, or simmering about life's injustices? Those mental predilections offer clues to default mental processes. One might observe a mental life obsessed with planning and abstract thought. Neither of those is bad, but neither are they always contextually appropriate.

This thinking about thinking, in turn, leads to more *cognitive flexibility* and more choice. This third-person perspective creates more choice in how people react to stimuli, which creates the possibility of different, perhaps more creative choices. David Rock, neuroscience author, calls this faculty "the director" and our mental lives a stage. The director makes sure that the right actors are on stage (in working memory) and that they are performing their correct parts.

Some of what enters the stage are emotional responses and habitual impulses. Having a strong "director" makes the practitioner a more accurate observer of her emotional life and impulses, and enhances the ability to *regulate emotions* and *inhibit impulses.* Those contribute to balance, maturity, wisdom, acceptance, and equanimity, by widening what Victor Frankl called "the gap between stimulus and response."

Mindfulness practices, finally, develop a special kind of *self-awareness.* Most people have completed psychological profiling of some kind in their career, revealing baseline psychological "resting states." However, self-awareness must include in-the-moment awareness or what McKinsey authors Boaz and Fox call "state awareness."[20] This state awareness is much more important than "profile awareness" (such as Myers-Briggs) because it informs the leader of their disposition *right now,* in the moment. Psychometrics, by comparison, are Self-Awareness 101.

Mindfulness practices develop *kindness* and *compassion.* Beginning meditators often slap themselves back to attention angrily and self-critically. "There I darned well go again." They might notice that they are not very kind to themselves and noticing this harsh inner voice is the beginning of self-compassion. Buddhists suggest that practicing this self-compassion is the ground of a much wider compassion (which they call loving kindness): Kinder to oneself means kinder to others.

Finally, mindfulness practice cultivates an ability to "be with" or accept what happens in the moment. When you sit back and reminisce about your life, it is almost a given that the most enjoyable and memorable moments are the ones in which you were completely present. Being "present" is associated with peak performance and

---

[20] Boaz, N., & Fox, E. A. (2004, Mar.). Change leader, change thyself. *McKinsey Quarterly.* Retrieved from http://www.mckinsey.com/insights/leading_in_the_21st_century/change_leader_change_thyself.

peak psychological states, as described by author Csikszentmihalyi in his seminal book *Flow: The Psychology of Optimal Experience.*

Acceptance of what "comes up" is, according to Eastern traditions, the root of *happiness*. In the words of mindfulness teacher Pema Chödrön,[21]

> In meditation we discover our inherent restlessness. Sometimes we get up and leave. Sometimes we sit there but our bodies wiggle and squirm and our minds go far away. This can be so uncomfortable that we feel it is impossible to stay. Yet this feeling can teach us not just about ourselves but what it is to be human...we really do not want to stay with the nakedness of our present experience. It goes against the grain to stay present. These are the times when only gentleness and a sense of humor can give us the strength to settle down... so whenever we wander off, we gently encourage ourselves to "stay" and settle down. Are we experiencing restlessness? Stay! Are fear and loathing out of control? Stay! Aching knees and throbbing back? Stay! What is for lunch? Stay! I cannot stand this another minute! Stay!

According to Chödrön, by learning to "be with" what happens in meditation, we strengthen the mental muscles of acceptance and perseverance, and become better able to deal with tumultuous conflict in real life.

The following list summarizes the substantial, but still largely anecdotal benefits, of mindfulness practices described above. I leave it to the reader to assess whether, if substantially accurate, those would be an enhancement to their business/leadership life:

- Control of attention and concentration
- Increased situational awareness
- Cognitive flexibility, choice
- Metacognitive faculties
- Increased (state) self-awareness

---

[21] Chödrön, P. (2007). *The places that scare you: A guide to fearlessness in difficult times.* Boston: Shamabala.

- Happiness
- Emotion and impulse regulation

One central feature of mindfulness practices is that they are *generative practices.* This means that they, and the associated benefits, *support the mastery of other skills* in the same way that strength, stamina, endurance, agility, and flexibility make learning and mastering physical skills (throwing, catching, hitting, swinging a golf club) easier. To be more specific, the enhanced awareness and control helps change other behaviors. For example, effectively countering cognitive biases requires a level of self-monitoring and cognitive flexibility; behavioral and habit change requires catching an old habit to replace it with a new one; influencing, you saw, requires nonjudgment and empathy for facts to have a chance; negotiation and conflict resolution require the ability to "be centered."

This has been an astonishing, I think, catalog of benefits. The healthy skeptic in all of us must wonder which are proven and which are overhyped. We turn now to see what science suggests about the truth of these descriptive/anecdotal benefits.

Science of Mindfulness Practices

Initial interest in mindfulness (and the practices which surround it such as meditation, yoga, and Tai chi) arose in alternative communities beginning at the start of the twentieth century, and accelerating in the 1960s. Saffron robes and long gray beards kept "serious" researchers away for decades. The few early studies found positive results for cardiovascular outcomes (blood pressure and heart rate) and stress reduction. Research then accelerated and researchers began to study mental health outcomes. Only at the beginning of this century did hundreds of researchers worldwide start to study high performance in the healthy and application of mindfulness in a business setting.

Still, high-quality research is hard to come by. Comparing meditators and nonmeditators, for example, will not yield useful results because the effect of meditation cannot be isolated from other lifestyle choices (are the meditators all vegan, cyclist, craftspeople with no stress). Studies need to teach people to meditate and contrast their results with randomly assigned control groups. But in long-term studies, people drop out, and short-term studies have their work cut out for them to generate the benefits. As with all new research areas, categorical answers are a work in progress.

Although we are interested in peak performance, and not redress of psychological pathologies, mindfulness produces many mental health benefits. These include prevention of depression relapse, addiction relief, control of ADHD behaviors, alleviation of stress-related medical conditions, pain management, and anxiety disorder.[22] These clinical effects attest to the general power of mindfulness practices to shift conditions that can be resistant to drug treatments and psychotherapies. By inference, if sitting quietly observing the breath improves the well-being of the distressed, we should wonder whether it develops peak mental performance in the healthy-minded.

Very recent research suggests we can do more than just infer. In a recent review, Professor Jeffrey Greeson, of Johns Hopkins, reviewed 52 of the most recent publications. His findings are summarized (along with selected others) in the following list:

- Emotional awareness, emotion labeling, correcting unpleasant mood states
- Increased positive affect (emotion) including kindness and compassion
- Lower levels of nonclinical anxiety, depression, and anger
- Problem solving (Ren et al., 2011)
- Creativity (Colzato, 2012)
- Increased attention, concentration, and meta-attention
- Executive attention (Tang et al., 2007)
- Increased emotional well-being, happiness, life satisfaction
- Equanimity, acceptance, nonreactivity

This brief summary of research findings correlates reasonably well with the anecdotal/descriptive benefits outlined above. We now turn to how, in greater detail, mindfulness practices work and, finally, how to using them in a corporate setting.

---

[22] Hussain, D., & Bhushan, B. (2010). Psychology of meditation and health: Present status and future directions. *International Journal of Psychology and Psychological Therapy*, *10*(3), pp. 439–451.

Where Can I Buy Some?

"When the mind becomes clean and tranquil, then there is no need to practice meditation; we will automatically be meditating always."
—Swami Satchidananda

Were any family of pharmaceuticals able to produce such a wide spectrum of interesting clinical and cognitive benefits, a dozen drug companies would each be investing billions to bring the first product to market. If it came in a pill, I would take it daily; would you?

Peculiarly, most people have a sense of what the mindful state feels like: *present, in the moment, in the zone,* or *in the flow.* Mindfulness practices are about achieving that state on demand, or getting back to it when far away.

The chief obstacle, say many businesspeople, is time. The Dalai Lama, über meditator, meditates for two 90-minute sessions per day. As an example to potential meditators who would give it a try, he sets a scary standard. I know that if I set myself a lofty target of 30 minutes per day, I will fail (because I have). I do not deal at all well with failure (part of the reason I should meditate in the first place), but rather than deal with my perfectionism, the prospect of (fear of) failure, for many years, I did little or nothing. Suggestions that I start again with 1, 2, or 5 minutes a day seemed wimpy.

Research has good news for people who think as I do. It seems that you do not have to have been meditating for 30 years to get the benefits. Y. Y. Tang, Professor at Texas Tech University, investigated new meditators in a corporate setting and found that after just one week of daily twenty minute sessions, the new meditators scored higher on tests of attention and mood, and had lower levels of the stress hormone cortisol.

Even more good news is that short bursts of meditation produce bursts of the mindfulness experience, and some practitioners even advertise the one-minute meditation, and the one-second meditation. Can you switch from autopilot, to being fully present just for a second? Some businesspeople have this minipractice just before starting a key meeting, wanting to bring their fullest awareness and attention to the proceedings. One Senior VP reported that he had trained himself to do this every time he touched a doorknob.

There is a certain false economy in passing up the chance to establish a personal practice. Each of us has our own daily distraction demons, and part of my own irrationality is the ability to spend five minutes mindlessly on Twitter, rather than five minutes mindfully giving myself a break (with all the attendant long-term benefits). Here, the hyperbolic discounting we found in Chapters 3 and 6, "Governance and the Psychology of Risk" and "Misunderstanding Human Behavior," respectively, makes us unwilling to invest a few minutes now for a hard-to-know future benefit.

Another obstacle newcomers stumble upon is the internal dialogue, "My mind is too frantic to meditate." That may be true, but if one believes the potential benefits, that is like saying I am too unfit to go to the gym, or too inflexible to stretch. Nobody hops off the couch and runs a 5k, nor do first-timers walk into a gym and bench-press 100 kilos. Setting ridiculously high initial standards and being unwilling to be a novice are the enemies of personal progress and change.

Looked at through the lens of economics, ten minutes per day would only have to make the rest of the other ten hours (550 minutes) 2 percent more pleasurable, productive, or less stressful to be worth the investment. Who can claim 98 percent productive efficiency over an entire day?

In building the habit, we can try some of the research on habit formation from Chapter 7, "The Science of Changing Behaviors." There we saw that "minihabits" were a way to develop constructive habits where the emphasis was on repetition rather than length. That means one minute done consecutively for seven days is much more valuable than one session of ten minutes on the weekend, because *for beginners, habit formation matters more.* In Chapter 7, you also saw the power of action triggers, linking a new behavior to an old one. In this case, the "when-then" action trigger might look like, "When I take off my shoes, then I will meditate for five minutes."

In a rather beautiful virtuous circle, the minihabit of meditation may bring the benefit of more conscious control of impulses, which can lead to greater power over more important habits. Could starting with one minute a day, and building gradually, unleash a sea of positive personal change?

Developing Mindfulness in Business

> *"Focus, clarity, creativity, compassion, and courage. These are the qualities of the mindful leaders I have worked with, taught, mentored, and interviewed."*

—Bill George, former CEO of Medtronic

Since 2005, all the (many dozens) of leadership programs I have designed have had a mindfulness component. We called it, secularly, "attention training" to slide it under the radar of skeptical senior leaders. One program that ran for several years was for 300 partners at KPMG. Following our 10- or 20-minute practice, they would report a sense of calm, a quieter mind, clarity of thought, disappearance of stressful thoughts, and that they were more present. They were intellectually sold on the benefits. Terrific! Practice at home 10 minutes a day for the duration of the program and the habit of this state of mind will become more permanent! Our encouragements that they might take this up were met with a sincere interest and solemn commitment, yet few gave it a serious sustained try in their lives.

Likewise, in a nine-day leadership program for HSBC bank, we introduced a mindfulness practice and used it daily during the program. Yet again, the enthusiasm and perceived value of the practice during the program was great, but there was very little take-up once people returned to their busy work lives.

Naturally, enjoying very close relationships with the program participants, we asked, "Why?" One reason stood head and shoulders above the rest. Habit. They knew it was good for them, they had felt its benefits—but after 25 years of throwing on a suit and dashing for the 6:43, and keeping their foot on the gas until evening collapse, the practice of stopping for even 1, 2, 5, or 20 minutes was too hard to initiate and sustain.

Fast-forward to Silicon Valley 2014 from London 2005, and Google's Search Inside Yourself program has benefited from twenty-first-century research and gets better take-up of the mindfulness practices. Much can be learned from their experience. In our programs, mindfulness was presented as an adjunct to "real" leadership material; in Google's, mindfulness is the focus. Google brought in world-famous psychologists and teachers, and linked the practice to neuroscience (much loved by the engineers). The culture at Google, though a long-hours culture, encourages novelty and individuality. In our earlier work, we missed the social and cultural dimension of behavioral change that Google seems to have captured.

With a program this popular, at a much-admired, high-growth, twenty-first-century business, and a well-selling book called *Search Inside Yourself,* perhaps mindfulness in business is an idea whose time has come. A few decades ago, people used to sneak off for five-minute smoke breaks a dozen times per day, and that was permitted by corporate cultures of the time. Perhaps it will become legitimate to take five-minute "sit breaks" in the near future. There are mindfulness programs at other admired companies such as Apple, Facebook, Twitter, eBay, Intel, Nike, LinkedIn, and General Mills.

Taking stock of the descriptive benefits outlined above, what would a corporate culture be like where those were constantly developed or even commonplace? The leader *as a human being* looks likely to benefit, but we have to draw our own inferences about leadership development based on those principles.

Conclusion

Could creating a growth culture out of growth mindsets be one of the things that makes resistance to change a thing of the past? I believe that older conceptions of resistance are too narrow and that the roots of change management (or organization development) in counseling psychology means that ideas such as, grief, loss, catharsis, denial, and repression are unhelpfully treated as truth rather than a very specific way of looking at people (psychologizing them). It is possible to create change-agile businesses where resistance to change is a foreign concept.

Multistakeholder dialogue and large-group interventions are a high-involvement method of engaging groups with fundamental disagreements about problem definition, expertise, and direction. Although they arose at the interface between business and society, where "social messes" are the rule, businesses can make use of the way they engage a large number of diverse stakeholders around a common vision and action plan.

Facts fail to influence people when their opposition is not factual; in fact, facts can backfire, strengthening opposition. Communications that affirm self-concept are more effective when persuading people using such motivated reasoning. When it comes to influencing hearts and minds, and changing behavior, the MINDSPACE framework neatly summarizes many of the most interesting research in changing hearts, minds, and behaviors and can be used as a checklist for stakeholder influencing and communication.

Finally, you saw that mindfulness training has benefits in healthy, highly productive people, including emotion and impulse control, cognitive flexibility, and increased focus. Many leading businesses are investing in mindfulness education to help leaders reduce stress and develop metacognitive faculties.

The final chapter now looks at change leadership and what the scientific perspective may have to offer.

9

Leading with Science

"Sparse and poor popularizations of science create ecological niches that pseudoscience promptly fills."

—Carl Sagan

Toward a Science-Based Craft

In this final chapter, I want to flesh out the concept "leadership as a science-based craft" that has been the backdrop for everything covered to date. In introducing that concept, I do not wish to denigrate any other aspect of leadership, nor compete with the dozens of other leadership models. I merely want to highlight a gap in what those models say and address a lack of balance in the treatment of leadership by business writers.

The idea of a science-based craft has parallels in other disciplines. Surgeons describe surgery as a craft, but the methods and procedures are based on robust scientific understanding of anatomy and physiology. Architecture is an aesthetic pursuit, and a craft, yet architects cannot ignore the basics from physics and mechanical engineering. Organizations are unfortunately less well understood than bodies and buildings, yet we must start a scientific revolution inside businesses that leads us toward practices that have a basis in science. The craft of business leadership today pays too little attention to the science of how humans tick and too much attention to folk and pop psychology.

What might this look like in practice?

- A much-respected project director makes an impassioned, well-argued presentation to continue a project that is already 60 percent over budget and 9 months late. Most of your leadership team colleagues, who approved the project, seem aligned. The director strengthens his case arguing that several unnecessary rounds of user testing and stakeholder engagement can be eliminated and that some of the 9 months can be caught up. You demur knowing that *escalation of commitment* is a powerful motivator, that *risk-seeking behaviors* multiply when projects are behind schedule, and that your colleagues are especially prone to *groupthink* because of *loyalty to this director* and have *reputational interest* having approved the initial budget. (In this situation, you conclude one of us is smarter than all of us and overrule the team.)

- An HR leader who you admire brings a proposal for an "agile innovation" training program. In this three-day course, 2,000 staff will learn the latest material on agile innovation from a famous professor at Ivy Towers School of Business. You ask (1) what is in the program *apart from theory*, (2) if there are behaviors, how will they *transfer to the workplace*, (3) how you will *measure the behavioral and financial benefits* (beyond happy sheets), and (4) what will be done to *support managers* attending in *breaking old habits* and forming the new "agile" ones.

- One practice you admire from leading organizations is staff being free to start "skunkworks" projects with 5 percent of their time. After consultation, the consultant brings you a draft of the policy—staff can opt-in, and choose one of 40 different projects. You (1) make the program *opt-out not opt-in* (because this will increase take-up), (2) *reduce the options* to six (because choices can deter action), and (3) will randomly *praise* one of the six project groups every week *(because intermittent incentives work better)*.

- A joint-venture in Tajikistan, according to your analysts, has an expected ROI of 35%. Their qualitative risk analysis has identified many risks, but all are green or amber. You realize that this is *extremistan* in Tajikistan (that single events will dominate average returns), that the analysts are prone to the *zero-risk bias*, and that the average ROI they propose is a poor measure of actual *risk-adjusted return* for the business.

Of course, these are hypothetical and a tiny subset of what twenty-first century science might suggest, but each of them has the potential to save many millions of dollars (which is a good day's work for most people). They represent the kind of thinking and the sort of knowledge that is not yet widespread.

Business versus Science: Two Examples

Science-based craft means basing decisions on the best available science, and may sound like an uncontroversial statement, but current practice is very far away from that ideal. I am continually amazed by two features of my own career that show how far there is to go.

I have spent more than three decades as a manager, director, and CEO/entrepreneur; in addition, I have spent the last two decades as a consultant dispensing advice on risk management, strategy, innovation, HR policy, leadership, and culture (at different times). *Not once* during that career has a client or colleague asked me whether I had any evidence to substantiate my recommendations. Could I prove what I was about to charge big bucks for would work?

The sad truth is that, if asked, the straight answer would have been "no"—I had stories aplenty, dozens of case studies, but no evidence other than anecdote. As scientists facetiously say, "the plural of anecdote is not data." The still sadder truth is none of my competitors could prove it would work either. For better or for worse, my recommendations (along with those of illustrious others such as McKinsey and IBM) fly under the scientific radar. My ideas were accepted by virtue of some combination of age, résumé, references, rhetoric, gravitas, or chutzpah on my part—or desperation and bad judgment on their part.

During that long career, I have interviewed for big jobs with grand-sounding titles such as "Director of Risk Management," "Assistant Dean," and "Managing Director." (A small compensatory benefit of the graying years is that one may be considered for such positions.)

Despite the fact that those interviewers (usually Human Capital specialists) should know better, the hundred or so interviews peppering my career were all in the "chat" format: "Talk me through your résumé," "What do you do with your free time?" "Tell us why you would like this job," "Did you like being a trader?" or "What were your biggest challenges?" My potential bosses were prepared to risk megabucks and megabudgets using an interview method that is little better than astrology at predicting performance: the unstructured interview.[1]

That should raise eyebrows. The standard "chat" interview, in the hands of an untrained interviewer, still used extensively for selecting staff, is almost uncorrelated with on-the-job performance, that is, not much better than rolling dice.[2] (Much better are assessment centers, work sampling, panel interviews, behavioral interviews, job sampling, structured interviews, and situational interviews—all of which require a little bit of work by HR, and a little bit of training and discipline from the interviewers.) As Stanford's Jeffrey Pfeffer says, "Hiring is another crucial workplace decision. Many studies show that unstructured, face-to-face interviews are biased; interviewers prefer candidates who are likeable, similar to them, and physically attractive—even if these qualities are irrelevant to performance."[3]

Businesspeople find this well-established truth very hard to swallow: Who does not pride themselves on being a good judge of character? Their confidence without competence makes take-up of selection methods that really work almost impossible. When Dr. Sigi Hoenle became the new head of recruitment for top Swiss bank UBS, he decided to change things using our team at PwC to design the process, the "competency-based behavioral interviews," and train the bankers in interviewing. Every banker thought their "gut feel" about

---

[1] These chat interviews were rarely combined with more predictive methods. Usually they were the only method of selection.

[2] There are 100 years of research and tens of thousands of studies. One landmark review, Wiesner and Cronshaw, placed the validity coefficient at .20 (with 1.00 being a perfect score).

[3] Pfeffer, J., & Sutton, R. (2011, Sep. 3). Trust the evidence, not your instincts, *New York Times*. Retrieved from http://www.nytimes.com/2011/09/04/jobs/04pre.html?_r=0.

people was a better judge than the "HR bureaucracy" to which they were being subjected. Bankers earning large, six-figure sums are not easily bludgeoned by HR: Compliance was nearly zero.

Let us consider the waste. How many unproductive "chat" interviews happen per day in the business world?[4] What does this cost businesses worldwide in terms of both bad hires and time wasted? This is just one example of a commonplace practice that defies all evidence that it does not work.

There are many more. Stanford Professors Pfeffer and Sutton, authors of *Hard Facts, Dangerous Half-truths & Total Nonsense*, artfully describe the roots of the problem:

> ...almost anyone can claim to be a management expert; a bewildering array of sources—Shakespeare, Billy Graham, Jack Welch, Tony Soprano, fighter pilots—are used to generate management advice... 1) managers are inundated with recommendations and information making separation of wheat from chaff difficult, 2) the quality of evidence is low ("you can get more information on your toothpaste or your cereal than on management interventions on which millions are spent"), 3) half-truths abound, and what works in one complex firm may not work in another, ... 4) personal beliefs (and self-justification) mean we think we know better than the science, 5) evidence is boring, stories sell books, and anecdotes are much more memorable.[5]

So far I have ducked the philosophical challenge—what do you mean by science, particularly science in business?

---

[4] They do produce social value, a sense of comfort for both parties, and an idea of "fit"—"is this person like us around here." (That fit, of course, can be a source of discriminatory bias.) There is also typically a prehire "social interview" process where new colleagues meet the candidate without much power to accept or reject.

[5] Pfeffer, J., & Sutton, R. (2006, Jan.). Evidence-based management. *Harvard Business Review*. Retrieved from https://hbr.org/2006/01/evidence-based-management.

What Is Science?

Despite my love of science, and ten years of post-high-school science education, I could not have defined science any better than Supreme Court Justice Potter's ham-fisted definition of pornography, "I know it when I see it." Although scientific discovery (reported by the media) surrounds us daily, and her offspring gadgets are interwoven with our lives, even trained scientists do not always understand what science is and is not. Science is *not* a corpus of rigid facts about the world: There is no such thing as a scientific fact (and only lay people and the media use this term). The "facts" are really theories; some just have more evidence than others. The statement "climate change is a fact" is false; it is a very good predictive theory based upon overwhelming expertise and evidence. (Even the theory of gravity is just a theory, and while it explains apples falling from trees, it has trouble explaining certain cosmological phenomena.)

If science is not a corpus of indisputable facts, what is it? It is an *experimental, social, learning process* for creating and revising a specific kind of knowledge about cause and effect. It is not infallible; in fact, one of the unique things about *scientific knowledge* is that it is constantly being revised. The idea that science is infallible or that only science produces knowledge is called *scientism*—which is a charge often levelled at people who argue as I do that we need to make more and better use of it in business and in society.

The learning process, science, is a *systematic* method for *creating knowledge* in the form of *explanations* and *testable hypotheses*. The scientific method has the following steps:

1. *Observe* phenomena in a detailed and systematic way. Speculate about how those phenomena are related.
2. Formulate a *hypothesis.* Create a model.
3. *Test* whether that hypothesis makes accurate predictions.
4. *Revise* or discard the hypothesis in the light of disconfirming observations.

As human beings, we perform Steps 1 and 2 in an unsystematic way daily, observing the world and trying to predict it. For example, we observe events and people acting in certain ways, and we generate hypotheses about the circumstances that create the behavior. As an example, autism is frequently diagnosed when children are between the age of one and two, and vaccinations are often administered during the same period. This leads distressed parents to conclude (using *post hoc ergo propter hoc* reasoning) that vaccination causes autism. (It does not, and this turns personal tragedy into a substantial public health risk as diseases eradicated decades ago come roaring back.) What do scientists do that human beings do not routinely do?

The Demarcation between Science and Prescience

This distinction might seem abstract, but I am going to claim that the business world is prescientific the way the natural sciences were before the Scientific Revolution[6] of the 1600s and 1700s. Every physics student learns of the Copernican revolution, which placed the Sun, and not the Earth, at the center of the Solar System. However, Copernicus did not *prove* any such thing. He hypothesized and proposed a model of how such a Solar System would behave, but in prescientific tradition, he left the proof for other astronomers. Proving his ideas took nearly one hundred years.

That is how prescientific (classical and medieval) great thinkers operated. They observed, had brilliant insights, dreamed up hypotheses and models, and generally made stuff up then stopped (after Step 2 of the scientific method). *The idea of testing a hypothesis, using our senses and rational faculties was what was revolutionary about the Scientific Revolution.* Even Aristotle developed scientific hypotheses that we know to be nonsense. For example, he believed that the function of the brain was to cool the blood, and that women had fewer teeth than men did. As philosopher Bertrand Russell quipped, "Aristotle could have avoided the mistake of thinking that women have fewer teeth than men, by the simple device of asking Mrs. Aristotle to keep her mouth open while he counted." In those days, and up to the time of Galileo, such testing of ideas was not commonplace.

---

[6] Because political revolutions happens in months or years, the term *revolution* is somewhat misleading when applied to science—because the *revolution* (as much as that term applies) took at least 200 years.

How Is Business Like Aristotelian and Copernican Science?

Take two excellent books, Kotter's *Leading Change* and Christensen's *The Innovators Dilemma*, as examples. Their frameworks are assembled from the authors' (substantial) experience, intellect, scholarly attitude, and superb skills at reducing complex phenomena to their essentials. The authors perform Steps 1 and 2 of the scientific process masterfully: (1) observing and speculating, and (2) hypothesizing and model building.

Where, though, is the testing and revision of hypotheses? If you cannot, or do not, test the model, how do we discriminate between Kotter's ideas and from those of my highly paid pseudoprofessor who had yet to finish college?

To prove Kotter's Step 1, "Establish a sense of urgency," you would have to prove that it was necessary (*that change would fail without it*). I am not sure that urgency is necessary, and the notion of "burning platform" (which is the kind of urgency often discussed) is utterly harmful (as discussed in Chapter 2, "From Change Fragility to Change-Agility"). Did Cisco "establish a sense of urgency" when they were acquiring one company per quarter? Do each of Google's product innovations require an injection of "urgency"? Perhaps Professor Kotter is right, about that step and the seven others, but there is no evidence other than an almost universal acceptance of the idea and anecdote.[7] Again, the plural of anecdote is not data, and overwhelming consensus is not proof. Humans have a long history of being unanimously wrong about many things.

What I mean by "business is prescientific" is that we grant validity to ideas without using science to validate them. This resembles pre-Enlightenment[8] science, more than what we understand to be science today. Pick a model, any model: Situational Leadership, Porter's Five Forces, McKinsey's 7-S, Theory Z management, Matrix management.

---

[7] I do not dispute the usefulness of some of the model, and can no more claim it is wrong than others may claim it is right. This is merely the assertion that the model's considerable insights have never been turned into hypotheses, tested, and revised.

[8] The core idea of the Enlightenment was to think for oneself, rather than place one's faith in the proclamations of authority (what Kings, the clergy, and the aristocracy would have us believe).

Which, if any of them, offer more than just anecdotal verification of their findings? They were all created using Steps 1 and 2 of the scientific method, but passed on Steps 3 and 4.

All those models are interesting ideas based on lots of observation. However, in the prescientific paradigm, when the predictive power of theories is not tested, and *little or nothing* is validated scientifically, how do we discriminate truth from fiction, good from bad, and useful from harmful? We rely on "face validity" (it looks about right), the source (how famous, which business school), popularity (the *New York Times* best-seller list), number of tweets or followers, testimony (what our friends think about it), and perhaps even how snappy the title is (never).

To return to our model from the introduction (shown in Figure 9.1), we have sometimes "hard-to-apply" academic research in the upper-left quadrant, pseudoscience and myth in the lower-left quadrant, and many useful yet unvalidated canonical change models in the lower-right quadrant. The project of science-based leadership is to work hard to make tools and models based on (sometimes arcane) academic research useful; to validate or discard the pseudoscience models of the lower left quadrant; to subject the commonly used models in the lower-right quadrant to much higher standards of evaluation; and to refine, pilot, and continue to validate tools in the upper-right quadrant.

Although science is not easy in complex human systems, we cannot afford to throw our hands in the air and give up. It might take decades, but it is a game worth playing and winning. It took one hundred years to prove Copernicus right (and about fifty to prove some of Einstein's theories). The fact that models and theories are hard to prove today, with today's research methods (and today's attitude toward evidence in business), should not prevent us from insisting upon its importance. Much nonsense persists in the change world (such as "unfreeze, change, refreeze") because they were introduced by someone of formidable intellect (like Kurt Lewin), and we change experts,[9] as practitioners/researchers, have been too intellectually lazy to challenge ideas from big-name sources.

---

[9] I mean to point the finger at myself in this criticism. For two decades, I have been talking about "burning platforms," and "unfreezing," and "sense of urgency."

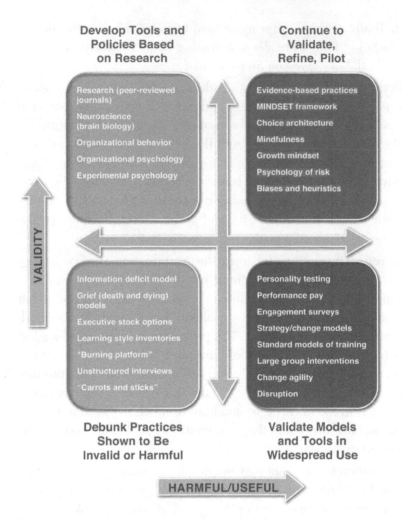

Figure 9.1 Change leadership needs to move toward increased validity and accountability even though it will take decades.

Figure 9.2 proposes the journey to "science-based craft." In my view, most businesses fall between levels one and two, but that many leading business are changing their culture and operating practices to ones where *experimentation, hypothesis testing,* and *analytics* drive decision making. The journey I propose, that many businesses have to make, begins by first stamping out antiscience and pseudoscience.

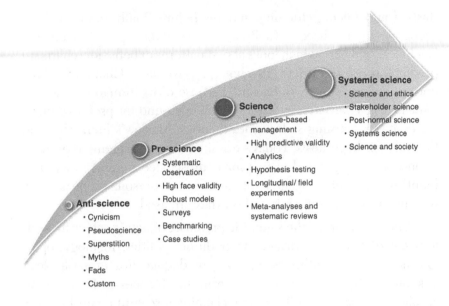

Figure 9.2 Evolution of a science-based craft.

Antiscience and Pseudoscience

"Primum non nocere." (First, do no harm.)

—Hippocractic Corpus

Before looking at the costs to business, what are antiscience and pseudoscience?

Pseudoscience pretends to be science. Sometimes it is benign, and sometimes it is harmful. I had dinner with a professional astrologer once who pulled out an 800-page book of scientific tables to tell me Neptune was an important influence in my birth, so I, of course, had daddy issues. He combined astrological pseudoscience with Freudian pseudoscience rather artfully. I recently had a debate with a world-famous nutritionist who claimed that the alkalinity (pH) of certain foods meant that they gave the body more oxygen. The food choices were sensible enough (green vegetables), but the science was pure *bubkes*. Even Steve Jobs, says biographer Walter Isaacson, eschewed the advice of friends and doctors, favoring pseudoscience therapies (fasting and juicing) for nine months before finally (and too late) accepting their advice.[10] In finance, a candidate pseudoscience is "technical analysis," which looks at past patterns of behavior (charts) to predict future stock prices. Psychology, as we say in Chapter 6, "Misunderstanding Human Behavior," because of its immature status as a science, is a particularly fertile breeding ground for pseudoscience: for example, learning styles, grief theories, Maslow's hierarchy, and the catharsis hypothesis. Today's candidates for management pseudoscience are exaggerated claims for neuroscience: "culture measurement" instruments, engagement surveys, and personality tests. How scientific these are depends on how they are used.

Antiscience drops the scientific pretense, rejecting scientific findings out of hand and preferring tradition, politics, ideology, opinion, nonscientific authority, folklore, or dogma. For example, lead is known to be a poisonous neurotoxin, but businesses kept lead in gasoline and paint for 60 years by claiming a scientific anti-business conspiracy was at work. When a snowy day hits New England and a climate change denier cites that as proof that tens of thousands of scientists are wrong, that is antiscience. (If there were good arguments against climate change, a snowy day would not be among them.) Recall that in the Deepwater Horizon case, one of the key actors, when asked why he ignored the model that suggested the well was in peril, offered some antiscience in his Congressional testimony: "... it is only a model." Doubtless true, but he forgot "and I'm only a human being," preferring his antiscience gut to the model's warnings. As mentioned in Chapter 8, "The Science of Changing Hearts and Minds," the antiscientist engages in "motivated reasoning," and rather than change his opinions in the face of evidence, he strengthens his views. This is not to say that science and scientists should always have the final say on every subject, but one of the most important public debates, *and one that must happen in business*, is "When do we trust science, and when do we look for answers elsewhere?"

What do antiscience and pseudoscience cost? Here are two examples: the first example from public policy, the next one from business.

---

[10] The five-year survival rate for Jobs' type of pancreatic cancer, if caught before metastasis and treated conventionally, is 87 percent.

The Financial Costs of Pseudoscience and Antiscience

Between 2006 and 2010, spending on performance based pay for teachers in the United States grew to $439 million from $99 million. The assumption is that failing schools and struggling students are caused (in some significant way) by lack of teacher motivation and that paying teachers more will motivate them. *Bubkes*. There is zero correlation between teacher performance-related pay and student performance.[11] Pay-for-performance schemes that make teachers accountable for results over which they have at best partial control simply demotivates them (and presumably drives good teachers away from "difficult" schools where they will find it hard to perform).

In business, the use of options to incentivize managers and drive company performance is widespread: 97 percent of S&P 500 companies granted options to their top executives.[12] Options cost shareholders money, so they ought to work, but Pfeffer and Sutton[13] report: "One review of more than 220 studies concluded that equity ownership had no consistent effects on financial performance." A study by Moody's concluded that incentive pay packages "can create an environment that ultimately leads to fraud and skew compensation strongly toward the most senior executives."[14] (In 1965, the CEO-to-worker compensation ratio was 18.3-to-1; by 2000, it was over 400-to-1.) Options may lead to risk-seeking behaviors, the sort of behaviors that caused the collapse of 2008, or focus executive attention on stock market perception and expectations and away from rational drivers of success—how things appear to Wall Street analysts and traders becomes a factor in decision making.

---

[11] There is a link between teacher pay (not performance related) and attracting high-quality teachers to the profession. See Loeb, S., & Page, M. (2000, Aug.). Examining the link between teacher wages and student outcomes. *The Review of Economics and Statistics, 82*(3), 393–408.

[12] Hall, B., & Murphy, K. (2003, Jun.). *The trouble with stock options.* (Working Paper–9784). Location: National Bureau of Economic Research

[13] Pfeffer, J., & Sutton, R. (2006). *Hard facts, dangerous half-truths, & total nonsense: Profiting from evidence-based management.* Boston: HBS Press, p. 11.

[14] Ibid, p. 10.

Equity options are not, by any means, a free ride that magically aligns executive behavior with shareholder interests.[15] Even if they definitively did so, it is not clear whether those kinds of incentive structures benefit anyone apart from the recipients. If the effect of options on motivation, or behavior, and on financial performance is questionable (or at least deeply contested), and the potential negative effects significant, how did 97 percent of S&P 500 companies adopt them?[16]

Many people believe that paying for performance will work in virtually any organization, so it is used again and again to solve problems, even where evidence shows it is ineffective. The evidence around individual performance-based pay in "knowledge" businesses suggests it reduces performance, not increases it.[17] By contrast, the evidence on the effectiveness of team-based compensation is much better.[18] Shifting from one to the other requires substantial changes to HR policies and systems, and HR departments have been slow to make the shift suggested by the evidence.

Saving Money by Stamping out Antiscience

To stamp out antiscience, we need to change culture, and culture change is partly changing the way we talk. When confronted by evidence, research, statistics, or science, the antiscientist will leap to one of the following logical fallacies:

---

[15] They are beneficial in attraction and retention, and they may be tax-efficient ways of compensating staff depending on current tax and accounting laws. However, they are only beneficial in attraction and retention because it is culturally accepted—the notion that they are good for performance appears to be fiction.

[16] They are probably stuck with them now because they are expected by senior hires, and few businesses seem courageous enough to drop them. Nobody thinks big Wall Street bonuses benefit the financial system (because of their effect on risk behavior), yet seven- and eight-figure bonuses are still part of the culture.

[17] For an illustrative review of a very hot topic (about which entire books are written), see Desai, M. (2012, March). The incentive bubble. *Harvard Business Review*.

[18] See Cacioppe, R. (1999). Using team-individual reward and recognition strategies to drive organizational success. *Leadership and Organizational Development Journal*, 20(6), pp. 322–331.

- **Appeal to tradition**—A deeply cherished practice is challenged by evidence (for example, "But we have always done it this way")

- **Appeal to personal experience**—A statistical finding is challenged with a personal anecdote (for example, "I know the engagement surveys suggest people are unhappy, but everyone I talk to seems fine")

- **Appeal to common sense**—This is usually used by people who know nothing about a topic (for example, "But everybody knows that individual bonuses drive performance")

- **Appeal to prejudice**—Used to criticize people and institutions, not methodologies (for example, "You can't trust this research; marketing always produces these crazy findings.")

- **Appeal to common practice**—Claiming what other businesses do must be correct (for example, "I see the ROI does not clear our hurdle rate, but all our competitors are investing here")

- **Appeal to uniqueness (also known as special pleading)**— Declaring our specialness renders us immune from the laws of probability or science (for example, "I know the average cost overrun is 45 percent, but this project is different")

It is not that statistics never lie, that research is never biased, that evidence is never misinterpreted, or that science is never wrong. It is *essential to challenge evidence*, but challenging a body of evidence with individual anecdote or opinion is pure hubris. Rooting out antiscience in business means rooting out those knee-jerk prejudices that humans have when confronted by facts that challenge their beliefs. Simply by stamping out those conversational antiscience modes of thinking, business will rely less on folklore and myths. One way to do that is to eliminate those antiscience modes of thinking.

Speculate for a moment on what you think the costs are, in your business, and in global business generally, of those modes of thinking and the resulting wasteful or harmful policies.

From Antiscience to a Scientific Mindset

"We need to overcome hunch and intuition with empirical evidence.... We can start with a hunch or strong belief, but we act on it through experiment.... We've gone from the introduction of experimentation as a technique to a culture of experimentation as a business discipline." (emphasis mine)

—Gary Loveman, CEO, Caesars Entertainment

Through the years of school and university, and long into our professional careers, we get rewarded for "knowing stuff" and communicating to others what we know and how much. This "know-it-all" persona is particularly prevalent in my own profession, consulting, where we get very large fees for imparting the benefits of our (self-proclaimed) gargantuan intellects and wisdom (requiring as Dilbert suggests, an auxiliary brain to carry it all around).

The scientific mindset, in ideal form, is the antithesis of this. Even though scientists typically know an enormous amount about their subject, their focus is principally on *what they do not know*, and *not* on what they do know. Richard Feynman, my favorite physicist, understood science and scientists as trading in degrees of uncertainty: "When a scientist doesn't know the answer to a problem, he is ignorant. When he has a hunch as to what the result is, he is uncertain. *And even when he is pretty darn sure of what the result is going to be, he is still in some doubt."*[19] The more you learn, the more you discover you do not know.

The scientific mindset is an ideal; not all scientists have it all the time, and many nonscientists do have it. It is particularly evident in children, as they tinker, explore, and experiment in their early years. There are three dimensions: skepticism, curiosity/wonder, and experimentation:

---

[19] From a lecture delivered to the National Academy of Sciences (U.S.) in 1955 entitled "The Value of Science," downloaded from the University of Washington Physics Department: http://www.phys.washington.edu/users/vladi/phys216/Feynman.html.

- **Skepticism**—Skepticism has been given a bum rap today, sometimes associated with a mind closed to new ideas of any kind, that is, confused with cynicism. Its original meaning was different—it meant not judging claims (either positively or negatively) until evidence was provided. The proper meaning of "I'm skeptical" is therefore closer to "I am not sure about that" rather than "I disbelieve." *Scientific skepticism* is a combination of this not-knowing, suspending judgment, while maintaining faith that exploration and experimentation can provide better answers. It seeks the Aristotelian mean between the extremes of gullibility (anything goes) and cynicism (nothing goes). It is metaphorically an immune system for ideas: When hyperactive, the immune system may reject useful transplants or kill existing cells (the autoimmune response); when underactive, too many harmful substances are allowed to prosper. I maintain that the immune system of the business community is insufficiently discriminating, allowing new ideas to enter because they are new, because they sound good, or because they come from someone popular.

- **Curiosity/wonder**—The spouse of scientific skepticism is the hunger for finding things out. This essential *curiosity* and the willingness to ask questions rather than proclaim expertise and knowledge is antithetical to many business rituals. (Replay a few meetings and assess the telling/asking ratio in your head as a thought experiment.)

This curiosity allows for the discovery of "unknown unknowns" and the finding of knowledge in surprising places. In 1928, Alexander Fleming's sandwich crumbs were clumsily dropped into his bacterial cultures, destroying weeks of work. He could have been forgiven for tossing both the cultures and the sandwich out in anger, but his deep curiosity about nature was triggered. Why would breadcrumbs kill bacteria? Something called faintly to him, and investigation of his breadcrumbs found that they were moldy, and the mold had a substance called penicillin—perhaps the greatest life-saving drug of all time.

The curiosity entails asking open questions as well as closed questions, which is one of the cultural shifts that are so important to extracting value from big data implementations. It allows discovery of new ideas in the "unknown unknowns" realm, as well as the "known unknowns."

- **Experimentation**—Experimentation is the antidote to skepticism, and the food that sates curiosity's hunger. Most businesses have areas where they experiment formally, in R&D, or in marketing, but shy away from experimenting with everyday rituals: email, meetings, calendar management, feedback, coaching, personal workflow, and work design. Those rituals that take up most of working life are great candidates for "hacks," but there is comfort in ritual. The reluctance to experiment, the desire (fantasy) to get things right the first time, is sometimes harmful. Churchill summed up the experimental mindset, "Success consists of going from failure to failure without loss of enthusiasm."

From Prescience to Evidence-Based Management (EBM)

A mere 120 years ago, medicine was pure craft—few of its practices were based on the still young biological sciences, and science (such as the germ theory of disease) only permeated the medical community slowly. Just as I regard the social sciences as relatively young compared to physics, biology, and chemistry, I regard business the way I regard nineteenth century medicine: still largely a craft and still reliant upon a great deal of superstition.

However, even 20 years ago, medical practice was thought of as "an art" and medical decisions were based on obsolete knowledge, expert opinion, personal experience, custom, and habit. (Sound familiar?) Medicine, because of its life-and-death nature and grounding in the hard sciences of biology and chemistry, ought to be very scientific (that is, evidence-based) in its approach, but until *evidence-based medicine* appeared on the scene in about 1998, medicine, too, was shy about subjecting widely-accepted practices to scientific scrutiny. Physicians treated with a particular surgery because they were good at it or comfortable with it, prescribed an antibiotic (or other drug) because patients expected it, or recommended diagnostic tests because doing so had become routine. Evidence-based medicine, "integrating *practitioner expertise* with the conscientious, explicit, and *judicious use of current best evidence* in business decision making," was a radical new idea that began to transform the way medicine is practiced.

The evidence-based idea is slowly spreading to other fields, including public policy, education, and now business. In medicine, progress has been slow but steady over the last two decades. Today, estimates for what percentage of procedures or prescriptions conform to the strictest standards for evidence are still only in the region of 35 percent. If I may hazard a guess, the uptake of evidence-based practices in business is less than 5 percent.[20]

Like doctors, business leaders can see what they do as art, or craft, rather than applied science—yet there is room for both. According to one of EBM's experts, Professor Rob Briner of the University of Bath, the essential criteria of the evidence-based decision (shown in Figure 9.3) include not just current (evidence-based) *theory*, but professional *experience*, hard *data* from the organizational context, and *stakeholder* concerns (which determine how easy or difficult implementation may be).

The typical leader today relies too heavily on professional experience, uses too little hard data, disregards too many stakeholders, and has too little good theory at his disposal.

This combination of science with professional judgment, feel, intuition, care, and hard data is the target at which we (as practitioners) have to aim to solve the problem of failing change, and the bigger problem generally of business waste. The trend is already established. Use of analytics is accelerating, and that means more data-driven decision making and fewer hunches. Evidence-based management complements analytics by adding validated cause-and-effect relationships between policies and effects.

---

[20] Nobody seems to know, which is, of course, part of the problem.

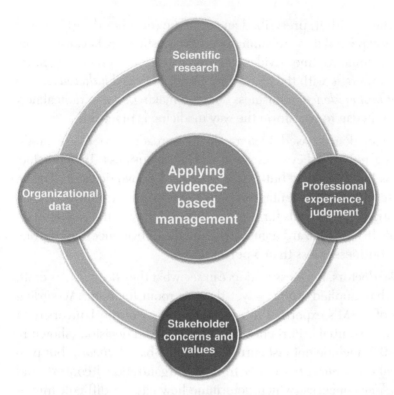

Figure 9.3 Evidence-based decision making weighs data, theory, experience, and stakeholders.

Types of Evidence

There remains the substantial question, one that has troubled very big thinkers for millennia, of what constitutes evidence. How do we know something works? Every time a leader pulls a lever to effect change in a business, she relies on a theory of cause-and-effect—that the lever she pulls, X, will produce the effect she wishes, Y. We want X to be based upon the best evidence available. So how do we know?

The pyramid shown in Figure 9.4 presents a frightening look[21] at what constitutes evidence in scientific circles, and just how far business has to go: We rely mostly on evidence from the bottom layers of the pyramid.

---

[21] This ranking is a generalization. A well-researched case study may provide better evidence than a poor-quality observational study further up the hierarchy.

Figure 9.4 Hierarchy of evidence.

Professional Experience

At the very bottom, the lowest quality of evidence, are the generalizations we make from *experience*. Human beings need to believe in themselves, so it is easy to persuade ourselves that what we do is effective, making us blind to how it may be ineffective. Cognitive biases, as we saw, skew perception in our favor. We are superb at recognizing patterns, yet we overdo this pattern recognition making up patterns (and cause and effect) to explain the workings of the world (the narrative fallacy). There is so little science used in business decision making that, as Carl Sagan feared, myths have found fertile ecological niches.

I once worked with an executive vice president at American Express who used to make his team of SVP reports compete with each other, sometimes asking two people to perform the same task (without telling them). His theory was "creating competition between team members increases productivity" and his "evidence" was (in effect) how successful he had been. He had risen far and fast in the Amex hierarchy and was tipped for promotion one day to the very top, yet could not see the chaos he caused and how he killed motivation around him. He was a clever and able leader in many respects, but deluded when it came to evaluating some of his own practices. As Taleb suggests in *Fooled By Randomness,* "...when things go our way we reject the lack of certainty."[22]

Expert Opinion

Next to the bottom is *expert opinion,* on which we rely extensively in business, from books, from business education, and from consultants. The critical questions are:

- How do you know someone is an expert? What makes them an expert?
- What is the source of the expert's expertise (if research, what kind, anecdotal, or more rigorous)?

Case Studies

Further up the hierarchy are *case studies,* an in-depth examination of a single company or scenario. There are several warring camps who debate how useful case studies are. I believe they are useful for teaching people how to apply general skills in context (where it matters), but I do not think case studies tell us much about cause and effect, and neither do I think a case study in one business says reliably what will work in another. I once ran a large culture change program for just one (of several dozen) business units at KPMG. The metrics (revenue per partner, average deal size, and total revenue) skyrocketed relative to all the other business units. Sadly, from my point of view, the new CEO was doing many (many) other things. I

---

[22] Taleb, N. (2005). *Fooled by randomness: The hidden role of change in life and in the markets.* New York: Random House. Ebook edition.

could not have said, "Hey, don't touch anything for a few years and let's see whether this culture change malarkey really works." Of all the projects in my consulting career, this one may have produced the most dramatic results, and it is a case study I am proud to share, but the quality of the evidence is still moderate.

Surveys and Benchmarking

Surveys are a more systematic way of gathering evidence. The evidence they gather is often opinion, and the plural of opinions is not data. They tend to be descriptive, and not directly aimed at producing cause-and-effect relationships (although they are used in that way). The most rigorous looking and very common kind of survey is benchmarking: the commonsense (but flawed) idea that studying practices in other businesses will help "at home." Professors Sutton and Pfeffer put it like this: "The logic behind what works at top performers, why it works, and what will work elsewhere is barely unraveled, resulting in mindless imitation... People copy the most visible, obvious, or frequently least important practices."[23]

Not all benchmarking is invalid, but caution must be used because it excludes contextual factors (other variables) that may be driving performance. In *The Halo Effect,* IMD Professor Phil Rosenzweig explains how surveys and benchmarking are flawed. He painstakingly shows how surveys of people in high-performing firms rate internal factors very positively, and in low-performing firms rate the same factors negatively. In other words, when your company is doing well (take Apple today, or Enron two decades ago), you are more likely to respond affirmatively to questions such as "my company rewards creativity and innovation," "my company has world-class talent practices," or "my company takes a strategic approach to supplier relationships."

Where might you be more engaged today, working for Samsung, which bounces from success to success in the mobile phone industry, or working for Research In Motion (that makes the BlackBerry) and struggling to survive? Now go back ten years, when BlackBerry was wiping the floor with competitors in the smartphone business—where

---

[23] Pfeffer & Sutton (2006), p 7.

would you have been more engaged, Samsung or Research In Motion? It is a small wonder that "research" finds that engagement is correlated with company performance!

In Rosenzweig's estimation, the researcher finds the correlations they look for. These so-called "predictive measures" of success are actually post hoc, halo-influenced, emotive judgments: "We are doing great, and I feel good about working here." He continues,

> How did Walmart become such a success? Perhaps it was the strategy of "everyday low prices," or a relentless obsession with detail, or a culture that gets ordinary people to do their best, or a sophisticated use of information technology in supply chain management, or bare-knuckled approach to squeezing suppliers...? Are some of these explanations right? Are all of them right? Which are most important? Do they only work in combination?[24]

Cohort Studies

Cohort studies are given a lot of credit for robustness by business practitioners. *In Search of Excellence* and *Built to Last* are two excellent books that reveal what is best about cohort studies, but also what is worst. The books do a great job of distilling corporate success and longevity down a few inspirational messages, such as "Create a strong, coherent organizational culture." These are excellent books, but nothing they say about cause and effect can be taken seriously, partly because of the halo effect, and partly because of the way they select high performers is unscientific.[25] Professor Freek Vermeulen of the London Business School offered the following critique:

> A common formula to create a best-selling business book is to start with a list of eye-catching companies that have been outperforming their peers for years. This has the added

---

[24] Rosenazweig, P. (2007). *The halo effect...and the eight other business delusions that deceive managers*. New York: Free Press. Ebook edition.

[25] Over which time period is high-performance relevant? Ten years? (Think of Research in Motion.) Twenty years? (Think of Enron.) Thirty years? (Think of Digital Equipment Corporation.)

advantage of creating an aura of objectivity because the list is constructed using objective, quantitative data (such as financial performance). Subsequently, the management thinker takes the list of superior companies and examines (usually in a rather less objective way) what these companies have in common. Surely—is the assumption and foregone conclusion—what these companies have in common must be a good thing?[26]

Unfortunately, even innocent-looking, commonsense type advice such as "strong organizational cultures drive performance" may be half-true. As Vermeulen says, "We now know from academic research that a strong culture is often the result of a period of high performance, rather than its cause."[27]

Perhaps the most damning critique of cohort studies is what happens to the "excellent" companies over time—several excellent companies went bust and while Peters and Waterman picked some winners (Walmart and Intel), they also picked some duds (Wang and Atari).

Observational Studies

Observational studies can be painstakingly conducted and examine correlations over long periods. Most people "know" that correlation does not prove cause. The observation "open umbrellas" is highly correlated with the observation "rain," but umbrellas do not cause rain. Police are observed in high-crime areas, and the correlation between frequency of police patrol and frequency of crime is very high—yet police do not cause crime. (Furthermore, if you try to decrease the crime rate by lowering the number of police, you will get a nasty surprise.) Real-world examples such as this make using correlation as a proxy for cause seem laughable, yet when you read

---

[26] Vermeulen, F. (2013, Aug. 23). Beware the sirens of management pseudo-science. *Harvard Business Review*. Retrieved from https://hbr.org/2013/08/beware-the-sirens-of-managemen.

[27] Ibid.

"scientific research studies show" in the business and wider media, you are usually (at best) reading a report of an observational study.

As you saw with engagement research, it is unclear which way the arrow of causation points. Yet, the employee engagement industry generates many hundreds of millions of dollars in survey and consultant fees worldwide. According to Professor Rob Briner of the University of Bath, 100 percent of the research (and they talk a lot about research) is from correlational studies.[28]

Controlled Experiment

At the very highest level of the evidence hierarchy, we have the controlled experiment and the meta-analysis (which aggregates the findings of many controlled experiments statistically). The controlled experiment is the most scientifically valid way to test a theory such as, if I do X, Y will happen. You do X to one group, nothing to the other, and see how often Y happens. If Y happens only when you do X,[29] you have excellent evidence that X causes Y (under the conditions of your experiment).

In medicine, the gold standard is the RCT (randomly controlled trial). People are randomly assigned to groups (and neither the researchers nor the subjects know who is in which group). Some are given the drug (or procedure) and others a sugar pill (or other placebo). Results are measured and if the drug performs better than placebo, we can have some confidence in it. Sampling is important, if you do this with too few subjects, you cannot be sure whether another factor caused the improvement. Using big samples irons out those random variations, but even professional researchers systematically underestimate the size of sample needed to establish a causal relationship with confidence.[30]

---

[28] Briner, R. (2013). What is employee engagement and does it matter?: An evidence-based approach. Institute for Employment Studies White Paper.

[29] Or happens much more.

[30] See Chapter 1 of *The Signal and the Noise*, by Nate Silver, for an excellent explanation (and the most interesting contemporary treatment of predictive statistics for lay people).

At the scale of entire businesses, the precision of a well-conducted RCT is impossible. You cannot "hold enough things still" to know that your intervention is the only effect (unlike the car being fixed by the mechanic). Nor can you build a big enough sample to iron out the substantial variations between different companies.

Fortunately, at a different scale, the level of teams or individuals, the disciplines of organizational psychology, social psychology, organizational behavior, and organizational development do conduct rigorous controlled experiments that produce findings with the kind of causal validity that we are after ("if you do X, Y will happen"). Such controlled experiments are also possible in marketing, particularly Internet marketing where your sample sizes may be in the tens of thousands. When experiments are run on large random samples, with control groups, and on testable hypotheses such as "structured, situational, behavioral interviews predict on-job performance better than unstructured, conversational interviews," you can be reasonably sure of your results.

The unfortunate fact is that few practitioners read the well-conducted research studies. Stories sell more books. The arid, nuanced, carefully worded conclusions of researchers seem boring next to immodest claims such as *The Revolutionary Book That Will Change the Way You Do Business* (*The Innovator's Dilemma*). This leaves us with a situation where the lower right (useful, not valid) of our validity versus usefulness diagram is heavily populated, the upper left (valid, but not useful) is heavily populated, and the upper right (valid and useful) is nearly an empty set.

I have painted a picture of a management world that uses evidence mostly from the bottom two rungs of the evidence hierarchy, management education that resembles the oral traditions of preliterate societies and a world where individual opinion counts for more than research.

Evidence-based management is the methodological adjunct to the scientific mindset (skepticism, curiosity, experimentation). The leader as scientist cannot just think like a scientist, she needs to act like one. The scientific method (evidence-based management) is an important way to do that.[31] In the opening chapter, I asserted two things about change knowledge——that it rested on weak foundations, but where it rested on stronger foundations, it was either in the wrong hands, or unused. What can a manager do to improve upon this situation?

Implementing Evidence-Based Management

EBM is not the idea that businesses drench themselves in basic research and hope to find something useful. It is, according to Rob Briner, about solving concrete problems and "pulling" research toward them. In gathering evidence about what might solve a specific problem, there will perhaps be a mixture of anecdote/experience, case-study, and stronger research that can be weighed for its relevance and usability. Critically, the most rigorous methods possible should be used to evaluate how well the decision or solution worked in practice.

The biggest problem implementing evidence-based management is that we cannot wait around for every policy or idea to be validated. (That will take decades.) We have to get on with delivering results. However, if you believe, as I do, that we cannot afford multibillion dollar businesses managing themselves on folklore (like preliterate indigenous societies), or on gurus (like medieval society where knowledge was held only by high-priests), surveys, benchmarking, and anecdotal studies (the kind of science performed before the scientific revolution in the 1600s), then perhaps you are ready for a change? *Science is principally a learning process*—an evidence-based learning process. In my view, we have not been learning. If there is any truth at all to the assertion that more than 50 percent of change programs fail, we are doing something wrong, and perhaps thinking about the whole matter in an entirely wrong way.

---

[31] This is not argument for blind acceptance of anything that bears the label research. As you will see shortly, that word is misused a great deal. Neither is this an argument that science can solve all problems today, or in the future. Science says nothing about morality (nor aesthetics, nor meaning, nor relationships, nor many cultural phenomena). Neither is *science-based craft* argument that the only criteria for evaluating a situation need be scientific, or that science is infallible (in fact, it is by definition fallible), and blind faith in the wrong kind of science is as harmful as blind faith in superstition.

Individual leaders can start small with some of these steps:

1. Observe where knowledge and expertise comes from. Whom do we trust and why? What are our typical standards for evidence?

2. Learn the essentials of what constitutes good evidence, mediocre evidence, and no evidence. When faced with a decision or policy choice, make a note to yourself into which category what you are doing falls.

3. Challenge consultants and advisers. They get paid a lot of money to sell you solutions. Begin asking, "What is the evidence base for what you are proposing?" In general, they will provide you with stories from other clients. Listen politely, and then ask again if they have any evidence.

4. We need more critical thinking. When we use long-standing metaphors, such as "burning platform," we must ask: Is the metaphor apt? Is it useful? Are there adverse consequences?

5. Confirm, verify, and criticize theories, *even those that are undisputed*. I spent a decade talking about "learning styles" and teaching Kotter's eight steps. I was horrified to discover that learning styles are a psychological myth, and my current critical reflection on the eight steps is that they are not all valid, and not always useful. (See Chapter 6.)

6. Be truthful about the scientific status of what we do. We have to do something on Monday morning, even if the evidence for what we do is not robust. We can be realistic about its scientific status; commit to the possibility of improving that scientific status even if it is not obvious how to do so.

7. Hold ourselves to higher standards of evaluation. Stanford's Jeffrey Pfeffer says, "Consultants get rewarded for selling work, sometimes rewarded for doing good work, and rarely—if ever—rewarded for evaluating whether their work actually improved things."[32]

8. Base what we do upon the best science available and not myth, pseudoscience, pop science, or fad theories. (See Chapter 6.)

---

[32] Pfeffer & Sutton (2006), p. 33.

9. Create cultures that insist on the scientific mindset, and using the scientific method. Gary Loveman, CEO of Caesars Entertainment, says, "You can get fired for three things, stealing, sexual harassment, and running an experiment without a control group."[33]

10. Steer management reading and management education toward evidence-based books and courses and away from the feel-good, or guru books. Skip the next inspirational conference on "Disruptive Innovation" or "Employee Engagement."

Still, you will face many problems. Even medicine, 20 years after EBM became a thing, still struggles with the attitudes of many physicians who prefer their own established practices to those shown to be better. Some doctors that I have interviewed (usually younger ones) embrace it wholeheartedly, and use their Web-enabled research skills to great advantage in patient care. Some older doctors feel otherwise, that evidence-based medicine may stifle innovation; some feel that the "art" is crowded out and some espouse antiscience views ("You can't really trust the research").

With the *gradual raising of standards,* individual managers can begin to transform their practices, and over time, entire organizations may be shifted in this helpful direction.

A few implementation troubles will be:

- Business culture is—at best—ambivalent, and sometimes hostile to evidence-based approaches. Your colleagues might not thank you for asking what evidence they may have that a certain practice adds value.

- There is a paucity of evidence-based practices available in most business sub-disciplines.

- Getting colleagues and team members to do their homework before they try something runs contrary to the prevalent tradition of intellectual laziness. (As Jack Welch said, "In God we trust, everybody else bring data."[34])

---

[33] Ibid., p. 15.

[34] Welch may have been quoting W. Edwards Deming (1900-1993), a management thinker many decades ahead of his time.

- People like their myths and prefer to think of management as *craft* and not *science.*

- Although *science* is a hot word today, it is overused, and misused. Internet articles frequently claim, "Science shows..." (no scientist would ever say that) and many people have their pet theories validated by what they read and disregard the rest.

Business desperately needs a go-to resource on evidence-based management, something like The Cochrane Collaboration which, founded 20 years ago, is the largest database of medical information in the world, reviewing the evidence base from everything from Vitamin C, to herbal remedies, to the most advanced surgical and medical protocols. Similar work is under way in the area of public policy; the goal of evidence-based policy is to make policy and spending decisions based *not on ideological or political grounds* (!), but on the basis of the best available evidence. There are several Web sites, but they are not yet (in my view) practitioner friendly. There are good books, particularly Pfeffer and Sutton's, but we need to have resources that help practitioners implement validated management practice, and that help validate (or discard) the management practices commonly used.

Despite the parlous state of evidence-based business today, I want to sell this as a 50-year culture change in the entire management/management advice industry, but one that will begin with leaders exacting higher standard from themselves, colleagues, and (mostly) advisers.

To repeat an earlier idea, although science is not easy in complex human systems, we cannot afford to throw our hands in the air and give up. It may take decades, but it is a game worth playing and winning.

Not 1920's Scientific Management, nor 19th Century Positivism

The possibility of scientific leadership (or even scientific management) being useful terms, describing ideas and practices such as data-driven approaches, analytics, evidence-based management, and the scientific mindset (for leaders), may have been forever destroyed by the work of F.W. Taylor, who seized the term "scientific manage-ment" to describe what he did. When I have shared this book's title and philosophy with various change and OD colleagues, some have asked whether the ideas were regressive, not progressive, pointing to Taylor and the positivists.

Taylor did measure and observe things systematically, performing time and motion studies of industrial laborers for whom he appeared to have complete contempt. "The science of handling pig-iron is so great that the man who is...physically able to handle pig-iron and is sufficiently phlegmatic and stupid to choose this for his occupation is rarely able to comprehend the science of handling pig-iron."[35] He also fudged data and made up "adjustments," and the intention of his work was to make smaller the iron cage of bureaucracy—to dehuman-ize and treat workers like animals (optimal levels of feeding, rest, and reward to extract the most from their flesh). Despite Taylor's misan-thropic intentions and dodgy research methods, I share his optimism that we might become increasingly rigorous in how we evaluate busi-ness practices. In that way alone could my philosophy be described as Taylorist.

Positivism was a late 19th century idea that what we can discover and prove with our senses all that was valid *and all that was important.* It was principally a rejection of supernaturalism, metaphysics, and rationalism. The idea was that all of the big and important questions of philosophy could be answered by science. The physicist Werner Heisenberg rejected positivism thus: "The positivists have a simple solution: the world must be divided into that which we can say clearly and the rest, which we had better pass over in silence. But can anyone conceive of a more pointless philosophy, seeing that what we can say clearly amounts to next to nothing? If we omitted all that is unclear we would probably be left with completely uninteresting and trivial tautologies."[36] What I share most with the positivists is their optimism that science will continue to push back the veil of ignorance; where

---

[35] For an excellent treatment, see Chapter 2, "The Pig Iron Tale," in *The Manage-ment Myth: Debunking Modern Business Philosophy,* by Matthew Stewart (2010, W.W. Norton).

[36] Nanshen, R.N. (1972). *Physics and beyond: Encounters and conversations.* New York: Harper and Row, p. 213.

I disagree most is with their hubris, that only subjects that are amenable to scientific enquiry have merit. The human sciences are less rigorous than the physical sciences, but to my mind, that makes them more interesting objects of study, and not less. I see that difference as one of maturity—the human sciences are both harder, and younger than the physical sciences. Perhaps unlike the positivists or Taylor, the core of my interest in science, and in how scientific thinking can improve business practices, is to reduce waste of resources that might be better spent improving the human condition, and to make businesses better places to work and the world that business inhabits a better place to live. Better leaders, better business, better planet.

Leadership, Reason, and Science

To be interested in how humans progress is to be interested in leadership: how we galvanize and connect the minds of those around us and achieve much greater than we can do alone, or than we can yet imagine. We want to characterize, understand, and get better at it and though Plato and Sun Tzu thought about it, it is a baby academic field (60 or 70 years).

There are contemporary perspectives, such as servant leadership, transformative leadership, conscious leadership, charismatic leadership, emotional leadership, authentic leadership, and level-5 leadership. Those contemporary characterizations lean toward leadership's (undeniable) spiritual and emotional dimensions. It is my view that the balance of contemporary discussion on leadership leans too heavily in that direction, and away from what it takes to lead strategizing, critical thinking, envisioning, directing, ideation, decision making, and analysis—the rational ("chess") aspect. This was an understandable and a necessary counterweight to earlier theories that seemed too rationalistic (for example, contingency, transactional, and trait theories). Some authors today even claim that those rational aspects are not really leadership, that leadership is entirely those relational/emotional matters.

When I witness catastrophic business failure (for example, the financial crisis of 2007/2008), missing rational faculties are at least part of the disaster's cause if not most of it. Leadership theories that ignore the rational may be as dangerous as leadership theories that ignore the emotional are callous. Motivated (ideological) reasoning, hubris, blind acceptance, cognitive error impaired rational business decisions at Lehman Brothers busted the 160-year-old bank. While there were moral dimensions to the collapse, it was principally a failure to act rationally.

Some disagree, claiming that excess rationality was at fault in such corporate disasters (and even in moral disasters such as colonialism and eugenics). For these critics, rationality includes a self-superior, blind faith in human reason that permits atrocity in its name. The perspective taken earlier (cognitive biases, complexity, uncertainty) underlines that *the most important dimension of that rationality is appreciating how fragile and limited our rationality can be*. We always have a stance, a position, a perspective—there is no perfectly objective and rational "view from nowhere." We can reason, but we cannot reason ourselves out of the picture. Rationality (the way described here) includes not *just seeing situations, but seeing ourselves seeing them*.

This emphasis on science and rationality does not, as is sometimes suggested, exclude caring about people. I believe, as did physicist Richard Feynman, that to understand something deeply is to care about it more. Understanding human biology and history only deepens appreciation for humanity; understanding ecosystems only increases the sense of wonder and duty to care for the planet; and understanding the cosmos only creates the experience of awe.

Leadership and Farsight

One transition people need to make when moving from manager to leader is to expand the horizon of time they consider from days and weeks to "think further" to years and decades. It is not enough to lead a change program; the "farsight" view proposed here is that leaders need to lead change differently, by focusing on creating an adaptable, agile organization that is not just well-positioned in this decade, but change-capable enough to respond and prosper in the decade beyond.

A good contemporary way of thinking about leadership is that is happens on two planes, a skills plane and a character plane. The character plane captures the essence of Gandhi and Mandela who did not attend skills courses on strategy, team leadership, and negotiation, but whose integrity, presence, ethics, vitality, emotional balance, cognitive agility, self-mastery, vision, commitment, authenticity, and rapport moved nations.

Despite teaching this model for 20 years, I do not think that this skills-character model explains everything we want from a leader. It does not pay sufficient attention to the future, the long view.

Some inventor-leaders seem to be less than exemplary on the skills-character scale: They were usually called "jerks" (mostly worse). Steve Jobs may be the best example. Jobs, says biographer Walter Isaacson, "revolutionized six industries, personal computers, animated movies, music, phones, tablet computing, and digital publishing."[37] Yet, Jobs has also been labeled narcissistic, impossible, erratic, cruel, control freak, and OCD. He neither had the business training we traditionally deliver (he studied calligraphy), nor many of the traditional character attributes from the softer side of leadership (for example, warmth, empathy, other-centeredness).

Much of Jobs' success may depend on the fit between his leadership style and the context in which he led. Leadership coaches and authors today lean very heavily away from the rational toward the emotional. In a recent conversation with one such global leadership expert, he asked (rhetorically) "Would you not rather be led by someone warm, than someone smart?" My response, and perhaps the response of Jobs' engineers was an emphatic "No!" Leadership experts must be very careful about projecting their values onto businesses and people as if they were "correct" visions of leadership—all our training in coaching, counseling, OD, humanistic psychology, and close ties with the self-help, personal growth, human potential, and spirituality movements create a very particular value set. We need to see that value set (call it spiritual, for want of a better word), for what it is—a cultural stance, rather than the orientation to which every leader must aspire.

---

[37] Isaacson, W. (2013). *Steve Jobs*. New York: Simon and Schuster. Ebook edition.

I think the Jobs kind of leader has something special outside the skills-character dimensions, and a dimension of leadership we need, one that builds cathedrals, pyramids, lands people on the moon, and builds today's business monuments—the corporations.

The word "farsight" almost captures the essence of this ability to read the future and create things for people who have not yet been born. Leaders with this faculty spot strategic niches, are skillful tacticians, reason through convoluted situations, make sense of complex patterns, and innovate exceptionally. This ability, to lead with the 10-, 20-, or 30-year view in mind is a rare thing. We remember Kennedy for his 9-year commitment to land on the moon, or Eisenhower for his vision of an Interstate Highway System (which took more than three decades to complete), or Konrad Adenauer and Jean Monnet for their 20-year vision of a united Europe (on a continent that had been at war for millennia). The drafters of the United States Constitution envisioned and saw the potential of a country that would endure for centuries. It is also worth remembering (for those who might cynically point to Europe as a bad example) that these continent-sized experiments in political collaboration take centuries to become stable—the U.S. was torn apart by war 80 years into its history. Nelson Mandela used to jog daily in his closet-sized cell while serving a life sentence. Why? Because, despite being 20 years into a life prison sentence, he was preparing to one day lead his country to freedom. (One might also notice that Mandela's focus on the future provides an inspiring context for in-the-moment personal development.) History may or may not judge Elon Musk either a great visionary, but the chutzpah of Space X's vision, "revolutionizing space technology with the ultimate goal of enabling people to live on other planets" is the kind of long-term perspective very rarely seen in business (and far less in politics).

This kind of leadership farsight, to my mind, leads with one eye on the yet-to-be-written history books. This history-making is the most inspirational type of leadership.

Can this farsight be developed? A novice chess player sees one move ahead, but by studying the game and patterns, she begins to formulate strategies more than ten moves ahead. We know that Bill Gates used to have a "think-week" to cultivate these faculties. Jack Welch used to try to safeguard an hour a day for uninterrupted reflection. Sadly, the two coaching questions that draw the blankest stares from my clients are:

- What is your five-year vision and strategy?
- What do you see as your role in building USA Incorporated, or UK PLC, or Deutscheland AG?

To reiterate a sentiment from the introduction, we need more business (and political) leaders who see beyond the urgent, and who, when they say "the next quarter" sometimes mean the next quarter century. We need to build more "cathedrals," those investments in our future that took half-a-century or longer to complete.

Conclusion—Science-based Leadership and Human Flourishing

Business has a pivotal role to play in continued human flourishing in this century (beyond the day-to-day role of employing people and supplying products they need). Businesses are also the chief consumers of resources, despoilers of habitats, spillers of oil, and poisoners of streams. Commercial pressures (or greed) may launch technologies (drugs, GMOs) before human or ecological safety is adequately established. Yet, if science has a part in securing our future, business must (as always) find a way to scale and deliver the science, through technology. This chapter, "Leading with Science" introduced what I believe to be imperatives, stamping out antiscience and pseudoscience, encouraging a scientific mindset, adopting evidence-based business practices, developing leadership rationality that is cognizant of its own limitations, and finally, leadership farsight.

Business leadership is as difficult a practical discipline as math, science, and philosophy are intellectual disciplines. Developing leaders along the lines suggested in *The Science of Successful Organizational Change* will reassert the importance of good decision making and strategizing (the "chess side") while remembering that reasons alone fail to achieve much (the "people side"). Agile organizations will require less change management firefighting, and the newest and most important change leadership role is creating those *complex adaptive systems* (agile businesses) that surf disruptions rather than getting "axed"[38] by the waves. We have a template for senior leadership development based on some new ideas in cognitive psychology, the psychology of risk, probability theory, complexity science, and analytics, where human beings (as business leaders) intersect with harder-edged subjects. Evidence-based approaches have made inroads in medicine and policymaking, and business should follow. Twenty-first-century human sciences are informing new tactical means of changing behaviors, hearts, and minds.

This is the great win-win for business and humankind: Ethical, efficient, agile businesses are good for human flourishing, and human flourishing is good for business. My hope, not just for business, but also for society, is that more science will nudge twenty-first-century business in the right direction.

---

[38] A heavy wipeout in surfing speak.

Bibliography

Baltic, S. (2013, Oct. 7). Liked or loathed, RUC wields broad influence. *Modern Medicine*. Retrieved from http://www.modernmedicine.com/content/ modernmedicine/modern-medicine-feature-articles/liked-or-loathed-ruc-wields-broad-influence

Batchelor, S. (1998). *Buddhism without beliefs: A contemporary guide to awakening*. New York, NY: Riverhead Books.

Berezow, A. (2012, Jul. 13). Why psychology isn't science. *Los Angeles Times*. Retrieved from http://articles.latimes.com/2012/jul/13/news/la-ol-blowback-pscyhology-science-20120713

Bernstein, P. (1996). *Against the gods: The remarkable story of risk*. New York, NY: Wiley and Sons.

Blenko, M. W., Mankins, M. C., & Rogers, P. (2010, Jul. 30). The key to successful corporate reorganization. *Forbes*. Retrieved from http://www.forbes.com/2010/07/30/corporate-reorganization-abb-ford-leadership-managing-bain.html

Bloch, M., Blumberg, S., & Laartz, J. (2012, October). Delivering large-scale IT projects on time, on budget, and on value. *McKinsey Quarterly*. Retrieved from http://www.mckinsey.com/insights/business_technology/delivering_large-scale_it_projects_on_time_on_budget_and_on_value

Boaz, N., & Fox, E. (2014, March). Change leader, change thyself. *McKinsey Quarterly*. Retrieved from http://www.mckinsey.com/insights/leading_in_the_21st_century/change_leader_change_thyself

Bridges, W. (2004). *Transitions: Making sense of life's changes* (2nd ed.). Cambridge, MA: Da Capo Press.

Briner, R. (2007, March). Is HRM evidence-based and does it matter? *Institute for Employment Studies*. Retrieved from http://www.cebma.org/wp-content/uploads/Briner-Is-HRM-evidence-based-and-does-it-matter.pdf

Briner, R. (2013). What is employee engagement and does it matter? An evidence-based approach. *Engage for Success*. Retrieved from http://www.engageforsuccess.org/wp-content/uploads/2014/03/Rob-Briner.pdf

Brown, B., Court, D., & Willmott, P. (2013, November). Mobilizing your C-suite for big-data analytics. *McKinsey Quarterly*. Retrieved from http://www.mckinsey.com/insights/business_technology/mobilizing_your_c_suite_for_big_data_analytics

Burkeman, O. (2014, May 10). This column will change your life: Hindsight—It's not just for past events. *The Guardian*. Retrieved from http://www.theguardian.com/lifeandstyle/2014/may/10/hindsight-in-advance-premortem-this-column-change-life

Cacioppe, R. (1999). Using team-individual reward and recognition strategies to drive organizational success. *Leadership and Organizational Development Journal*, 20(6), 322–331.

Camillus, J. C. (2008, May). Strategy as a wicked problem. *Harvard Business Review*. Retrieved from https://hbr.org/2008/05/strategy-as-a-wicked-problem

Cermak, J., & McGurk, M. (2010, July). Putting a value on training. *McKinsley Quarterly*. Retrieved from http://www.mckinsey.com/insights/organization/putting_a_value_on_training

Chabris, C. (2013, Sep. 29). Book review: *David and Goliath* by Malcolm Gladwell. *Wall Street Journal*. Retrieved from http://www.wsj.com/articles/SB1000142405270 2304713704579093090254007968

Chitta, K. (2014). Change agility: *Leadership, transformation, and the pursuit of purpose*. Charleston, SC: Createspace.

Chodron, P. (2001). *The places that scare you: A guide to fearlessness in difficult times*. Boston, MA: Shambala.

Cialdini, R. (2006). *Influence: The psychology of persuasion* (Revised). New York, NY: Harper Business.

Cohen, M. D., March, J. G., & Olsen, J. P. (1972). A garbage can model of organizational choice. *Administrative Science Quarterly*, 17(1), 1–25.

Collier, A. (1994). *Critical realism: An introduction to Roy Bhaskar's philosophy*. London, England: Verso.

Collins, J. (2001). *Good to great: Why some companies make the leap…And others don't*. New York, NY: Harper Business.

Collins, J., & Porras, J. (1994). *Built to last: Successful habits of visionary companies.* New York, NY: Harper Business.

Colzato, L., Ozlurk, A., & Hommel, B. (2012). Meditate to create: The impact of focused-attention and open-monitoring training on convergent and divergent thinking. *Frontiers in Cognition*, 3, 116–129.

Cook, J., & Lewandowsky, S. (2011, Nov. 5). The debunking handbook. Retrieved from http://www.skepticalscience.com/Debunking-Handbook-now-freely-available-download.html

Csikszentmihalyi, M. (1990). *Flow: The psychology of optimal experience*. New York, NY: Harper Collins.

Cullinan, G., Rovit, S., & Tymms, A. (2003). Organising for deal success. *European Business Journal*. Retrieved from http://www.bain.com/Images/EBJ_Organising_for_deal_success.pdf

Dai, G., De Meuse, K., & Tang, Y. (2013). The role of learning agility in executive career success: The results of two field studies. *Journal of Managerial Issues*, 25(2), 108–131.

Davenport, T. (2012, August). The human side of Big Data and high-performance analytics. Retrieved from https://www.ndm.net/datawarehouse/pdf/Research_Human_Side_of_Big_Data_and_High_Performance_Analytics.pdf

Davenport, T. (2014). *Big Data at work: Dispelling the myths, uncovering the opportunities*. Boston, MA: Harvard Business Review Press.

Davenport, T., & Manville, B. (2012). *Judgment calls: 12 stories of big decisions and the teams that got them right.* Boston, MA: Harvard Business Review Press.

Dean, J. (2010). *Making habits breaking habits.* London, England: Oneworld.

Desai, M. (2012, March). The incentive bubble. *Harvard Business Review.* Retrieved from https://hbr.org/2012/03/the-incentive-bubble

Dolan, P., Hallsworth, M., Halpern, D., King, D., & Vlaev, I. (2009). Mindspace: Influencing behavior through public policy. Institute for Government (UK). Retrieved from http://www.instituteforgovernment.org.uk/sites/default/files/publications/MINDSPACE.pdf

Duhigg, C. (2012). *The power of habit: Why we do what we do in life and business.* New York, NY: Random House.

Dweck, C. (2006). *Mindset: The new psychology of success.* New York, NY: Random House.

Eagle, N., & Greene, K. (2014). *Reality mining: using Big Data to engineer a better world.* Cambridge, MA: MIT Press.

Easly, D., & Kleinberg, J. (2010). *Networks, crowds, and markets: Reasoning in a highly connected world.* Cambridge, England: Cambridge University Press.

Ekvall, G. (1991). The organizational culture of idea-management: A creative climate for the management of ideas. In J. Henry, & D. Walker, *Managing Innovation* (pp. 73–79). London, England: Sage Publications.

Ellenberg, J. (2014). *How not to be wrong: The power of mathematical thinking.* New York, NY: Penguin.

Fitts, A. S. (2013, October 10). The Gladwellian debate: Why are we still listening to Malcom Gladwell's cherry-picked gospel? *Columbia Journalism Review.* Retrieved from http://www.cjr.org/the_observatory/the_gladwellian_debate.php

Flyvbjerg, B., Bruzelius, N., & Rothengatter, W. (2003). *Megaprojects and risk: An anatomy of ambition.* Cambridge, England: Cambridge University Press.

Flyvbjerg, B., Landman, T., & Schram, S. (2012). *Real social science: Applied phronesis.* Cambridge, England: Cambridge University Press.

Fodor, J., (2009, Sep., 30) Diary. *London Review of Books,* 21(19), 68–69.

Fricke, M. (2007, April). The knowledge pyramid: A critique of the DIKW hierarchy. *Journal of Information Science,* 35(2), 1–13.

Furnham, A. (2004). *Management and myths: Challenging business fads, fallacies, and fashions.* Basingstoke, England: Palgrave Macmillan.

Gardner, H. (2006). *Changing minds: The art and science of changing our own and other people's minds.* Boston, MA: Harvard Business School Press.

Gawande, A. (2009). *The checklist manifesto: How to get things right.* New York, NY: Metropolitan Books.

George, B., (2013, Mar. 22). Resilience through mindful leadership. *Huffington Post.* Retrieved from http://www.huffingtonpost.com/bill-george/resilience-through-mindfu_b_2932269.html

Gibbons, P. (2000). Spirituality at work: Definitions, measures, and validity claims. In J. Biberman, & M. Whitty, *Work and spirit.* Scranton, PA: University of Scranton Press.

Gilson, L., Lim, H., Luciano, M. & Choi, J. (2013). Unpacking the cross-level effect of tenure diversity, explicit knowledge, and knowledge sharing on individual creativity. *Journal of Occupational and Organizational Psychology*, 86(2), 203–222.

Gigerenzer, G. (2014, Fall). *Risk savvy: How to make good decisions.* New York, NY: Viking.

Gneezy, U., Meier, S., & Rey-Biel, P. (2011, Fall). When and why incentives (don't) work to modify behavior. *Journal of Economic Perspectives*, 24(4), 191–210.

Goldacre, B. (2008). *Bad science.* London, England: Fourth Estate.

Greeson, J. (2009, January). Mindfulness research update 2008. *Complementary Health Practice Review*, 13(1), 10–18.

Gribben, J. (2002). *Science: A history.* London, England: Penguin.

Gross, P., Levitt, N., & Lewis, M. (1996). *Flight from science and reason (annals of the New York Academy of Sciences).* New York, NY: New York Academy of Sciences.

Grove, A. (1999). *Only the paranoid survive: How to exploit the crisis points that challenge every company.* New York, NY: Crown Business.

Guise, S. (2013). *Mini habits: Smaller habits, bigger results.* San Bernadino, CA: CreateSpace.

Haidt, J. (2005). *The happiness hypothesis: Finding modern truth in ancient wisdom.* New York, NY: Basic Books.

Hall, B., & Murphy, K. (2003, June). The trouble with stock options. *(Working Paper–9784) National Bureau of Economic Research,* Retrieved from http://www.nber.org/papers/w9784

Hamill, P. (2013). *Embodied leadership: The Somatic approach to developing your leadership.* London, England: Kogan Page.

Hamilton, S., & Micklethwait, A. (2006). *Greed and corporate failure: The lessons from recent disasters.* Basingstoke, England: Palgrave.

Harris, J., Davenport, T., & Morison, B. (2010, September). *Analytics at work: Smarter decision, better results.* Boston, MA: Harvard Business Review Press.

Heath, C., & Heath, D. (2010). *Switch: How to change things when change is hard.* New York, NY: Broadway.

Heath, C., & Heath, D. (2013). *Decisive: How to make better choices in life and work.* New York, NY: Crown Business.

Heckler, R. (2007). *In search of the warrior spirit: Teaching awareness disciplines to Green Berets* (4th ed.). Berkeley, CA: Blue Snake Books.

Heelas, P. (1996). *The new age movement: The celebration of the self and the sacralization of modernity.* Cambridge, England: Blackwell.

Hoffman, J., (2009, Sep. 13). Why can't she walk to school? *New York Times*, p. ST1.

Hughes, M. (2011, Dec. 16). Do 70 percent of all organizational change initiatives really fail? *Journal of Change Mangagement, 11*(4), 451–464.

Hume, D., Colby Biggs, L., & Nidditoh, P. (1978). *A treatise of human nature.* Oxford, England: Oxford University Press.

Hunter, S. T., Bedell, K., & Mumford, M. (2007). Climate for creativity: A quantitative review. *Creativity Research Journal, 19*(1), 69–90.

Huskins, M., Kaplan, J., & Krishnakanthan, K. (2013, August). Enhancing the efficiency and effectiveness of application development. *McKinsey Quarterly.* Retrieved from http://www.mckinsey.com/insights/business_technology/enhancing_ the_efficiency_and_effectiveness_of_application_development

Hussain, D., & Bhushan, B. (2010). Psychology of meditation and health: Present status and future directions. *International Journal of Psychology and Psychological Therapy, 10*(3), 439–451.

Ingersoll, C., Locke, R., & Reavis, C. (2012, Apr. 3). BP and the Deepwater disaster of 2010. Retrieved from https://mitsloan.mit.edu/LearningEdge/CaseDocs/10%20 110%20BP%20Deepwater%20Horizon%20Locke.Review.pdf

Isaacson, W. (2013). *Steve Jobs.* New York, NY: Simon and Schuster.

Jackson, B. (2001). *Management gurus and management fashions.* London, England: Routledge.

Johnson, S. (2001). *Emergence: The connected lives of ants, brains, cities, and software.* New York, NY: Scribner.

Jones, D., & Elcock, J. (2001). *History and theories of psychology: A critical perspective.* London, England: Arnold.

Jorgensen, H., Owen, L., & Neus, A. (2013). Making change work. *IBM Future of Enterprise.* Retrieved from http://www-935.ibm.com/services/us/gbs/bus/pdf/ gbe03100-usen-03-making-change-work.pdf

Jurado, M., & Rosselli, M. (2007, September). The elusive nature of executive functions: A review of our current understanding. *Neuropsychological Review, 17*(3), 213–233.

Kahane, A. (2012). *Transformative scenario planning: Working together to change the future.* San Francisco, CA: Berrett Koehler.

Kahneman, D. (2011). *Thinking fast and slow.* New York, NY: Farrar, Strauss and Giroux.

Kahneman, D., & Klein, G. (2009, September). Conditions for intuitive expertise: A failure to disagree. *American Psychologist, 64*(6), 515–526.

Kahneman, D., & Tversky, A. (1974, Sep. 27). Judgment under uncertainty: Heuristics and biases. *Science, 185*(4157), 1124–1131.

Kegan, R., & Lahey, L. L. (2009). *Immunity to change: How to overcome it and unlock the potential in yourself and your organization.* Boston, MA: Harvard Business School Press.

Kellaway, L. (2013, Apr. 9). Where others failed: Top 10 fads. *Financial Times.* Retrieved from http://www.ft.com/cms/s/2/3c7f1e40-a03e-11e2-88b6-00144feabdc0. html#axzz3WVOyc0Qp

Keller, S., & Aiken, C. (2011, Aug. 14). The inconvenient truth about change management: Why it isn't working and what to do about it. *McKinsey Quarterly*. Retrieved from http://www.scribd.com/doc/133684297/McKinsey-The-Inconvenient-Truth-About-Change-Management#scribd

Klein, G. (2008, June). Naturalistic decision making. *Human Factors*, *50*(3), 456–460.

Knight, F. (1921). *Risk, uncertainty, and profit*. Evergreen Books.

Kohn, A. (1993). *Punished by rewards: The trouble with gold stars, incentive plans, A's, praise, and other bribes*. Boston, MA: Houghton Mifflin.

Kotter, J. (1996). *Leading change*. Boston, MA: Harvard Business Review Press.

Kotter, J. (2014). *XLR8: Building strategic agility for a faster moving world*. Boston, MA: Harvard Business Review Press.

KPMG. (2008). Many enterprise risk management programs lack fundamentals: KPMG survey of internal auditors and boards. Retrieved from http://www.kpmg.com/US/en/services/Advisory/risk-and-compliance/internal-audit-risk-and-regulatory-compliance/Pages/enterprise-risk-management.aspx

Kuhn, T. (1962). *The structure of scientific revolutions*. Chicago, IL: University of Chicago Press.

Lally, P., van Jaarsveld, C., Potts, P., & Wardle, J. (2010, October). How habits are formed: Modelling habit formation in the real world. *European Journal of Social Psychology*, *40*(6), 998–1009.

Laloux, F. (2014). *Reinventing organizations*. Brussels, Belgium: Nelson Parker.

Latham, G. (2011). *Becoming the evidence-based manager: Making the science of managment work for you*. Boston, MA: Davies Black.

Lee, D., & McCrary, J. (2006, Jul. 1). Crime, punishment, and myopia. *National Bureau of Economic Research*. Retrieved from http://www.nber.org/papers/w11491

Lilienfeld, S., Steven, L., Ruscio, J., & Beyerstein, B. (2010). *50 great myths of popular psychology: Shattering widespread misconceptions about human behavior*. Oxford, England: Wiley-Blackwell.

Loeb, S., & Page, M. (2000, August). Examining the link between teacher incomes and student outcomes. *The Review of Economics and Statistics*, *82*(3), 303–408.

Lorenz, J., Rauhut, H., Schweitzer, F., & Helbing, D. (2011, May 31). How social influence can undermine the wisdom of crowd effect. *Proceedings of the National Academy of Sciences*, *108*(22), 9020–9025.

Macnamara, B. N., Hambrick, D. Z., & Oswald, F. L. (2014, August). Deliberate practice and performance in music, games, sports, education, and professions: A meta-analysis. *Psychological Science*, *25*(8), 1608–1618.

Meadows, D. (2008). *Thinking in systems: A primer*. White River Junction, VT: Chelsea Green Publishing.

Meng-Tang, C., Goleman, D., & Kabat-Zinn, J. (2014). *Search inside yourself: The unexpected path to success, happiness (and world peace)*. New York, NY: HarperOne.

Miller, D., & Hartwick, J. (2002, Oct. 1). Spotting management fads. *Harvard Business Review*. Retrieved from https://hbr.org/2002/10/spotting-management-fads

Morgan, G. (2006). *Images of organization.* London, England: SAGE.

Morgeson, F., Campion, M., Dipboye, R., Hollenbeck, J., Murphy, K., & Schmitt, N. (2007). Reconsidering the use of personality tests in personnel selection contexts. *Personnel Psychology, 60*(3), 683–729.

Nanshen, R.N. (1972). *Physics and beyond: Encounters and conversations.* New York, NY: Harper and Row.

October, what a month! (2012, Oct. 22). *The Quant Monitor.* Retrieved from http:/// www.quantmonitor.com/october-what-a-month/

Owen, A., Hampshire, A., Grahn, J., Stenton, R., Daiani, S., Burns, A. H., & Ballard, C. (2010, Jun. 10). Putting brain training to the test. *Nature, 465* (7299), 775–778.

Owen, H. (1997). *Open space technology.* London, England: Berrett-Koehler.

Peters, T., & Waterman, R. (2006). *In search of excellence: Lessons from America's best-run companies.* New York, NY: Harper Business.

Pfeffer, J., & Sutton, R. (2006, January). Evidence-based management. *Harvard Business Review.* Retrieved from https://hbr.org/2006/01/evidence-based-management.

Pfeffer, J., & Sutton, R. (2006). *Hard facts, dangerous half-truths, and total nonsense: Profiting from evidence-based management.* Boston, MA: Harvard Business School Press.

Pfeffer, J., & Sutton, R. (2001, Sep. 3). Trust the Evidence, Not Your Instincts. *New York Times.* Retrieved from http://www.nytimes.com/2011/09/04/jobs/04pre.html

Pillay, S. (2011). *Your brain and business: The neuroscience of great leaders.* Upper Saddle River, NJ: FT Press.

Pinker, S. (2009, Nov. 7). Malcolm Gladwell, eclectic detective. *New York Times.* Retrieved from http://www.nytimes.com/2009/11/15/books/review/Pinker-t.html?pagewanted=all

Pollock, R., & Jefferson, A. (2012, August). Ensuring learning transfer. Retrieved from http://www.astd.org/Publications/Newsletters/ASTD-Links/ASTD-Links-Articles/2012/08/Ensuring-Learning-Transfer

Powell, W. W. (1990). Neither market nor hierarchy: Network forms of organization. *Journal of Organizational Behavior, 12,* 295–336

Pronovost, P., & Hales, B. (2006). The checklist: A tool for error management and performance improvement. *Journal of Critical Care, 21*(3), 231–235.

Przybylski, R. (2008, February). What works? Effective recidivism reduction and risk-focused prevention programs—A compendium of evidence-based options for preventing new and persistent criminal behavior. Retrieved from http://www.colorado.gov/ccjjdir/Resources/Resources/Ref/WhatWorks2008.pdf

Ren, J., Huang, Z., Luo, J., Wei, G., Ying, X., Ding, Z., Wu, Y., & Luo, F. (2001, October). Meditation promotes insightful problem-solving by keeping people in a mindful and alert conscious state. *Science China - Life Sciences, 54*(10), 961–965.

Roberto, M. (2007). *Why great leaders don't take yes for an answer.* Upper Saddle River, NJ: Pearson Education.

Robertson, B. (2015). *Holacracy.* New York, NY: Macmillan.

Robinson, D. (1986). *An intellectual history of psychology.* Madison, WI: University of Wisconsin Press.

Rock, D. (2009). *Your brain at work: Strategies for overcoming distraction, regaining focus, and working smarter all day long.* New York, NY: Harper Collins.

Rock, D., & Page, L. J. (2009). *Coaching with the brain in mind: Foundations for practice.* New York, NY: Wiley.

Rosenzweig, P. (2007). *The Halo effect…and the eight other business delusions that deceive managers.* New York, NY: Free Press.

Satel, S., & Lilienfeld, S. (2013). *Brainwashed: The seductive appeal of mindless neuroscience.* New York, NY: Basic Books.

Schroeder, S., & Frist, W. (2013, May 23). Phasing out fee-for-service payment. *New England Journal of Medicine, 368*(21), 2029–2032.

Senge, P. (1994). *Fifth discipline fieldbook: Strategies and tools for building a learning organization.* New York, NY: Crown Business.

Siegal, D. (2007). *The mindful brain: Reflection and attunement in the cultivation of well-being.* New York, NY: WW Norton.

Silver, N. (2012). *The signal and the noise: Why so many predictions fail—But some don't.* New York, NY: Penguin.

Smil, V. (2008). *Global catastrophes and trends: The next fifty years.* Cambridge, MA: MIT Press.

Smith, M. E. (2002, January). Success rates for different types of organizational change. *Performance Improvement, 41*(1), 26–45.

Smith-Barrow, D. (2013, May 22). Where America's top CEOs went to school. *U.S. News and World Report.* Retrieved from www.usnews.com/education/best-colleges/articles/2013/05/22/where-americas-top-ceos-went-to-school

Snowden, D., & Boone, M. (2007, November). A leader's framework for decision making. *Harvard Business Review.* Retrieved from https://hbr.org/2007/11/a-leaders-framework-for-decision-making

Stewart, M. (2009). *The management myth: Debunking modern business philosophy.* New York, NY: Norton.

Taleb, N. N. (2005). *Fooled by randomness: The hidden role of change in life and in the markets.* New York, NY: Random House.

Taleb, N. N. (2007). *The black swan: The impact of the highly improbable.* New York, NY: Random House. Kindle edition.

Taleb, N. N. (2012). *Antifragile: Things that gain from disorder.* New York, NY: Random House.

Taleb, N. N. (2015). *Silent risk.* Draft manuscript. Retrieved from http://www.fooledbyrandomness.com/

Tang, Y., Yinghua, M., Wang, J., Fan, Y., Feng, S., Lu, Q., & Posner, M. (2007, August). Short-term meditation training improves attention and self-regulation. *Proceedings of the National Academy of Sciences, 104*(43), 17152–17156.

Tetlock, P. (2006). *Expert political judgment: How good is it? How can we know?* Princeton, NJ: Princeton University Press.

Thaler, R., & Sunstein, C. (2009). *Nudge: Improving decisions about health, wealth, and happiness*. New York, NY: Penguin.

Thornton, D. (2011, Sep. 11) The rhetoric of neuroscience. *Wired Magazine*. Retrieved from http://www.wired.com/2011/08/the-rhetoric-of-neuroscience/

Trousselard, M., & Steiler, D. C. (2014, December). L'histoire de la mindfulness a l'epreuve des donnees actuelles de la litterature: Questions en suspens. *Encephale*, *40*(6), 474–480.

Twitchell, S., Holton, E., & Trott, J. (2008, Oct. 22). Technical training evaluation practices in the United States. *Performance Improvement Quarterly, 13*(3) 84–109.

Uttal, W. (2003). *The new phrenology: The limits of localizing cognitive processes in the brain*. Cambridge, MA: MIT Press.

Varian, H. (2013). *Beyond Big Data*. San Francisco, CA: National Association of Business Economists.

Vermeulen, F. (2013, Aug. 23). Beware the sirens of management pseudoscience. *Harvard Business Review*. Retrieved from https://hbr.org/2013/08/beware-the-sirens-of-managemen

von Clausewitz, C. (2012). *On war*. San Bernadino, CA: CreateSpace.

Waldrop, M. (1992). *Complexity: The emerging science at the edge of order and chaos*. New York, NY: Simon and Schuster.

Wagner, K., Taylor, A., Zablit, H., & Foo, E. (2014, Oct. 28). A breakthrough innovation culture and organization. *BCG Perspectives*. Retrieved from https://www.bcgperspectives.com/content/articles/innovation_growth_digital_economy_breakthrough_innovation_culture_organization/

Wallace, B., & Shapiro, S. (2006, October). Mental balance and well-being. *American Psychologist, 61*(7), 690–701.

Walsh, R., & Shapiro, S. (2006, April). The meeting of meditative disciplines and western psychology. *American Psychologist, 61*(3), 227–239.

Weisbord, M. (2012) *Productive workplaces: Dignity, meaning, and community in the 21st century* (3rd ed.). New York, NY: Pfeiffer.

Why do projects fail?. Qantas (2008). Retrieved from http://calleam.com/WTPF/?p=2347

Wiesner, W., & Cronshaw, S. (2011, August). A meta-analytics investigation of the impact of inteview format and degree of structure on the validity of the employment interview. *Journal of Occupational Psychology, 61*(4), 275–290.

Wilber, K. (1995). *Sex, ecology, and spirituality: The spirit of evolution*. Boston, MA: Shambhala.

Wood, R. (2000). *Managing complexity: How businesses can adapt and prosper in the connected economy*. London, England: Economist Books.

Woodward, J. (1981). *Industrial organization: Theory and practice*. Oxford, England: Oxford University Press.

Index